# OBJECTIVE
## CAE
**Second edition**

Felicity O'Dell    Annie Broadhead    Teacher's Book

CAMBRIDGE UNIVERSITY PRESS

CAMBRIDGE UNIVERSITY PRESS
Cambridge, New York, Melbourne, Madrid, Cape Town,
Singapore, São Paulo, Delhi, Tokyo, Mexico City

Cambridge University Press
The Edinburgh Building, Cambridge CB2 8RU, UK

www.cambridge.org
Information on this title: www.cambridge.org/9780521700580

© Cambridge University Press, 2008

This publication is in copyright. Subject to statutory exception
and to the provisions of relevant collective licensing agreements,
no reproduction of any part may take place without the written
permission of Cambridge University Press.

First published 2002
6th printing 2006
Second edition published 2008
4th printing 2012

Printed in the United Kingdom by Short Run Press, Exeter

*A catalogue record for this publication is available from the British Library*

ISBN 978-0-521-70057-3 Self-study Student's Book
ISBN 978-0-521-70056-6 Student's Book
ISBN 978-0-521-70059-7 Workbook
ISBN 978-0-521-70060-3 Workbook with Answers
ISBN 978-0-521-70058-0 Teacher's Book
ISBN 978-0-521-70062-7 CD (audio) Set

Cambridge University Press has no responsibility for the persistence or
accuracy of URLs for external or third-party internet websites referred to in
this publication, and does not guarantee that any content on such websites is,
or will remain, accurate or appropriate. Information regarding prices, travel
timetables and other factual information given in this work is correct at
the time of first printing but Cambridge University Press does not guarantee
the accuracy of such information thereafter.

Cover concept by Dale Tomlinson and design by Jo Barker

Produced by Kamae Design, Oxford

# Contents

| | |
|---|---|
| Map of Book | 4 |
| Exam information | 8 |
| **Unit 1** Getting to know you | 10 |
| **Unit 2** Keeping in touch | 14 |
| **Unit 3** The real you | 18 |
| **Unit 4** Acting on instructions | 22 |
| **Unit 5** Dear Sir or Madam | 26 |
| Units 1–5 Revision | 29 |
| Test 1 | 30 |
| **Unit 6** Speak after the tone | 37 |
| **Unit 7** Running a successful business | 41 |
| **Unit 8** Best thing since sliced bread | 45 |
| **Unit 9** You live and learn | 49 |
| **Unit 10** I have a dream | 53 |
| Units 6–10 Revision | 57 |
| Test 2 | 58 |
| **Unit 11** Read all about it | 64 |
| **Unit 12** In a nutshell | 68 |
| **Unit 13** Leaf through a leaflet | 72 |
| **Unit 14** Views from the platform | 76 |
| **Unit 15** If you want to know what I think … | 80 |
| Units 11–15 Revision | 83 |
| Test 3 | 84 |
| **Unit 16** Raving and panning | 91 |
| **Unit 17** Do it for my sake | 95 |
| **Unit 18** May I introduce … ? | 99 |
| **Unit 19** Feeding the mind | 103 |
| **Unit 20** Answers on a postcard | 107 |
| Units 16–20 Revision | 110 |
| Test 4 | 111 |
| **Unit 21** Travel broadens the mind | 118 |
| **Unit 22** Under the weather | 122 |
| **Unit 23** I'm afraid I really must insist | 126 |
| **Unit 24** News and views | 130 |
| **Unit 25** Powers of observation | 134 |
| Units 21–25 Revision | 137 |
| Test 5 | 138 |
| **Unit 26** Natural wonders | 145 |
| **Unit 27** The open window | 149 |
| **Unit 28** Weighing up the pros and cons | 154 |
| **Unit 29** A testing question | 159 |
| **Unit 30** Why should we employ you? | 164 |
| Units 26–30 Revision | 167 |
| Test 6 | 168 |
| Photocopiable tapescripts | 179 |
| Photocopiable activities | 183 |

# Map of Objective CAE Student's Book

| TOPIC | GENRE | MAIN EXAM SKILLS | GRAMMAR | VOCABULARY |
|---|---|---|---|---|
| **Unit 1**<br>**Getting to know you**<br>10–13<br>People and places | Introductions | Speaking and Listening | Conditionals | Collocations<br>Adjective-noun, adverb-verb, adverb-adjective |
| **Exam folder 1** 14–15 | | Paper 3 Use of English: 1<br>Multiple-choice gap fill | | |
| **Unit 2**<br>**Keeping in touch** 16–19<br>Making contact | Informal letters | Writing and Speaking | Prepositions and adverbs | Multiple meanings |
| **Writing folder 1** 20–21 | | Informal letters | | |
| **Unit 3**<br>**The real you** 22–25<br>Career paths | Interviews | Speaking | Wish and if only<br>It's time, would rather/sooner | Idioms<br>Verb + the + object |
| **Exam folder 2** 26–27 | | Paper 3 Use of English: 2<br>Open gap fill | | |
| **Unit 4**<br>**Acting on instructions**<br>28–31<br>Memory techniques | Instructions | Use of English | Modals: may, might, can, could | Prefixes and suffixes |
| **Writing folder 2** 32–33 | | Essays | | |
| **Unit 5**<br>**Dear Sir or Madam**<br>34–37<br>Dream jobs | Formal letters | Writing and Listening | Relative clauses | Connotation<br>Positive, negative and neutral |
| **Units 1–5 Revision** 38–39 | | | | |
| **Unit 6**<br>**Speak after the tone**<br>40–43<br>Communications technology | Phone messages | Speaking | Phrasal verbs | Collocations<br>Have, do, make and take |
| **Exam folder 3** 44–45 | | Paper 3 Use of English: 3<br>Word formation | | |
| **Unit 7**<br>**Running a successful business** 46–49<br>The world of work | Reports | Writing | Cause and effect | Multiple meanings |
| **Writing folder 3** 50–51 | | Formal letters | | |
| **Unit 8**<br>**Best thing since sliced bread** 52–55<br>Inventions | Describing objects | Reading, Listening and Speaking | Modals: must, should, ought to, shall, will, would | Positive and negative adjectives |
| **Exam folder 4** 56–57 | | Paper 3 Use of English: 4<br>Gapped sentences | | |

| TOPIC | GENRE | MAIN EXAM SKILLS | GRAMMAR | VOCABULARY |
|---|---|---|---|---|
| **Unit 9**<br>You live and learn 58–61<br>Further study | Academic texts | Writing and Speaking | Participle clauses | Word formation |
| **Writing folder 4** 62–63 | | Reports and proposals | | |
| **Unit 10**<br>I have a dream 64–67<br>Social change | Speeches | Listening | Future forms | Metaphors and idioms |
| **Units 6–10 Revision** 68–69 | | | | |
| **Unit 11**<br>Read all about it 70–73<br>Fashion | Magazine and newspaper articles | Listening and Speaking | Direct and reported speech | Collocation |
| **Exam folder 5** 74–75 | | Paper 3 Use of English: 5<br>Key word transformations | | |
| **Unit 12**<br>In a nutshell 76–79<br>Dreaming | Short stories | Writing | Past tenses and the present perfect | Adjectival order |
| **Writing folder 5** 80–81 | | Reviews | | |
| **Unit 13**<br>Leaf through a leaflet 82–85<br>Leaving home | Information pages | Listening | *-ing* forms | Verbs with the *-ing* form |
| **Exam folder 6** 86–87 | | Paper 1 Reading: 1<br>Themed texts | | |
| **Unit 14**<br>Views from the platform 88–91<br>Language development | Lectures | Listening and Use of English | The passive<br>*To have/get something done* | Word formation |
| **Writing folder 6** 92–93 | | Information sheets | | |
| **Unit 15**<br>If you want to know what I think … 94–97<br>Family life | Expressing opinions | Speaking | The infinitive | Agreeing and disagreeing |
| **Units 11–15 Revision** 98–99 | | | | |
| **Unit 16**<br>Raving and panning 100–103<br>The arts | Reviews | Speaking | Articles and determiners | Collocation |
| **Exam folder 7** 104–105 | | Paper 1 Reading: 2<br>Gapped text | | |
| **Unit 17**<br>Do it for my sake 106–109<br>Persuasion | Proposals | Writing and Speaking | Language of persuasion | Multiple meanings |
| **Writing folder 7** 110–111 | | Set texts | | |

| TOPIC | GENRE | MAIN EXAM SKILLS | GRAMMAR | VOCABULARY |
|---|---|---|---|---|
| **Unit 18**<br>**May I introduce ...?**<br>112-115<br>White lies | Small talk | Writing and Speaking | Cleft sentences and other ways of emphasising | Collocations and longer chunks of language |
| **Exam folder 8** 116–117 | | Paper 1 Reading: 1, 3 and 4<br>Multiple choice and multiple matching | | |
| **Unit 19**<br>**Feeding the mind**<br>118–121<br>Food, pictures and science | Talks | Listening and Writing | Emphasising | Word formation |
| **Writing folder 8** 122–123 | | Articles | | |
| **Unit 20**<br>**Answers on a postcard**<br>124–127<br>Mini sagas | Competition entries | Writing | Hypothesising | Idioms |
| **Units 16–20 Revision** 128–129 | | | | |
| **Unit 21**<br>**Travel broadens the mind** 130–133<br>Trips and travel | Travel writing | Writing and Speaking | Range of grammatical structures | Word endings |
| **Exam folder 9** 134–135 | | Paper 2 Writing: 1 and 2 | | |
| **Unit 22**<br>**Under the weather**<br>136–139<br>Climate change | Interpreting facts and figures | Reading and Speaking | Linking devices | Collocations |
| **Writing folder 9** 140–141 | | Descriptive writing | | |
| **Unit 23**<br>**I'm afraid I really must insist** 142–145<br>How to complain | Formal letters | Listening, Writing and Speaking | Phrasal verbs | Language for complaining |
| **Exam folder 10** 146–147 | | Paper 4 Listening: 2<br>Listening for specific information | | |
| **Unit 24**<br>**News and views** 148–151<br>Stories in the news | Investigative journalism | Listening | Linking devices | Homophones |
| **Writing folder 10**<br>152–153 | | Formal writing | | |
| **Unit 25**<br>**Powers of observation**<br>154–157<br>Research methods | Academic texts | Writing and Speaking | Complex sentences and adverbial clauses | Formal and informal language |
| **Units 21–25 Revision** 158–159 | | | | |

MAP OF OBJECTIVE CAE STUDENT'S BOOK

| TOPIC | GENRE | MAIN EXAM SKILLS | GRAMMAR | VOCABULARY |
|---|---|---|---|---|
| **Unit 26**<br>**Natural wonders** 160–163<br>Beauty spots | Travel articles | Writing | *Like, alike, as, so* and *such* | Idioms |
| **Exam folder 11** 164–165 | | Paper 4 Listening: 3 and 4<br>Multiple choice and<br>multiple matching | | |
| **Unit 27**<br>**The open window**<br>166–169<br>Personality traits | Fiction | Reading and Listening | Emphasising | Chunks |
| **Writing folder 11**<br>170–171 | | Informal writing | | |
| **Unit 28**<br>**Weighing up the pros<br>and cons** 172–175<br>Air transport | Discursive articles | Writing, Reading and<br>Listening | Adverbials expressing<br>opinion | Word formation |
| **Exam folder 12** 176–177 | | Paper 5 Speaking:<br>The whole paper | | |
| **Unit 29**<br>**A testing question**<br>178–181<br>Education | Debates | Reading | Gerunds and infinitives | Collocations |
| **Writing folder 12**<br>182–183 | | Descriptive, narrative and<br>discursive articles | | |
| **Unit 30**<br>**Why should we employ<br>you?** 184–187<br>Job interviews | Interviews | Writing and Speaking | Using a range of structures | Using a range of<br>vocabulary |
| **Units 26–30 Revision** 188–189 | | | | |
| **Grammar folder** 190–207 | | | | |

When you see this icon in the Student's Book it means that this language area has been identified in the Cambridge Learner Corpus (CLC) as an area in which learners often need extra practice. The CLC is a collection of over 100,000 exam scripts from Cambridge ESOL providing over 28 million words of data, and it shows the real mistakes candidates have made in their exams. The mistakes the authors focus on are typical of learners at this level and that is why the course provides further practice in using these features of the language accurately.

# Content of the CAE Examination

The Cambridge Certificate in Advanced English examination consists of five papers, each of which is worth 20% of the exam total. It is not necessary to pass all five papers in order to pass the examination. There are five grades: Pass – A, B, C; Fail – D, E. As well as being told your grade, you will also be given a statement of your results which shows a graphical profile of your performance on each paper.

## Paper 1 Reading   1 hour 10 minutes

There are four parts to this paper and they are always in the same order. Each part contains one or more texts and a comprehension task. The texts used are from newspapers, magazines, journals, books, leaflets, brochures, etc.

| Part | Task Type | Number of Questions | Task Format | *Objective CAE* Exam Folder |
|---|---|---|---|---|
| 1 | Multiple choice | 6 | You read three short texts relating to the same theme and have to answer two multiple-choice questions on each. Each question has four options, A, B, C and D. | 6 (86–87) |
| 2 | Gapped text | 6 | You read a text from which paragraphs have been removed and placed in jumbled order after the text. You decide where the missing paragraphs fit in the text. | 7 (104–105) |
| 3 | Multiple choice | 7 | You read a text followed by multiple-choice questions with four options. | 8 (116–117) |
| 4 | Multiple matching | 15 | You read a text preceded by multiple-matching questions. You match a prompt from one list to a prompt in another list, or match prompts to elements of the text. | 8 (116–117) |

## Paper 2 Writing   1 hour 30 minutes

There are two parts to this paper. Part 1 is compulsory as you have to answer it in 180–220 words. In Part 2 there are five questions, two of which relate to set texts. You must write an answer of 220–260 words to one of these five questions.

| Part | Task Type | Number of Tasks | Task Format | *Objective CAE* Writing Folder |
|---|---|---|---|---|
| 1 | article report proposal letter | 1 | You are given a situation and some information which you need to respond to. You may be given two different pieces of material which you need to use in your answer. | 1 Informal letters (20–21) 3 Formal letters (50–51) 4 Reports and proposals (62–63) 8 Articles (122–123) 10 Formal writing (152–153) 11 Informal writing (170–171) |
| 2 | article report review essay letter proposal information sheet competition entry contribution to a longer piece (only the first four from this list used for set text tasks) | Choose 1 from a choice of four tasks. | You are given a choice of tasks which specify the type of text you have to write, your purpose for writing and the person or people you have to write for. | As for Part 1 but also: 2 Essays 5 Reviews 6 Information sheets 7 Set texts 9 Descriptive writing 12 Descriptive, narrative and discursive articles

Exam Folder 9 (134–135): Writing, 1 and 2 |

## Paper 3 Use of English 1 hour

There are five parts to this paper, which tests your grammar and vocabulary.

| Part | Task Type | Number of Questions | Task Format | *Objective CAE* Exam Folder |
|---|---|---|---|---|
| 1 | Multiple-choice gap fill mainly testing vocabulary | 12 | You choose which word from four choices fills each of 12 gaps in a text. | 1 (14–15) |
| 2 | Open gap fill, mainly testing grammar | 15 | You fill each of 15 gaps in a text with one word each. | 2 (26–27) |
| 3 | Word formation | 10 | You form an appropriate word, using the given prompt word which has the same root, to fill each of the gaps in a text. | 3 (44–45) |
| 4 | Gapped sentences | 5 | You are given sets of three sentences, each of which has a one-word gap. For each set you have to think of one word which can be used appropriately in all three sentences. | 4 (56–57) |
| 5 | Key word transformations | 8 | You read a given sentence, and then complete a second sentence so that it has a similar meaning to the first one. You can use between three and six words, including one word which is given. | 5 (74–75) |

## Paper 4 Listening 40 minutes

There are four parts to this paper. All the listening texts are heard twice. The texts used are a variety of types. In some parts you hear just one speaker; in others more than one speaker.

| Part | Task Type | Number of Questions | Task Format | *Objective CAE* Exam Folder |
|---|---|---|---|---|
| 1 | Multiple choice | 6 | You hear three short extracts and have to answer two multiple-choice questions on each. Each question has three options, A, B and C. | 10 (146–147) |
| 2 | Sentence completion | 8 | You hear a text and have to write a word or short phrase to complete sentences. | 10 (146–147) |
| 3 | Multiple choice | 6 | You hear a text and have to answer multiple-choice questions with four options. | 11 (164–165) |
| 4 | Multiple matching | 10 | You hear a series of five short extracts. There are two matching tasks focusing on the gist and the main points of what is said, the attitude of the speakers and the context in which they are speaking. | 11 (164–165) |

## Paper 5 Speaking 15 minutes

There are four parts to this paper. There are usually two of you taking the examination together and two examiners. This paper tests your grammar and vocabulary, interactive communication, pronunciation and how you link your ideas.

| Part | Task Type | Time | Task Format | *Objective CAE* Exam Folder |
|---|---|---|---|---|
| 1 | Three-way conversation between two students and one of the examiners | 3 minutes | The examiner asks you both some questions about yourself and your interests and experiences. | 12 (176–177) |
| 2 | Individual 'long turn' with brief response from partner | 4 minutes | You are each given some visual and written prompts and the examiner will ask you to talk about these for about a minute. You are asked to give a short response after your partner has finished their 'long turn'. | 12 (176–177) |
| 3 | Two-way interaction between students | 4 minutes | You are given some visual prompts for a discussion or problem-solving task and you discuss these prompts with your partner. | 12 (176–177) |
| 4 | Three-way interaction between students and one of the examiners | 4 minutes | The examiner asks you questions relating to topics arising from Part 3. | 12 (176–177) |

# 1 Getting to know you

| Genre | Introductions |
|---|---|
| Topic | People and places |

| Speaking and Reading | People and places |
|---|---|
| Grammar | Conditionals |
| Reading | Cultural behaviour |
| Vocabulary | Collocations (adjective-noun, adverb-verb, adverb-adjective) |
| Listening | Meeting people |

**Workbook contents**

| Reading | Putting paragraphs into gaps, vocabulary |
|---|---|
| Vocabulary | Collocation |
| Writing | A description |
| Grammar | Conditionals |

## SB pages 10–13

Throughout the Teacher's Book guidance is given relating to the length of lesson: **SV** (short version) and **LV** (long version). The **SV** gives an indication of what can be cut out of the lesson if time is short or which parts could be set for homework. The **LV** gives suggestions on what could be developed and provides extension activities where appropriate.

> **Lesson planning**
> **SV** Grammar 3 could be set for homework
> **LV** See extension activities in the Speaking and Reading section

## Speaking and Reading

Introduce Unit 1 by asking students questions such as:

*Which English-speaking country do you know the most about?*
*Are you curious about other countries and cultures?*
*To what extent is learning about countries and their cultures part of learning a language?*

Generate a class discussion using these questions and establish that in order to appreciate a language fully, some knowledge of its culture can be an advantage. However, do not spend too much time on the discussion at this point as it is important to move on to the questions in the Student's Book and establish a lively pace.

1 The aim of tasks 1 and 2 is to generate interest in places. It allows students to bring their own knowledge to the group.

If this is your first lesson with the group, you may prefer to do question 1 as a whole-group activity. Alternatively, you could ask students to do question 1 in small groups. As you go through the answers, elicit students' knowledge of the places shown.

> **Answers**
> a The Blue Mosque, Istanbul, Turkey
> b The Great Wall of China
> c The Eiffel Tower, Paris, France
> d The White House, Washington DC, USA
> e Christ the Redeemer statue on Corcovado, Rio de Janeiro, Brazil

### **E**xtension activity

The ideas in questions 1 and 2 could be developed further by asking the students to prepare questions about countries they know. This could be part of a long-term project in which students research an English-speaking country.

2 Ask the students to read the extracts quickly and match them to the cities listed in the box. Explain that it is not necessary to understand every word in the extracts. If you have extra time, you could exploit the vocabulary in the extracts further.

> **Answers**
> a Cambridge, UK   b Sydney, Australia   c Cape Town, South Africa   d Cairo, Egypt   e Buenos Aires, Argentina

### **E**xtension activity

Students write a text describing a town they know well either in groups in class or for homework.

### **T**eaching extra

Promote learner independence by eliciting and thereby acknowledging what students already know. Guide them to find out background information or information about the language for themselves.

3  Go through the introduction to the quiz and then ask students to work in small groups to discuss their answers.

**Answers**
1 b  2 c  3 a  4 c  5 b  6 a

### Teaching extra

Throughout the course try to develop students' sensitivity to register. Check that they have recognised either informal or formal register by talking about the speakers, their relationship and the situation. Ask students to produce language in another register where appropriate.

4  Ask students to work with a partner and discuss the questions.

5  Ask students to work with a different partner and discuss the questions. When they have finished, elicit phrases from the class for question a and write them up on the board.

**Suggested answers**
*Would you mind if I asked ...   Do you mind if I ask ...*
*I don't mean to be personal but could I ask you ...*
*I hope you don't think it's rude but could I ask you ...*
*I wonder if you'd mind telling me ...*

Many people show their interest in listening to a speaker by making eye contact, leaning a little towards the speaker and using facial expressions such as nodding or shaking their head. Then there may be lots of *ahas*, *ums* and *yeahs*. Asking students to act out their suggestions for question b can be fun.

**Suggested answers**
*Sounds interesting/brilliant/awful* etc.   *I see.   Go on.*
*Oh really?   Wow!   Cool!   What!*
Short questions: *Do you? Have you?* etc.
Follow-up questions which develop what the speaker has just said.

6  The Exam spot draws attention to the fact that social English is helpful both in real life and in Part 1 of the CAE Speaking test (Paper 5). Go through the Exam spot with the students and ask them to prepare some questions to find out more about their partner. Point out that the questions can be phrased openly, e.g. *Tell me something about your family*. If necessary, give some examples such as *What do you like to do in your free time? What sort of job do you hope to do in the future?*

# Conditionals

The Grammar folder at the back of the Student's Book provides explanations and further examples. The grammar here is covered on page 190.

1  Read out the example of the second conditional and then refer to the table of conditional forms. Ask students to complete the rest of the table.

**Answers**

| Type | Tense – *if* clause | Tense – main clause | Use |
|---|---|---|---|
| zero | present simple/ continuous | present simple/ continuous | to talk about common states or events |
| first | present simple/ continuous | *will* *to be going to* present simple/ continuous | to talk about possible states or events |
| second | past simple/ continuous | *would* + infinitive without *to* | to talk about a situation which is hypothetical or very unlikely to happen |
| third | past perfect | *would have* + past participle | to talk about the past and say that now it is impossible to do anything about it |

2  This exercise introduces some of the more advanced forms of conditionals.

**Answers**
a If you experience any difficulties, I'll be available to help you.
b If it hadn't been for Jane's intervention, the meeting would have gone on far too long.
c I'll turn on the air conditioning if it makes you feel more comfortable.
d If you take your seats, ladies and gentlemen, the concert will begin.

3  Ask students to work on their own and then check their answers with a partner.

**Answers**
1 otherwise   2 Given   3 If so   4 unless   5 Provided

**GETTING TO KNOW YOU**

## Reading

1. Ask students to discuss questions a–c with a partner. Ask them to make notes of the main points of their discussion so that they can report back to the rest of the class when they have finished. Encourage cross-cultural awareness during the discussion.

2. Ask students to read the text and then answer the questions.

> **Answers**
> a Many British people tend to try to avoid potential personal conflict by backing off and allowing the other person a way out without causing embarrassment. On the other hand, confrontation is acceptable on large public occasions.
> b letting off steam
> c in response to an offer to avoid conflict

3. Ask students to discuss the questions in small groups.

> **Suggested answer**
> a It can be dangerous to make sweeping statements about a nationality as every nation is made up of a wide range of individuals. General statements will probably be untrue for at least some of the people. If the characteristics are negative, it may be offensive to voice them.

## Vocabulary

Go through the Vocabulary spot which explains what collocation is.

1. Refer back to the reading text *Close encounters of the British kind* and point out the examples of collocations given. Then ask students to work in pairs and find some more examples.

> **Suggested answers**
> to offer a way out   to express their true feelings
> the immediate linguistic consequence
> taking a middle route   engaging in open conflict
> make errors   unfamiliar environment

2. Ask students to work with a partner or in small groups. If this is the first time your students have done this sort of exercise, go through the example carefully. If students need further help as they are doing the exercise, give them the first letter of each missing word.

> **Suggested answers**
> a ring  b give, grant, ask  c mild  d genuine, heartfelt, sincere, warmest  e realise  f bear, cause, endure, feel, inflict, kill, soothe, stand, suffer

## Listening

Go through the information in the Exam spot. This task is slightly different from the CAE exam as here there are only seven options. (The CAE exam has eight options to choose from.) This should make it slightly easier for students.

1. Ask students to look at the pictures of places and as a class speculate about where these places might be and what it would be like to be there.

   Go through the instructions in 1. Play the recording and ask students to match the speakers to the pictures.

> **Answers**
> 1 C   2 E   3 B   4 A   5 D

2. Ask students to read through the topic headings. Play the recording again and ask students to match the speakers to the topics. In the exam students have to do both tasks as they listen to the text twice.

> **Answers**
> 1 E   2 C   3 F   4 A   5 G

3. Ask students to discuss this question in small groups or as a class. If you have extra time, you could encourage students to talk about some of their own adventures.

## Tapescript

**Speaker 1:** We went to some incredible places, a place which has the most famous mosque in the whole of North Africa. We went in and then some boys came and, well, they wanted to show us around. Well, we were a bit dubious but they did anyway. After that, they asked us to come to a carpet museum, and they said, really, you have to see that, it's wonderful, there are old Tunisian carpets. So we decided to go with them. And guess what! The museum turned out to be a carpet shop, owned by the father of one of the boys. And of course, he wanted to sell us a carpet. We actually didn't want to buy one because we didn't have enough space in our backpacks, but finally he managed to persuade us to buy one. So my friend, yeah, she bought one.
To thank us for that, the boys guided us around the town and we ended up going down these really narrow alleyways, and we had no idea where we were because this whole city was like a maze. Then we came to a house and we realised it was the house of one of the boys and we were invited in by his family and we had tea, coffee, nice biscuits, and it was a really, really good experience.

GETTING TO KNOW YOU

**Speaker 2:** My story is actually a bit bizarre. I was going to Florida and first we took a plane to New York and then to Florida and during the trip from New York to Florida I felt that I had to go to the bathroom. And in front of me there was a girl, she was about, perhaps twenty-five, very good-looking, who went into the bathroom, but she didn't lock the door, it was still on the er, … it wasn't completely locked. And I thought that maybe I should knock on the door and tell her that her door wasn't completely closed, but I didn't. And I also had a funny feeling that this wouldn't turn out well. And I was right because about thirty seconds later the door flew open and there she was on the loo, and she gave out a loud shriek and me and the rest of the queue just stood there in disbelief, totally in shock.

**Speaker 3:** Four years ago I went to Indonesia with my parents and my sister, which was, of course, a very beautiful holiday. First, we went to Sumatra and er, there we met a man who wanted to show us his village. So we went off with him. The village was very small, perhaps five hundred inhabitants, maybe less. And it was very special because the people there had never seen tourists before. So they acted like, yeah, they treated us like very special people, which we aren't, of course. They were a bit shy at first but then somehow we managed to communicate, and what I realised is that people, good people, are the same perhaps the world over.

**Speaker 4:** Well, with a few friends from my rowing club, we went on a weekend in the middle of winter in Holland. When we got there we couldn't even get out on the water, it was way too cold and we were in this big, er, shed, the size of a football pitch. There was no heating, the water was coming through the roof. The whole time it was windy and terrible. We went there by bike and it was about three hours, I think. And we just, you know, went on automatic pilot and went on and on and on. And in this shed we couldn't get warm and people started getting really irritable and we started fighting over stupid, stupid things, for example, who has to cook dinner, who has to do the dishes, and we were really nasty to each other. And we had to sleep all together in one corner otherwise we'd freeze to death. There were about twenty-five of us all huddled together, trying to sleep and hating each other.

**Speaker 5:** Whenever people talk about dolphins, they always say they're very intelligent creatures but I never really grasped the idea of how intelligent they are until this summer when I went to Zanzibar, which is a little island off Africa. And one of the things I did there was actually swimming with dolphins. When you go there, there are a few locals and you go on a boat with them, and even before you've seen anything their enjoyment really rubs off on you. They're laughing all the time and when they find some dolphins, they're really proud of themselves because they've found some dolphins and they know that you're really going to love it. What you have to do then is, you have to jump in the water, when the boat stops you jump in the water, and if you're lucky, the dolphins come straight at you, and then they dive really deep in the water so you can't see them any more. They hide themselves and then they come back. And when you see the look in their eyes, you see they're just making fun of you! And for me that's proof of how smart dolphins really are.

# Exam folder 1

## SB pages 14–15

## Paper 3 Part 1
## Multiple-choice gap fill

Remind students that there is a full description of the CAE exam on pages 8–9 of the Student's Book. Paper 3 has five parts and candidates have 1 hour to complete the paper. The Exam folders can be studied by students on their own outside class, but notes are given below for a mini-lesson in class.

Explain that the test focus in Paper 3 Part 1 is vocabulary. Point out that the general area of vocabulary can be subdivided into categories such as phrasal verbs, collocations and idioms and that the exam tests a range of different vocabulary areas.

Go through the examples of the types of words and expressions which can be tested. If you have a dictionary of collocations and a dictionary of phrasal verbs, it would be useful to show them to the students at this point. Then go through the Advice box. This gives students strategies for tackling this part of Paper 3.

Go through the task *Aunt Margaret's kitchen*, asking students to follow all the steps in the Advice box.

**Answers**
1 A  2 B  3 D  4 B  5 B  6 C  7 D  8 A  9 C
10 D  11 D  12 B

# 2 Keeping in touch

| Genre | Informal letters |
|---|---|
| Topic | Making contact |

| Speaking 1 | Keeping in touch |
| Writing | Informal letters |
| Grammar | Prepositions and adverbs |
| Vocabulary | Multiple meanings |
| Listening | Note taking |
| Speaking 2 | Developing what you want to say |

**Workbook contents**

| Writing | Informal letter |
| Reading | Analysing approaches to organisation, summarising |
| Grammar | Prepositions |

## SB pages 16–19

**Lesson planning**

SV  Grammar 2 or 3 could be set for homework
LV  See extension activities in the Grammar and Listening sections

## Speaking 1

1 Ask students to work with a partner to discuss questions a–c, which introduce the topic of the unit. Leave time for a class round up of the students' discussions.

## Writing

Go through the information in the Exam spot. Explain that if you know who the intended reader is, it should be clear which style, formal or informal, is suitable for the letter. It is also important that the purpose for writing is clear to the reader.

1 The aim of this question is to raise awareness about the reasons for writing informal letters. Ask the students to read through the letter quickly and answer question 1. Elicit the answer from the whole class.

**Answers**
to give information about finishing exams
to thank a friend for a present
to give information about a holiday

2 Ask students to work with a partner and to read the letter again in order to answer questions a–g.

**Answers**
a This letter does not give an exact address. The writer wants to draw attention to the fact that she is on holiday in Scotland rather than give the traditional house number, street and town. In many informal letters, English people will just write the name of their town as a short form of the address. The date in this letter is written as *Midsummer* rather than the traditional day, date and year. It is common to leave out the year in informal letters.
b beginnings: *Dear Sarah, Hello Sarah*, endings: *See you, Love and kisses, Lots of love, All the best*
c it resembles spoken English, e.g. *Anyway, what I really wanted to say was ...*
informal vocabulary, e.g. *nightie* instead of *nightdress*
slang, e.g. *swipe* instead of *steal/take*
d use of dash to indicate a pause
brackets to denote an aside
exclamation marks and rhetorical questions to engage the reader
e yes
f She wrote *PS* (postscript) followed by the information she had forgotten.
g Paragraph 1  I've gone from the stress of exams to the quiet of a holiday in a remote place.
Paragraph 2  Thank you for the present/T-shirt.
Paragraph 3  I'm going to explore other parts of the island tomorrow.

3 This question is very similar to the type of question candidates could find in the CAE Writing test (Paper 2). Here the points to be included in the reply are very clearly indicated with bullet points. The number of words required in the examination is approximately 250, but here the focus is more on content and style than on length. Students could work with a partner, in small groups, as a class with you writing up their sentences on the board or the question could be set as homework. It depends how much guidance your students need.

## Prepositions and adverbs

The grammar here is covered on page 190 of the Grammar folder.

1 Go through the introduction in the Student's Book.

2 This exercise could be set for homework.

> **Answers**
> a on the phone  b married to  c (from) sleeping
> d from / for  e on my way, at home
> f suffer from, in the summer  g in a rut
> h for next to nothing  i throughout the country
> j on time  k to the pub, under age  l as a teacher
> m on duty

3 Make sure that students read the whole text first before they start to fill the gaps. This technique will stand them in good stead for the exam.

> **Answers**
> 1 to  2 in/for  3 in  4 about  5 to  6 off  7 up
> 8 at  9 of  10 until/to  11 in  12 from  13 among/in
> 14 aside/away/down  15 with  16 of

### ⓔ xtension activity

Ask students to find another text, preferably from an authentic source and ask them to rewrite a passage deleting the prepositions and adverbs. They can then give their passage to another student to complete.

### ⓣ eaching extra

Encourage students to read in English. They could read either graded readers or authentic texts such as novels, short stories or magazines. Students can then use these sources for extension activities such as the one above.

4 Answering questions a and b reinforces the notion that all texts have been written to convey meaning or feelings; they should not be seen merely as exam practice. Questions c and d round off this section by personalising the situation for students.

> **Answers**
> a It was difficult to read the handwriting, so *bladder* was confused with *ladder*.
> b They usually reacted strongly (*indignant uproar*). The mother accepted that she would have to read out the long letter to everyone (*sigh of resignation – unfurled the twenty odd pages*).

## Vocabulary

Go through the Vocabulary spot, which explains what is meant by multiple meanings. Point out that an awareness of this feature of English vocabulary can help students to build up a richer vocabulary. Encourage them to check for multiple meanings when they look up words in the dictionary.

If your students find this exercise difficult, you could give them the first letter of the missing word and/or the number of letters in the missing word.

> **Answers**
> a foot  b last  c power  d round  e answer  f ran

## Listening

1 The aim is to provide a model of authentic native speech in an area similar to Part 1 of the CAE Speaking test (Paper 5). Encourage speculation about the two women's lives based on the pictures of them.

2 Ask students to work with a partner; one is to listen for Rebecca's answers and the other for Amanda's answers. Play the first part of the recording (up to *That's about it*). When they have finished making notes, students exchange the information. Encourage them to write key words, not full sentences.

| Answers Question | Main idea | Extra information |
| --- | --- | --- |
| *Rebecca* | | |
| Where are you from in England? | Nottingham | in the East Midlands |
| Have you studied any foreign languages? | French and German at school | a little bit of Italian in Italy |
| *Amanda* | | |
| Where are you from in England? | Bath | near Bristol |
| Have you studied any foreign languages? | Spanish | very difficult so gave up |

**KEEPING IN TOUCH**

Further details can be found in the tapescript. Accept any correct details. The aim is for students to see that answers are usually developed.

3 Point out that it will not be possible to write down everything students hear so notes will be sufficient.

**Answers**

| Topic | Main idea | Extra information |
|---|---|---|
| *Rebecca* | | |
| hobbies | wants to do self defence and dancing | wants new hobbies – only reading and music now |
| future hopes and dreams | be rich; have a donkey sanctuary; another degree, travel | when she's sixty on a Greek island; in History then Masters degree |
| living or working abroad permanently | yes | for a few years, somewhere sunny, warm and relaxed |
| earliest memories of school | Maths problem | couldn't watch TV with other students; went home; was told off by everyone |
| *Amanda* | | |
| hobbies | theatre; pictures; dancing | not much time for hobbies; thrillers/suspense; Middle Eastern dancing and yoga; didn't like yoga |
| future hopes and dreams | be happy | further studies, PhD when older |
| living or working abroad permanently | yes | end days in foreign country – different work ethos |
| earliest memories of school | school report | opened it instead of parents, was hit by teacher |

### Extension activity

Photocopy the tapescript and ask student to highlight the phrases which the women use to develop their answers.

The tapescript is on pages 179–180.

4 Ask students this question to round off the activity.

## Speaking 2

The aim here is to encourage students to develop their spoken answers.

1 If possible, elicit answers from the class as a whole and write up the students' suggestions on the board.

> **Suggested answer**
> A good communicator asks questions, takes turns, listens, develops answers and uses appropriate body language.

2 Ask students to read the Exam spot, then to work with a partner and suggest how answers to the questions could be developed.

> **Suggested answers**
> a size of city, facilities/amenities
> b pleasure, future job, studies
> c places visited/cinema/theatre/concert – why it was interesting
> d work, study, family, travel, ambitions

3 Ask students to work in groups of three. Go through the instructions in the Student's Book. Make sure time is allowed for feedback either within groups or to the class as a whole.

4 This question is included here so that students know how they are going to be assessed for the Speaking test. See Teaching extra (below) for further information.

### Teaching extra

All details about the CAE examination can be found at http://cambridgeesol.org.uk.
The assessment criteria for speaking are:

**Grammar resource**
Students are awarded marks for the accurate and appropriate use of a range of both simple and complex forms.

**Vocabulary resource**
Students are expected to use a range of vocabulary to meet the task requirements, for example, to speculate and exchange views.

**Discourse management**
Examiners are looking for evidence of the candidate's ability to express ideas and opinions in coherent, connected speech.

**Pronunciation**
Students are assessed on their ability to produce both individual sounds and prosodic features, i.e. linking of words, stress and intonation to convey intended meaning. Examiners are looking for the production of comprehensible sentences and communicative ability.

**Interactive communication**
Examiners are looking for the use of strategies to maintain interaction, e.g. conversational turn-taking.

# Writing folder 1

## SB pages 20–21

## Informal letters

1 This activity can be done with the whole class or in small groups.

> **Answers**
> a a friend writing to a friend – giving news about holiday plans – promising to tell him/her about the holiday when he/she returns
> b a friend writing to a friend – saying thank you for a present
> c a friend writing to a friend – regretting the fact that the friend could not go to a party as he/she was ill – giving news about who was at the party and hoping the friend will get better soon

2 The aim is for students to become aware of the features of informal letters.

> **Suggested answers**
> Choice of vocabulary: phrasal verbs, informal vocabulary, idioms, phrases with *get*, *take*, *have*, etc.
> Grammatical features: reported speech, contractions, direct questions, etc.
> Length of sentences: a mixture of short and long sentences
> Linking words: informal linking words to improve the flow of the language and link ideas between the paragraphs
> Punctuation: exclamation marks (to show surprise), dashes (to show a pause or change of thought), brackets (to show something is an aside or was forgotten)

3 Remind students that they do not need to write addresses in the exam.

> **Suggested answers**
> a 24 Sturton Street, Chelmsford, CH3 4RB *or* Glasgow
> b 3/6/08 *or* Mon 5th
> c Dear Jose *or* Hi Sarah!
> d main body of letter
> e Lots of love / Bye for now
> f Andrea / John

4 It can be very useful for students to build up a stock of set phrases to use or adapt in the CAE Writing test (Paper 2).

5 Encourage students to read the question and plan carefully. Students could work in pairs or small groups to prepare the first draft of the letter. If you would like to highlight one aspect of writing, e.g. linking devices, you could ask students to highlight examples of that feature. Ask students to write approximately 250 words.

When students exchange their first drafts, encourage constructive criticism and a keen eye for errors. Draw their attention to the Advice box.

# 3 The real you

| | |
|---|---|
| Genre | Interviews |
| Topic | Career paths |

| | |
|---|---|
| Speaking 1 | Interviews with famous people |
| Reading | Interview with a model |
| Listening | Interview with a soap opera star |
| Grammar | Wish / if only, it's time, would rather/sooner |
| Vocabulary | Idioms (verb + the + object) |
| Speaking 2 | Role play |

**Workbook contents**

| | |
|---|---|
| Reading | Supply questions for answers |
| Vocabulary | Vocabulary from the reading text |
| Grammar | I wish, I'd rather, If only, It's time, asking questions |

## SB pages 22–25

### Lesson planning
- **SV** Grammar 2 and Vocabulary 2 or 4 could be set for homework
- **LV** See extension activities in the Speaking 1 and Grammar sections

## Speaking 1

### Extension activity

If you have any copies of this kind of magazine, bring them into the class to generate interest. If a story concerning a famous person has recently broken, you could refer to it and discuss it.

1 Ask students to work with a partner to discuss the questions. Allow time for class feedback if possible.

## Reading

### Teaching extra

Prediction exercises help bridge the gap between the classroom and real life. In real life we usually have impressions of people before we really get to know them or we can have a good guess at the content of an interview. Prediction exercises help students bring this ability or knowledge to their second-language learning.

1 If necessary, give an example of the sort of question we might expect an interviewer to ask a model, e.g. *What are your beauty secrets?*

   Tell the students that the interviewer is a woman and ask them to predict some other questions she might ask the model. When the students have run out of ideas, write their suggestions up on the board and leave them there until you have read the text.

2 Read the text quickly. Ask students which questions on the board were asked. Even if the question is not the same, if it covers the same topic, tick it off. Then ask the students what other questions were asked.

3 Allow time for students to discuss their answers and then go through them with the whole class. Try to elicit more information than the questions demand, e.g. *Why was coming from Denmark significant?*

### Answers
a her family upbringing
  the fact that she comes from Denmark
b She just went in, did the job and then left.
c She went to Paris while the fashion show was on so she met people in the fashion business.
d photography
e She has worked with many great photographers and some of their experience has rubbed off on her. She also knows what it feels like to be photographed.
f She has her own magazine and the idea was that she should be the creative director but she just wants to write and take some of the photographs.
g Men are intimidated by female models until they start talking to them.

4 Ask students to work with a different partner and discuss questions a–e.

## Listening

1 Elicit the meaning of the phrase *to have one or two skeletons in the cupboard* (i.e. to have secrets which would cause embarrassment if they were known) and ask students what kind of past they think David Burns might have had. Write up the suggestions on the board and generate interest in hearing about this actor. Suggested skeletons in the cupboard could be:
   - unhappy relationships
   - problems at school
   - crime
   - problems in childhood.

   Leave the suggestions up on the board until you have listened to the interview.

2 Listen to the interview and then check which problems in his life David Burns talks about. Check what was said against the suggestions on the board.

> **Answers**
> school life, a person who helped him, fans, his working relationship with a director, his marriage, his daughter

3 Ask students to listen again for how the phrases a–k are used in context. They should try to work out the meaning.

> **Teaching extra**
>
> Promote the habit of deducing meaning from context, which in turn promotes learner independence. When students do look words up in a dictionary, encourage them to take note of the multiple meanings (see Unit 2).

4 If practical, after listening, encourage students to walk around the classroom to try to find a student who can help them with some of the words they do not know. Have some English-English dictionaries available for students to check the meanings and make yourself available if all other means fail.

> **Answers**
> a a person in the public eye is written about in newspapers and seen on TV
> b a person who hurts or frightens others
> c an unkind remark made intentionally to annoy and upset someone
> d situation where things go wrong and it feels as if nothing can be done to prevent it
> e became aware of a person's feelings and situation
> f playing the role of bad people who harm others or break the law
> g a nervous/anxious person
> h it can become very unpleasant
> i unable to stop thinking about something
> j I wanted all the public attention for myself
> k it's a secret

5 and 6 Ask students to work with a partner to discuss these questions.

## Tapescript

**Interviewer:** With me today in the studio is David Burns, who freely admits that he has had a troubled past. And when I read through this potted biography; a difficult childhood, married to a fellow soap opera star, a relationship with a famous actress, an 11-year-old daughter from a subsequent relationship … all I can say, David, is that your life has been a roller coaster. It's no wonder you're constantly in the public eye. Do you think it all started in your teenage years?

**David:** I think it all stemmed from when I was at school. When I was about 14 I was picked on by a bully. One day he went too far with a taunt about my mother. I snapped; I really laid into him.

**Interviewer:** What happened?

**David:** Oh, there was a big fuss at school and I was branded a troublemaker. My mum began to think she couldn't cope with me. Things were going from bad to worse.

**Interviewer:** And how did you get out of that downward spiral?

**David:** I was lucky. A drama teacher we had really tuned into me. She said I could choose to go whichever direction I wanted. I could continue playing truant, getting into trouble or I could make something of myself. She said I had talent. Was I prepared to ignore that for a life of trouble and misery?

**Interviewer:** I wonder if directors see that tough upbringing because the irony is that you've specialised in playing villains …

**David:** I've always been an edgy person. I can bring that out if the part demands it. I've got a dark side. People say they can see an element of that in my eyes.

**Interviewer:** And how does that affect your fan mail? Does it mean that people think they don't like you as a person as well as the parts you play?

**David:** Er, I get a very mixed reception. There are fans that write very complimentary letters, saying I'm good-looking and that sort of thing, but then there are those who seem to become obsessed and it can turn nasty.

**Interviewer:** What do you mean?

**David:** Well, for example, a fan became obsessed, sort of jealous, and she caused me a lot of problems. She didn't like anyone in the TV series getting near me. She'd send 50 letters every week and pictures from the show with everyone cut out except me. Then she wrote to another

THE REAL YOU

cast member saying she knew I had a daughter. That's when I went to my producer who contacted the police and social services got involved.

**Interviewer:** Tell us about your experience in *Joseph And The Amazing Technicolor Dreamcoat* …

**David:** I played the lead role. I did it for two years – and then I got sacked. The director saw I was getting a lot of attention. I think it was thought I was hogging the limelight. It may have been internal politics, but I wasn't even given the chance to give my final performance.

**Interviewer:** And tell us about your marriage to your fellow soap opera star Julia Watts …

**David:** Looking back, I don't think we were destined to grow old together. We just didn't know it at the time. But she's a great actress. She could be in the soap for another 20 years. She's brilliant in it. We've each said things in the press which I'm sure we both regret. I was offered a fortune to tell my story, but I'm not interested. But when she was in another TV series which did quite well, she couldn't give an interview without having a go at me.

**Interviewer:** And what about your daughter, Sarah?

**David:** She's 11 and she's very beautiful and assured. Her mother, Carol, was a model. We separated a couple of years ago, but we've always put Sarah first. She lives with Carol and I see her every other weekend.

**Interviewer:** Will you ever marry again?

**David:** Yeah, I hope so. I'm in a relationship with someone who's not in show business. But my lips are sealed on that. All I'll say is that I do believe in marriage.

## Wish and *if only*

The grammar here is covered on page 191 of the Grammar folder.

Go through the introduction to the *wish* and *if only* section.

1  In order to establish the grammatical forms which can follow *wish* or *if only*, ask students to complete sentences a–i. If necessary, go through the first sentence as an example.

**Answers**
a had started
b had / had had
c would come / came / had come
d to inform
e to be disclosed
f were/was
g would brighten up / had brightened up
h wouldn't ask / didn't ask / hadn't asked
i had known

### Extension activity

If you would like to spend more time on *wish* or *if only*, write up the following headings on the board and go through sentences a–i completing the grid.

| | Form | Time reference | Feelings |
|---|---|---|---|
| a | past perfect | past | regret |
| b | past simple | present/past | a wish for change; regret |
| c | would | present/future | regret, dissatisfaction, impatience |
| d | infinitive | present and future | X |
| e | passive infinitive | present and future | X |
| f | unreal past | present | regret |
| g | would | present/future | regret, dissatisfaction, impatience, irritation |
| h | wouldn't/ past simple | present | dissatisfaction, impatience, irritation |
| i | past perfect | past | regret |

2  Encourage a class discussion to consolidate the use of structures after *wish* and *if only*.

## It's time, would rather/sooner

1  This exercise establishes which structures are possible after *It's time* and *would rather/sooner*.

**Answers**
*It's time* + **a** and **e**
*I'd rather/sooner* + **b** and **e**
**c** and **d** are not correct with either structure

2  This exercise could be set for homework. Ask students to read through the whole text first to get the gist of it.

**Answers**
1 had / would have  2 read  3 woke
4 had been born  5 to do

3  Point out that students should use *It's time*, *I'd rather* or *I'd sooner* when appropriate.

## Vocabulary

Refer students to the Vocabulary spot on page 24, then go through the introduction to this section pointing out the pattern of the idiom (verb + *the* + object).

1   Students can check the answers and meaning with each other, in a dictionary or with you.

**Answers**
a 4   b 1   c 6   d 2   e 3   f 5

2   This exercise could be set for homework.

**Answers**
1 test the water   2 delivered the goods
3 called the shots   4 saw the light

3   Ask students to work with a partner or in small groups to discuss these questions. The aim is to encourage students to check the meaning of unknown words and phrases, to be more independent and to develop good learning strategies.

4   This exercise could be set for homework.

**Answers**
1 c   2 e   3 a   4 d   5 b

## Speaking 2

1   Students should work with a partner. Make sure that students do not all choose the same person.

2   If your class is quite big, you may prefer to have two interviewers working together and two famous people together. As the students are working on their questions, go round and encourage a variety of question styles, such as direct questions, open questions and polite questions. Remind students that they should not mention the interviewee by name because the other students are going to try to guess who is being interviewed.

3   Set up the role play. Ask students to do their interview in front of the class. You could also either record or video the interviews, telling students that they can vote on the best chat show. Ask students to guess who they think the interviewees are.

4   Ask students this question as a round up.

# Exam folder 2

## SB pages 26–27

## Paper 3 Part 2
## Open gap fill

Go through the introduction to this task type.

1   Ask students to complete sentences a–j.

**Answers**
| | | |
|---|---|---|
| a | preposition | of |
| b | reflexive pronoun | herself |
| c | linking device | whereas/while |
| d | determiner | every |
| e | verb | need |
| f | relative pronoun | which/that |
| g | linking device | whether/if |
| h | possessive pronoun | its |
| i | part of phrasal verb | out |
| j | linking device | Although/Though |

2–5   Go through questions 2–5 as these give students the strategy for dealing with this task type.

6   Go through the Advice box with students, then ask them to complete the text.

**Answers**
| | | |
|---|---|---|
| 1 | which | pronoun |
| 2 | as | linking device |
| 3 | its | possessive pronoun |
| 4 | turns | part of phrasal verb |
| 5 | thus/so/therefore | linking device |
| 6 | When/Once | linking device |
| 7 | something | pronoun |
| 8 | whether | linking device |
| 9 | can/may | modal verb |
| 10 | into | preposition |
| 11 | from | preposition |
| 12 | Also/Moreover/Furthermore | linking device |
| 13 | this/our | determiner |
| 14 | without | preposition |
| 15 | let/allow | verb |

# 4 Acting on instructions

| Genre | Instructions |
|---|---|
| Topic | Memory techniques |

| Listening 1 | Following instructions |
| Speaking | Giving instructions |
| Reading | Tips and techniques for improving memory |
| Grammar | Modal verbs: *may, might, can, could* |
| Writing | Giving instructions |
| Listening 2 | Instructions over the phone |
| Vocabulary | Prefixes and suffixes |

**Workbook contents**

| Use of English | Part 1 multiple-choice gap fill |
| Reading | Grouping words under headings |
| Writing | A recipe |
| Vocabulary | Prefixes, suffixes, irregular plurals |
| Grammar | Modals: *can, could, may, might* |

## SB pages 28–31

**Lesson planning**

SV  Grammar 3 or the Writing section could be set for homework

LV  See extension activities in the Listening 1 and Reading sections

## Listening 1

1  Use the first question to introduce the unit. Discuss with students the stressful situations illustrated in the pictures.

2  Ask students to do the exercises as they listen. Play the recording once only.

## Tapescript

Gently lean your head to one side. Breathe in. Hold for three seconds and then breathe out. Repeat to the other side.

Lift your arms up from your sides to above your head and hold for three seconds. Breathe in. Place your arms behind your head and breathe out. Repeat twice.

Bend your foot upwards, spread your toes and hold for three seconds. Point your foot downwards, clenching your toes and hold for three seconds. Repeat twice.

3  Ask students to work with a partner to discuss the questions. Prompt them to think of other grammatical forms that could be used to give instructions. If necessary, play the recording again.

**Answer**
The imperative is used in the example. This could also be expressed using a polite request.

### Extension activity

Elicit from students what makes good clear instructions. This can act as a useful link to the next Speaking activity. The instructions need to be precise, use the exact words, and the order must be clear. Linking devices are very important. Elicit the type of linking words which would be appropriate, e.g. *Firstly, secondly, then, next, finally, while*.

## Speaking

1  Students could work with a partner to establish the correct sequence.

**Answers**
1 e  2 b  3 g  4 c  5 a  6 d  7 f

2  If you think your students would prefer to talk about something else, let them choose their own subject or give other suggestions, e.g. how to use the transport system in their home town.

## Reading

1  Introduce the reading text by asking students to work with a partner and discuss questions a–c. Leave time for class feedback before going on to question 2.

2  Read through the tips and then ask students to discuss with a partner which recommendations are the most effective and why. This encourages students to give a natural response to the reading, which is what they would do in their own language.

### Extension activity

You might like to initiate discussion on some of the tips which you think are particularly useful for language learning and ask students how they could apply them to learning English.

3 This question could be discussed as a class or in small groups.

> **Extension activity**
>
> You could also talk about how students are keeping notes of their language learning, which will be of use for revision before the CAE exam.

4 Go through the instructions for this activity making sure that everyone understands that Group A reads 1, Group B reads 2 and Group C reads 3. This will lead on to an information gap activity so it is important that students only read their text, although they all read the introduction.

5 Students exchange information when they have regrouped.

6 If the majority of students are interested in one of the techniques, try to encourage its use throughout the course.

## Modals: *may, might, can, could*

The aim is to draw attention to the range of uses of some common modal verbs. The grammar here is covered on pages 191–192 of the Grammar folder. Go through the examples together.

1 Ask students to work with a partner and go through question 1.

> **Answers**
> a ability   b offer   c negative certainty   d request
> e order   f theoretical possibility   g permission

2 Elicit the difference in meaning in the pairs of sentences.

> **Answers**
> 1a The use of *could* suggests a general ability; the person could always get into the house by the back door.
> 1b The use of *was able to* suggests that the person is referring to one specific achievement/occasion.
> 2a She may get here ...   *may* is used for possibility
> 2b May I use ...   *May* is used for asking for permission (formal)
> 3a She might get here ...   *might* is used for possibility (smaller possibility than *may*)
> 3b Might I make a suggestion?   *Might* is used for asking tentatively for permission (formal)

3 Point out the perfect form *might have* + past participle and the continuous form *might be* + *-ing*. Go through the two examples which relate to the pictures and elicit other possibilities from students.

> **Suggested answers**
> a He might have been caught in the rain.
> b She might have just passed her exam.
> c She might have fallen over.
> d They might have just had an accident.
> e She might be marking some homework.
> f He might be paying off a debt.
> g They might have got lost.

## Writing

You might like students to work in pairs and prepare this writing task in class first. Alternatively, you could set it for homework. If you think it is necessary, go over the main points regarding giving instructions: layout, grammatical structures, choice of vocabulary, linking devices and clarity so that students are sure of what they should do. Encourage students to choose a subject which they find interesting.

## Listening 2

1 Elicit students' experience of talking to machines when they phone a company.

> **Answers**
> 1 *Phoning the cinema*
>   a press 1
>   b press 2
> 2 *Phoning an airline*
>   a press 2
>   b press 4
>   c bring your flight details and some form of identification with a photograph on it
> 3 *Phoning a telephone and Internet provider*
>   a call 0800 952 43 43 or visit the website at www.askstl.com
>   b press 2 to speak to the fault management centre
>   c press 5 to speak to Telesales

## Tapescript

1 Thank you for calling MovieMax Booking Information Service. Please press the star key on your telephone twice now. If you wish to book for *Cast Away*, please press 1 now, otherwise stay on the line for all other films. If at any time during the call you make a mistake and want to change the previous selection, press the star key. If you wish to book for *Cast Away*, press 1. If you wish to book for any other film and know the details, press 2. If you'd like information, press 3.

**ACTING ON INSTRUCTIONS**

2 Thank you for calling PanAir, Europe's low fares airline now available for easy booking on *PanAir.com*. If you are using a Touch-Tone phone, please select one of the four following options. For timetable information, please press 1. If you wish to make a booking, press 2. For general enquiries, press 3. Or to book a last-minute promotional offer, press 4. If you are not using a Touch-Tone phone, please hold the line and a PanAir agent will be with you shortly. Please note that PanAir is now a ticketless airline. In order to check in all you need are your flight details and a form of photo ID. A receipt will be sent to you but it is not necessary for check-in. Thank you for calling PanAir.

3 Hi, thanks for calling STL. Please listen carefully to the following options which are designed to help us assist you with your call. If your call is regarding information for our exciting new Internet service, STL World, which is available through your PC or even through your TV, please call our exclusive hotline number on 0800 952 43 43, that's 0800 952 43 43. Alternatively, visit our website at *www.askstl.com*. If you would like to make a payment by credit or debit card, please press 1 on your telephone key pad. If you need to report a fault on your service, including the Internet, please press 2 to speak to our fault management centre. If you have an enquiry about an existing account and would like to speak to a representative, please press 3. If you would like to change the channels you currently subscribe to, please press 4 to leave your account details. If you are not an existing customer and would like information about the services we offer, please press 5 to speak to Telesales. For all other enquiries, please hold while we transfer you to a customer service representative.

2 Generate discussion of this topic according to how interested your students are in it.

## Vocabulary

> **Teaching extra**
>
> In Part 3 of the CAE Use of English test (Paper 3), the words which candidates have most difficulty with are often those which require them to add a prefix or suffix. In many cases, this may be because candidates have not read the text for meaning.

1 Refer students to the Exam spot, then go through the introduction with the class.

Ask students to work with a partner and put the words under the correct heading. Check if the meaning of any of the words is unknown before students do the exercise.

**Answers**

| dis- | il- | im- | in- |
|---|---|---|---|
| disappear | illogical | immature | inaccessible |
| discontinue | illiterate | imprison | insensitive |
| distrust | | impolite | inconclusive |
| | | immaterial | |

| ir- | non- | mis- | un- |
|---|---|---|---|
| irresistible | non-iron | mislead | unbelievable |
| irregular | non-smoker | mistrust | untimely |
| | | | unexpected |

2 Use the table to elicit the rules for the use of *im-*, *il-* and *ir-*.

**Answers**
a *im*  b *il*  c *ir*

Go through the introduction to suffixes with the class.

3 Ask students to work with a partner and put the words under the correct heading. Check if the meaning of any of the words is unknown before students do the exercise.

**Answers**

| -able | -ation | -ency | -ful |
|---|---|---|---|
| photocopiable | emancipation | emergency | deceitful |
| countable | dramatisation | frequency | careful |
| employable | recommendation | tendency | respectful |
| arguable | | | |
| recommendable | | | |
| respectable | | | |
| reliable | | | |

| -ly | -less | -ment | -ness |
|---|---|---|---|
| timely | countless | judg(e)ment | rudeness |
| rudely | timeless | employment | calmness |
| frequently | speechless | argument | |
| calmly | careless | | |
| | pointless | | |

4 Enlarge and make copies of the suffix cards (in the Photocopiable activities section at the back of the book on page 183) according to the number of students in your group. Cut up the suffix cards, giving five to ten cards to each pair or small group of students. Write the teacher's words on individual cards. Shuffle the teacher's words and read them out one by one. If a student has the suffix for the word read out, they should hold up their card and say the complete word. If it is right, the student gives the card to you. If the word is wrong, they keep the card. The first student to hand in all their cards is the winner.

You could also ask students to work in groups and make their own word cards to play the game again at a later date. Alternatively, you could ask one of the students to read out the teacher's words.

**ACTING ON INSTRUCTIONS**

# Writing folder 2

## SB pages 32–33

## Essays

You might like to introduce this Writing folder by asking your students to think of examples of school/academic essays they have written where they had to express their opinion and argue the case.

1. In order to help students to plan essays, first look at the *Content* column of the table, explaining that this is what is typically included at each stage of an essay. Then ask the students, in pairs, to choose from the list of purposes and write them in the appropriate place in the *Purpose* column.

2. In the table, students should tick the purposes that have been included in the sample essay.

> **Answers (1 and 2)**
>
> | Stage of essay | Content | Purpose |
> |---|---|---|
> | Introduction | General statement<br>Definition(s) – optional<br>Scope of essay | 1 To introduce the reader to the topic ✓<br>2 To explain what is understood by some key words/concepts<br>3 To tell the reader what you intend to cover in this essay ✓ |
> | Body | Arguments<br>Evidence | 4 To express important ideas ✓<br>5 To support ideas with examples ✓ |
> | Conclusions | Summary<br>Relate the argument to a more general world view | 6 To remind the reader of the key ideas ✓<br>7 To underline the writer's point of view ✓ |

3. Highlight the importance of using linkers in writing (and speaking) – they act as signposts for the reader so that he/she can follow your line of argument.

> **Answers**
> while, On the one hand, In addition, for example, On the other hand, and the like, because, and, In my opinion, Moreover
>
> Most of the linkers are formal; *and the like*, *and* and *because* are less formal.
>
> *On the one/other hand*, *In addition*, *for example*, *In my opinion* and *Moreover* are followed by a comma.

4. Students could work in small groups straight away to complete the table or you could work with the class as a whole, eliciting some ideas and writing them up on the board. You could then let students work in small groups to complete the table.

> **Example Answer**
> - Who is the reader? my teacher
> - Style? Formal
> - Length? 250 words
>
> | Stage of essay | Content | Purpose |
> |---|---|---|
> | Introduction | – More people are studying English<br>– English, Spanish, Chinese as world language?<br>– Discuss ways in which it will be easier<br>– Examine what we may lose | 1 To introduce the reader to the topic<br>2 To tell the reader what you intend to cover in this essay |
> | Body | For one language<br>Everyone learns at young age – easy (eg bilingual children)<br>Travel: easier to make arrangements, get help, get info, meet people<br>Study: easier to follow any course, anywhere (but not always poss – visas etc.)<br>Better job prospects<br>Might lose:<br>Cultural identity<br>Thrill of travel | 3 To express important ideas<br>4 To support ideas with examples |
> | Conclusion | Many activities will be easier but keep cultural identity/traditions | 5 To remind the reader of the key ideas<br>6 To underline my point of view |

# 5 Dear Sir or Madam

| Genre | Formal letters |
| --- | --- |
| Topic | Dream jobs |
| Speaking | Formal letters |
| Reading | The secrets of writing business letters |
| Writing | A job application |
| Vocabulary | Connotation (positive, negative and neutral) |
| Grammar | Relative clauses |
| Listening | A dream job |
| **Workbook contents** | |
| Grammar | Relative clauses |
| Vocabulary | Connotation |
| Use of English | Part 1 multiple-choice gap fill |
| Writing | A formal letter |

## SB pages 34–37

**Lesson planning**

SV  Writing 5 and Vocabulary 3 could be set for homework

LV  See the extension activity in the Speaking section

## Speaking

1 Answering question a will establish what we mean by formal letters and highlight the importance of the purpose of a letter. Answers to question b may depend on the age and mother tongue of your students.

2 Ask students to read the extracts from formal letters and to decide on the purpose of each letter. Draw attention to formal set phrases, e.g. *on behalf of …* and formal vocabulary, e.g. *commence*.

**Answers**
a to express sympathy for a person's ill health
b to apologise for an awkward situation
c to remind someone about an unpaid invoice
d to offer someone employment
e to introduce a colleague
f to request information

3 Point out that the position of the sender's address can vary as some companies have their name and address on headed paper, often at the top of the page in the centre. However, when an individual is sending a formal letter, this is a common layout.

**Answers**
a 2  b 6  c 1  d 4  e 7  f 3  g 5

### Extension activity

Students plan and write the rest of this letter, describing the items which went missing. They should complain that they have heard nothing from the hotel since they left, and outline the course of action which they will take.

4 Point out to students that these salutations are used in British English but there are other forms, mainly in American English, which students may see, e.g. *Yours truly*. If we open a formal letter with *Dear (name)*, we close it with *Yours sincerely*.

## Reading

1 You could brainstorm the 'secrets' of writing business letters as a whole class first, writing students' suggestions up on the board. Then ask students to work with a partner and to match the headings with the 'secrets'.

**Answers**
1 f  2 c  3 e  4 g  5 h  6 d  7 b  8 a

2 Ask students to work with a partner. Allow time for class feedback for discussion of the main points.

## Writing

Go through the Exam spot and point out that in the CAE Writing test (Paper 2), students may be asked to write an informal and/or formal letter so it is very important that they can distinguish between the two. Remind students of their discussions in the Speaking section.

1 Go through the advertisement for the job with the students. They will first have to identify what qualities and skills are needed for the job.

**Answers**
up-to-date knowledge on travel options, excellent organisational skills, IT literate, good communication skills, self-motivation, organisation, ability to work to deadlines, good numeracy

2 Students plan their letter with a partner in response to the job advertisement.

3 Students then compare their plans and decide on the best ideas.

4 Ask students to write the first draft of the letter in pairs. Monitor them as they work, checking layout, punctuation and language. Students should then swap first drafts with another student.

5 Students write the final draft in class if time permits, so that a good final version is produced which can then be kept as an example. Alternatively, this could be set for homework.

6 To round off the writing section, get students to talk about the job in small groups, giving reasons why it would or would not appeal to them.

## Vocabulary

Go through the Vocabulary spot with students to make sure that they understand the concept of connotation.

1 Ask students what they know about Dian Fossey, then encourage them to read the text quickly and answer the questions.

**Answers**
a false  b true  c false  d false  e false

2 Ask students to work with a partner and classify the words under the headings.

**Answers**

| Positive | Negative | Neutral |
|---|---|---|
| mansion | shack | house |
| praise | judgment | evaluation |
| state-of-the-art | new-fangled | modern |
|  | nosy | inquisitive |
| courageous | foolhardy |  |
| innocent | gullible | naive |

3 This exercise could be set for homework.

**Answers**
1 sound  2 steely  3 solitude  4 detailed
5 keen  6 intriguing

## Relative clauses

Most students at this level will have studied relative clauses before but the omission of the relative pronoun and the position of prepositions provide advanced practice. The grammar here is covered on pages 192–193 of the Grammar folder.

1 Use these sentences as a diagnostic tool to assess your students' knowledge of these structures.

**Answers**
a defining relative clause
b non-defining relative clause

2 Work through the differences in meaning with the students.

**Answers**
a This sentence means that *all* government officials wanted to convert gorilla habitats to farmland.
b This sentence means that only *some* government officials wanted to convert gorilla habitats to farmland.

3 Ask students to work with a partner if they find this exercise difficult.

**Suggested answers**
- Leakey gave the job to the person who showed the most determination.
- Fossey's PhD, which she obtained from Cambridge University, was based on her research in Africa.
- Fossey lived with gorillas in an area which is on the mountain slopes of the Democratic Republic of the Congo.
- Fossey, who had spent many years in Africa, met her untimely death there.

4 Elicit from students that we can leave out the relative pronoun when it is the object in its clause.

5 This exercise could be set for homework.

**Answers**
a Dian lived in a hut which had no electricity. (no alternative)
b The film of the story of her life made an impact ~~that~~ many people will never forget.
c The story ~~which~~ she told in the film made Dian Fossey a household name.
d The clothes ~~that~~ she wore in the jungle were old and worn.
e The place where she grew up has a different sort of beauty. (no alternative)
f The place ~~that~~ she grew up in is known to few, even in the USA.
g The people who made the film about Dian immediately realised the remarkable effect ~~that~~ her story has on whoever sees it.

> h She had an inspirational quality which defies analysis. (no alternative)
> i Her animals were often the only 'people' ~~that~~ she talked to for days on end.
> j Dian had an intimate relationship with the land, which to a large extent determined the way ~~that~~ she lived.

6 Ask students to rewrite the sentences in formal style, paying particular attention to the position of the prepositions.

> **Answers**
> a This is the area of research on which he is working.
> b Here are some new statistics in which you will be interested.
> c Is this the advertisement for the job for which you are applying?
> d Is this the experiment about which you were reading?
> e Is this the person with whom you have entered into correspondence?
> f She received a reply from the editor to whom she sent her paper.
> g Social Sciences is the category into which his work falls.
> h The college has cancelled the conference for which you wanted to enrol.

# Listening

1 The aim of the pre-listening questions is to get students thinking about the topic and to make the interview more interesting and accessible. After students have had enough time for their discussion, get some class feedback.

Go through the Exam spot and explain that sentence completion is one of the listening task types in the CAE Listening test (Paper 4).

2 Ask students to try to predict possible words which could fill the gaps.

3 Play the recording once and then ask the students to compare their answers. Play the recording again and remind students to check that the whole sentence makes grammatical and semantic sense.

> **Answers**
> a a camera crew  b calm  c sixth  d petrol
> e sponsors  f boat  g at university

## Tapescript

**Interviewer:** The darkness refuses to lift over the racetrack and the rain is beating against the windows of the motorhome. A tiny white race suit is hanging in the corner but the young man sat back on the sofa is not ready for it yet as he rubs his eyes and comes to terms with the fact that he could still be snuggled up in bed instead of putting himself on display yet again at such an unearthly hour. James, how did you get yourself into this business?

**James:** Well, it's all down to Frank Weston. He took a calculated risk with me when I was completely unknown. And then, as you know, it was a rapid change for me as I suddenly became famous.

**Interviewer:** How has your family coped with your fame and I suppose their fame too?

**James:** Well the fame thing doesn't bother me, most people don't disturb me when they see me eating in a restaurant or something like that but I think my mum finds it a bit unsettling, you know, having to deal with a camera crew every time she comes out of the house. And in fact, my sisters now, they don't come down to the track to see me race, they watch me on TV at home.

**Interviewer:** Your father has shown great faith in you, hasn't he?

**James:** Well, I think both of us have had many doubts at times about my talent but he reckons it's being calm which makes the difference between champions and the rest. He's amazing too; he's become really hardened to the constant attention. And he's the one who has to watch from the sidelines. I think that must be a lot worse than doing the race.

**Interviewer:** Yes, you had a scary moment in Australia, didn't you?

**James:** Yeah, I'd qualified twenty-first and in the race got up to sixth position before my car gave out. It was real scary. You've only got split seconds to make life and death decisions. In an instant I knew something had gone wrong with the car and then you've got to get off the track and out of the way of the other drivers as fast as you can.

**Interviewer:** And you did it. But from an early age you proved that you've got what it takes.

**James:** Oh, I don't know. When I left school as a teenager it was just hard work. I went from track to track around Europe. And, yeah, I suppose when I had to live in Italy and Belgium on my own it was a bit tough, but my dad was a great support. There were loads of funny times then too. I remember once my father had to borrow money for petrol so that I could get home for a race in Scotland. And that's only a couple of years ago.

**Interviewer:** Things are very different now; you've got sponsors queuing up to take you on and make you a millionaire.

**James:** And I've already got more money than I'd ever dreamed of. And I'm trying to be sensible with the money but I must admit to one or two indulgences.
**Interviewer:** Yes, I've heard about the Ferrari in the garage and the BMW sports car. What's next on the list?
**James:** You make me sound irresponsible and I suppose to many people I must seem that way. But it's strange what money and fame can do to you. I mean it just seems normal to me now to have all those things and, in fact, next on my shopping list is a boat. I'd love that, to have it somewhere hot.
**Interviewer:** Does this mean that you have nothing or little in common with your old school friends now?
**James:** When I go back home I still meet up with my old mates but lots of them have moved on too, they're at university in different places so I only get to see them when they have holidays and they're back at home too. I suppose at our age people are moving around a lot and doing different things. I don't think my situation is any different. It's just that I've changed jobs. But when we meet up we still talk about the same things.
**Interviewer:** He might just be a lad with his mates but on Sunday he will be the new young star of Formula One, driving in front of five hundred million TV viewers.

4  Round off the Listening section with a class discussion.

# UNITS 1–5 Revision

## SB pages 38–39

## Topic review

Ask students to work with a partner to discuss questions a–j. The aim of this exercise is to encourage students to recycle the vocabulary and structures they have covered in the preceding units in a personalised way.

## Grammar

1  If you think your students will need more guidance to complete the text, you could give them the root of the verb required.

**Answers**
1 could say   2 hadn't come / wasn't / weren't
3 go / we went   4 could have come / had come / were
5 grew   6 had come / were

2  When checking the answers, check that students have understood what type of word is required and go through the meanings of the distractors.

**Answers**
1 D  2 B  3 C  4 A  5 D  6 A  7 C  8 B  9 C
10 D  11 C  12 D

## Vocabulary

1  Ask students to work with a partner. Make English–English dictionaries available for the students if possible.

**Suggested answers**
a  sit, take, pass, fail   b  enter   c  forces, laws, wonders
d  clear, creative, great, lateral, logical, muddled, original
e  accumulate, amass, have, honour, pay off

2  Ask students to complete the sentences with an appropriate word formed with a prefix or suffix.

**Answers**
a  misled   b  shatterproof   c  popularity   d  boyhood
e  underdone   f  reclaim   g  heartless

3  Point out to students that the connotation of a word depends on the context where it is used, so the following words might not always carry a negative connotation.

**Answers**
Words with negative connotations: simplistic, shack gorge/gobble, aggressive, criticism
Words with positive connotations: a challenge, inexpensive, inquisitive, childlike, innocent

4  This exercise allows students to use connotation in a very personalised way.

5  Encourage students to read the whole biography first for gist.

**Answers**
1 in/for   2 with   3 across/onto   4 from   5 on
6 to   7 into   8 with   9 in   10 at   11 on
12 to/of   13 at/from   14 in   15 for/in

# TEST 1

## Paper 1 Part 1

You are going to read three extracts which are all concerned in some way with names.
For questions 1–6, choose the answer (**A**, **B**, **C** or **D**) which you think fits best according to the text.

# What's in a name?

In England alone there are around 45,000 different surnames and the sources from which names are derived are almost endless: nicknames, physical attributes, counties and trades. Tracing a family tree involves looking at lists of these names – this is how we recognise our ancestors when we find them.

Before the Norman Conquest of Britain, people did not have hereditary surnames: they were known just by a personal name or nickname. When communities were small each person was identifiable by a single name, but as the number of inhabitants grew, it became necessary to identify people further – leading to names such as John the butcher or Henry from Sutton. Over time many names became corrupted and their original meaning is now not easily seen.

After 1066, the Norman barons introduced surnames into England. Initially, the identifying names were changed or dropped at will, but eventually they began to stick and to get passed on. So, trades, nicknames, places of origin became fixed surnames. By 1400 most English families had adopted the use of hereditary surnames.

Many individuals and families have changed their names or adopted an alias at some time in the past. This could be for legal reasons, or simply on a whim, but points up the fact that although the study of surnames is vital in family history research, it is all too easy to place excessive emphasis on them.

It is important to be aware that both surnames and forenames are subject to variations in spelling, and not only in the distant past. Standardised spelling did not really arrive until the 19th century, and even in the present day, variations occur.

1 The author explains that, in Britain, people began to have more than just one name as a result of
  A the increase in bureaucracy.
  B the increase in population.
  C the desire to pass on family history.
  D the need to get a register for work.

2 The aim of this text is to
  A encourage readers to research their family history.
  B advise family researchers to go back to before 1400.
  C demonstrate how easy it is to change one's name.
  D warn researchers not to rely too heavily on surnames.

# Naming your domain

You've come up with the invention of all time; you're going to conquer the world and make a fortune. Your next step is to set up a domain on the internet where you can start conducting your business. Now you just need to find the perfect name for it. You go to the internet and start punching in clever names, along with their many variations, only to find that all the good ones are seemingly taken.

Given that approximately 50 million .COM names are already registered, it's not surprising that all the short snappy names are taken. Your chances of hitting on a good three-letter name or acronym are close to zero. To get one of these, your only recourse would be to haggle with whoever has already registered the name you fancy and see if you could get him to hand it over – for a certain sum of course.

It's even worse if you're thinking of a name with just two letters. If you want one of the 676 possible two-letter sequences, for instance for an acronym or abbreviation, you're out of luck: they're all taken. So you have to get smart. Think about adding a digit. Trouble is, quite often the look of it just doesn't work – so think about a dash. It can fit in with lots of clever designs for logos and so on. One company has a domain name with punctuation written out in words – 'full stop'. Rather confusing, don't you think? No, concentrate on the visual impact of your name.

3 According to the writer, the best way of getting a good name with three letters is
  A to try to buy one from someone else.
  B to think of something really unusual.
  C to keep trying variations of the letters.
  D to think of a clever acronym.

4 The writer recommends registering a name which includes
  A a dash.
  B punctuation written as full words.
  C letters and numbers.
  D only two characters.

# The nuts and bolts of writing

We all know what William Shakespeare had to say about a name in *Romeo and Juliet* – that "a rose by any other name would smell as sweet". Maybe so for flowers, but not for characters. How would Shakespeare's play have worked as *Howard and Brunhilda*? Lacks a certain resonance, doesn't it?

A character's name is the first clue we give the reader about this individual we want them to care about, to love, to hate – but above all to follow. It is also perhaps the biggest clue. A number of studies have shown that a paper submitted to a panel of teachers will generally fare better if the student's name on it is a currently more popular name than the same paper with an unpopular or old-fashioned name.

A pregnant friend maintains that naming her child-to-be is more difficult than my naming a character, because she doesn't know what kind of person her child will become. True, but that also gives the child an opportunity to mould the name to his/her personality and accomplishments, to go against our expectations.

Selecting a name for our characters, I maintain, is more difficult than naming a baby because we are trying to convey not only what the person can become, but what s/he is and has been. That's a lot of weight for a few syllables to carry.

5 What point is the writer making when he quotes Shakespeare?
  A Shakespeare knew a lot about flowers.
  B Shakespeare was a clever playwright.
  C Shakespeare's characters are believable because of their names.
  D Shakespeare favoured the use of names in the titles of his plays.

6 The aim of the text is to
  A draw authors' attention to the importance of the names of their characters.
  B alert teachers to the dangers of favouring a child because of his name.
  C advise parents-to-be to wait until a child is born before naming him.
  D explain to readers that names change little over time.

# Paper 2 Part 1

You **must** answer this question.

You were in Britain recently and went on an organised visit to see the musical *Joseph and the Amazing Technicolor Dreamcoat*, which you enjoyed very much. You have just read a review in the newspaper which criticises the musical in very strong terms. You have spoken to some of the other people who went to see the musical to find out what they thought.

Read the review from the newspaper. Then, **using the information provided**, write the letter outlined below.

---

## A night out to remember – but perhaps for the wrong reasons

*Joseph and the Amazing Technicolor Dreamcoat* is advertised as 'The Show of the Century'. It is very interesting that they do not say which century as I found the show rather faded and old-fashioned.

While I admit that the writer of the musical is recognised as a modern genius, I am afraid the cast let him down. They seemed under-rehearsed and dare I say even bored. It is very difficult for an audience to appreciate a show when the cast are not giving their best.

The scenery looked as though it had been put together on a shoestring rather than the lavish production which the advertising blurb promised. In fact, the photos in the advertisement for the show do not look anything like the performance I saw.

I really felt sorry for the people who had seats in the balcony as they must have found it difficult to see anything, sitting so far away from the stage.

All in all, a very disappointing and expensive night out!

---

**Comments from people on trip**

- The show far surpassed my expectations.

- Our balcony seats meant we were able to get a good view of the whole stage and so we got the full impact of the colourful show.

- I'd never seen such a huge orchestra. There were several really famous musicians playing; the quality was first class.

- Obviously no expense had been spared on set design; it changed from scene to scene and it was truly amazing.

- Considering we bought the cheapest seats, I think it was a memorable evening. I wouldn't have believed I could see such a show for only £15.00.

- The poster of the show I saw looked great but a poster cannot show how brilliant it is in reality. There's nothing like going there and being involved.

- I just couldn't believe the singers. They were putting their heart and soul into every note. I don't know how they manage to create such energy.

Now write a **letter** to the editor of the newspaper (about 250 words), correcting the inaccuracies in the newspaper review. You should use your own words as far as possible. You do not need to include addresses.

# Paper 3 Part 1

For questions **1–12**, read the text below and then decide which word best fits each space. The exercise begins with an example (**0**).

## LONDON – THE STUDENT'S CAPITAL?

London is the city which seems to (**0**) ...*draw*... people like a magnet from across the country every year, not to (**1**) ............... from around the world. London is cool, fashionable and multi-cultural. For the (**2**) ............... student, it is the most incredible arts, academic and entertainment Mecca.

London is one of the few real student capitals of the world. Despite the grime, the (**3**) ............... costs, the troublesome transport system, and the (**4**) ............... sensation of living with eight million people, students (**5**) ............... to the city's universities.

However, rents are steep, with students paying around £75 a week for a room in a (**6**) ............... house. Halls of (**7**) ............... are a little over this price – but of course include meals and bills.

Work is plentiful at the moment though, so a part-time job should be easy to (**8**) ............... across, and there are all sorts of graduate opportunities with the best (**9**) ............... of pay in the country. The London institutions try to play (**10**) ............... the cost of (**11**) ............... so as not to (**12**) ............... off future students, but there is no doubt about it, London costs money and you will be looking at a sizeable debt on graduating.

| 0 | **A** catch | **B** bring | **C** draw | **D** grasp |
|---|---|---|---|---|
| 1 | **A** say | **B** include | **C** utter | **D** mention |
| 2 | **A** budding | **B** bidding | **C** blooming | **D** blithering |
| 3 | **A** peak | **B** high | **C** money | **D** extreme |
| 4 | **A** overestimated | **B** overawed | **C** overwhelming | **D** overloaded |
| 5 | **A** stem | **B** wave | **C** pounce | **D** flock |
| 6 | **A** divided | **B** parted | **C** shared | **D** separated |
| 7 | **A** residence | **B** accommodation | **C** dormitories | **D** wards |
| 8 | **A** put | **B** get | **C** do | **D** come |
| 9 | **A** rates | **B** terms | **C** conditions | **D** means |
| 10 | **A** up | **B** at | **C** out | **D** down |
| 11 | **A** life | **B** living | **C** live | **D** livelihood |
| 12 | **A** set | **B** run | **C** write | **D** put |

# Paper 3 Part 2

For questions **1–15**, complete the following article by writing each missing word in the correct space. **Use only one word for each space**. The exercise begins with an example (**0**).

## THE HILLS ARE ALIVE WITH THE SOUND OF MUSIC

For the past eight years, (**0**) ....*many*.... of the world's leading classical musicians (**1**) .................... gathered in Switzerland's glitziest ski resort to play, to teach and socialise. (**2**) .................... this were all, it would be the ultimate classical music insiders' club. But the attraction of Verbier, (**3**) .................... charm and relevance, is (**4**) .................... it is also home for three weeks to (**5**) .................... than 100 young musicians from 31 countries, starry-eyed about meeting the masters and getting a crash course at the highest possible level. Conductors of the world's top orchestras are (**6**) .................... hand to get the young musicians into shape, coaxing fine performances of (**7**) .................... daunting challenges as Mahler's Third Symphony and Brahms' First Symphony.

Verbier is the creation of the Swede, Martin Engstroem, (**8**) .................... for many years was a leading agent. He wanted to run his (**9**) .................... festival and, (**10**) .................... some of the best contacts in the business, it was (**11**) .................... hard to find a Swiss ski resort looking for a summer boost, rich villa owners keen to open their houses to musical celebrities and stars used to (**12**) .................... indulged. Engstroem is the most relaxed and charming of men, (**13**) .................... in his way he is a dictator. The music heard at Verbier (**14**) .................... to be to his classical taste with (**15**) .................... a note of the contemporary.

# Paper 4 Part 1

You will hear three extracts. For questions **1–6**, choose the answer (**A**, **B** or **C**) which fits best according to what you hear.

### Extract One

You hear a woman giving a talk to business students.

1 What criticism does she make of much of the advice given to business students about social conversations?
   A  It has the wrong focus.
   B  It is too general.
   C  It is ineffective.

2 When referring to body language she makes the point that most people
   A  need special training to be convincing.
   B  reflect the body language of others.
   C  cannot disguise their true feelings.

### Extract Two

You hear a producer talking to a colleague about a new TV sports presenter.

3 Why were some people hesitant to appoint this new presenter?
   A  He lacked experience in sports journalism.
   B  His interviewing technique was inappropriate.
   C  He didn't seem to be a team player.

4 What will the new presenter have to change about himself?
   A  the way he speaks
   B  the way he looks
   C  the way he moves

### Extract Three

You hear a man talking about buying a lighthouse to live in.

5 How did he get to know about the lighthouse when it was for sale?
   A  He was looking for a home for when he got married.
   B  It was said that a celebrity was living in it.
   C  It was part of something he had to do for his job.

6 Why did it take so long to renovate it?
   A  Too many regulations had to be complied with.
   B  It was too costly to do all the work at once.
   C  Original materials were difficult to source.

# TEST 1 Key

## Paper 1 Part 1

1 B  2 D  3 A  4 A  5 B  6 A

## Paper 3 Part 1

1 D  2 A  3 B  4 C  5 D  6 C  7 A  8 D  9 A  10 D
11 B  12 D

## Paper 3 Part 2

1 have  2 If  3 its  4 that  5 more  6 on
7 such  8 who  9 own  10 with / having  11 not
12 being  13 but / although  14 tends / has
15 scarcely / hardly / barely / not

## Paper 4 Part 1

1 A  2 C  3 C  4 B  5 C  6 A

## Tapescript

### Extract 1

There are numerous articles, language units and seminars on how to start a conversation with people you don't know, how to keep the conversation going and how valuable it is to network. All terribly laudable but, as an extremely busy person, you may actually more often find yourself in the position of wanting to get out of a conversation because you have one hundred and one other things you ought to be doing. And frankly, Mr X is more than a tad dull!

When you're at a conference and you get stuck with someone, you may think you're being nice and polite by standing there smiling back at them, nodding and pretending to be interested but, in fact, only the best of actors can get away with that. For most of us, the smile turns into a gruesome plastic grin, our eyes dart around the room as we search for a get-out, or even worse, we crane our necks to see the nearest watch or clock.

### Extract 2

A: Hiring Tony certainly raised a few eyebrows – you can't gloss over the fact that he has a reputation for going it alone and producing a story that no one else knows anything about.

B: Yes, but it wasn't the courageous move it might appear. He had form as a sports reporter. What really sells him, though, is his love of the sport, a genuine fan who congratulates himself on being the local team's most devoted supporter.

A: It's that and his very un-presenter-like manner. Tony doesn't interview people, he chats to them. It's a simple difference which has proved very disarming.

B: Yes, I know. He's quietly-spoken, self-deprecating and desperate to learn. There haven't been any complaints about him, just emails decrying his beard and scruffy haircut.

A: When he's speaking he's almost as animated as the players in the football match. I know the camera crew have a job keeping up with him.

B: That's part of his engagement with sport. I wouldn't take that away for anything.

A: Absolutely.

### Extract 3

Well, there was a lighthouse for sale and as a reporter I was sent to cover it – it was rumoured that someone famous might be buying it. When it didn't reach its reserve at auction, curiosity got the better of me: I got the keys and went with my fiancée to look at it. It was an empty shell. Just a 40-metre chimney with eight floors linked by vertical steel ladders. It had no water. No toilet.

But it's a very beautiful piece of architecture. It's got a copper roof, huge granite floors and two-metre thick walls. We bought it, but with no idea how much it would cost to turn it into a dwelling, and no planning permission. We were young and stupid and in love with each other and the building. Initially the dream was to bring up our kids and live in the lighthouse. But the bureaucracy took the gloss off. It took nearly ten years to complete.

# 6 Speak after the tone

| Genre | Phone messages |
| Topic | Communications technology |

| Speaking 1 | Telephone technology |
| Listening | Answering machine messages |
| Grammar | Phrasal verbs |
| Vocabulary | Collocations (*have*, *do*, *make* and *take*) |
| Speaking 2 | The schwa |
| Reading and Speaking | Communications technology |

**Workbook contents**

| Reading | Putting paragraphs into gaps |
| Grammar | Phrasal verbs |
| Vocabulary | Collocations (*do*, *have*, *make*, *take*) |

## SB pages 40–43

### Lesson planning
- **SV** Grammar 2 or 3 could be set for homework
- **LV** See extension activities in the Listening and Vocabulary sections

## Speaking 1

1 Ask students to discuss these introductory questions in pairs or small groups. Allow time for feedback relating to each of the questions.

Some telephone services may not be universally familiar:

- Voice mail is an electronic message-taking service used by businesses.
- An answering machine is a recording machine that is switched on when someone is not at home or a business is closed.
- A mobile is a mobile phone (the word *phone* is often not now used in the phrase – NB this is called a cellphone in American English).
- A bleeper is a device which makes a noise to indicate that someone is trying to contact you and you must go to an ordinary phone (it is typically used to contact doctors, e.g. in a large hospital).
- A videophone is a system which allows people talking on a phone to see as well as hear each other.
- A WAP phone is a kind of mobile phone which also allows the user to have Internet access.
- Text messaging is sending written messages from one mobile phone to another.
- A call waiting service allows you to hear if someone else is trying to contact you when you are on the telephone.
- A ring back service helps if you are ringing someone who is engaged. It makes an automatic connection for you when the person you are trying to contact puts the phone down.
- Dialling 1471, etc. allows you to hear the number and time when someone last tried to contact you on the phone.
- The speaking clock is a telephone service in the UK which states the precise time when dialled.

## Listening

1 Ask students to read through the questions, then play the recording once. Students should compare their answers in pairs.

### Answers
a Her boyfriend had decided he had got tired of her and wanted to end their relationship.
b She dialled an automatic recorded message from his phone while he was away for a month and then left the phone off the hook.
c It is a matter of opinion whether it was effective or not, but it must have been satisfying in that it would have resulted in an enormous phone bill for her ex-boyfriend.

## Tapescript

Oh, talking of revenge, I read about a great one once. There was this girl, she'd been dumped by her boyfriend, 'cos he'd decided he'd gone off her and he told her to move her things out of his flat before he got back from a business trip. I think he was going to the States for a month or something. Anyway, she moves her stuff out straightaway but before she leaves, she picks up the phone and dials the speaking clock. Then she leaves the phone off the hook while the clock goes on speaking the time to an empty flat. 'At the third stroke, it'll be ten twenty-five and thirty seconds …' So the boyfriend finds it when he returns four weeks later. You can imagine what the bill was like after a solid month of phone calls. Even at local rates, it'd be huge! That must have been really satisfying for the dumped girl!

2   Play the messages straight through once and ask students to take down as much information as they can. Play the recording again message by message for students to complete the information and then check their answers.

The tapescript is on page 180.

> **Answers**
>
> 1  For:           Andy
>    From Name:     Eddie
>         Number:   245908
>    Message:
>    Does history project have to be handwritten or can it be typed? Please ring back before 7 (has to go out then).
>
> 2  For:           Michael Removals
>    From Name:     Robert Smith
>         Number:   0207 562 4957
>    Message:
>    Recommended by Richard Johnstone. Wants to know charges and availability to move a few things on 22nd or 21st. Is moving beds, chests of drawers, fridge, washing machine, etc. out of house (moving about one mile). Also could you plumb in washing machine for him?
>
> 3  For:           Nicky
>    From Name:     Leila
>         Number:   not given
>    Message:
>    Just wants a gossip. (Jo's resigned – wants to tell you why!)
>
> 4  For:           Nicola Smith
>    From Name:     Paolo
>         Number:   0802 334 567 (mobile)
>    Message:
>    Your seminar next Tuesday to start at 11 and finish 3.30 (with lunch in middle) rather than 2–5. Group really on the ball, need loads of stretching activities. Best if doing things rather than listening. Nice but hard work. Ring with any queries.
>
> 5  For:           Michael
>    From Name:     John
>         Number:   not given
>    Message:
>    Bob's stag party tonight meeting in *Red Lion* NOT *Slug and Lettuce*
>
> 6  For:           Andy
>    From Name:     Alex
>         Number:   not given
>    Message:
>    Has new PlayStation game. Do you want to go round this evening at 7 and play it?

> **Extension activity**
>
> Copy the cards in the Photocopiable activities section at the back of the book on page 184, fill in an appropriate name (of another student in the class) and give one to each student. Allow time for students to think about exactly what they should say. Remind them that they need to start by saying clearly who the message is for. Then, if you have access to an answering machine, ask them to ring up and record their message. If you do not have access to an answering machine, ask students in turn to record their messages on a tape recorder either in the language lab or in the classroom. Listen to the tape and give feedback to the students on how successfully they recorded their messages.

## Phrasal verbs

1   Give students a photocopy of the tapescript which is in the Photocopiable tapescripts section at the back of the book on page 180. Ask students to highlight the phrasal verbs in the tapescript and put them on the board. Note that some of them are repeated in several conversations.

> **Answers**
>
> 1  Please could you *ring* me *back*?
>    I've got to *go out* at 7-ish,
>    so I hope you *get back* before then.
> 2  into a house I'm going to *rent out*
>    Would you be able to *plumb* those *in* for me as well?
>    Could you *get back* to me
> 3  when you *get back*
>    I'll *fill* you *in* on all the gory details
> 4  it'll be *broken up* by lunch
>    *Ring* me *back* if you've got any queries.
> 5  If you haven't *turned up* by 8.15
> 6  Do you want to *come round*

Point out that there is quite a high concentration of phrasal verbs because the English used is fairly informal spoken English where phrasal verbs are typical.

2   Students work through the exercise individually or in pairs.

> **Answers**
>
> a out  b through  c up  d through  e on
> f over/on  g up  h off  i off, up

3   Ask students to match the two parts of the dialogues, then check the answers together.

> **Answers**
>
> b 1  c 6  d 7  e 4  f 10  g 9  h 3  i 8  j 5

SPEAK AFTER THE TONE

## Vocabulary

Check that all students are clear about the concept of collocation (words that are frequently used together).

1. Students can work individually or with a partner on this exercise. Suggest that they do the ones they are sure about first and leave the rest for the moment.

   When students have done all the ones they are sure about, check the answers as a class. Then suggest students use dictionaries to deal with any remaining items (if necessary).

   **Answers**

   | *have* | *do* | *make* |
   |---|---|---|
   | a baby | the cooking | a cake |
   | a go | someone a favour | a mistake |
   | a party | your best | a phone call |
   | dinner | the housework | an effort |
   | fun | your homework | an excuse |
   |  |  | dinner |

   | *take* | both *have* and *take* |
   |---|---|
   | a photo | a bath |
   | hold of | a chance |
   | part | a nap |
   | someone seriously | a phone call |
   | someone's word for it | a shower |

2. Ask students to complete the gaps individually and to check their answers with a partner.

   **Answers**
   a do  b make  c has/takes  d make
   e take  f have  g do

> **Extension activity**
>
> As homework, students prepare more sentences with blanks using some of the collocations they have been working with. These can then be used by other students in the class as follow-up or revision of the useful collocations practised in this section.

## Speaking 2

1. Ask students to read the tapescript and identify the sounds that would normally be pronounced as schwa. These are underlined in the tapescript below. Play the recording while students read aloud at the same time. If you have access to a language laboratory, then this exercise can usefully be done there.

   **Answers**
   Oh, talking o̱f revenge, I read a̱bout a̱ great one once. There wa̱s this girl, she'd been dumped by her boyfriend, co̱s he'd decided he'd gone off he̱r and he told her to̱ move her things out o̱f his flat before he got back from a̱ business trip. I think he wa̱s going to̱ the States fo̱r a̱ month or something. Anyway, she moves he̱r stuff out straighta̱way but before she leaves, she picks up the phone and dia̱ls the speaking clock. Then she leaves the phone off the̱ hook while the̱ clock goes on speaking the̱ time to̱ a̱n empty flat. 'At the̱ third stroke, it'll be ten twenty-five and thirty seconds …' So the̱ boyfriend finds it when he returns four weeks late̱r. You ca̱n imagine what the̱ bill wa̱s like after a̱ solid month o̱f phone calls. Even a̱t local rates, it'd be huge! That must ha̱ve been really satisfying fo̱r the̱ dumped girl!

## Reading and Speaking

1. Ask students to read through the text and then answer the questions.

   **Answers**
   a Because the writer is writing on a train and is working with a very small keyboard. Both of these factors make it difficult for him to press the correct keys.
   b I am writing this on the train. I am writing this, not just on the train, but on my telephone on the train. My telephone is simultaneously picking up my email and I have just ordered a book from the Cambridge University Library, via their website. All on my telephone! Isn't technology wonderful?
   c The writer tells us that he has a phone with Internet connection and that he has a Macintosh Powerbook G3 computer. He thinks both are wonderful and clearly finds it very exciting that they can do what they do.
   d Telephone communications have changed a great deal in the writer's lifetime. He can remember when homes typically had at most one phone. This was fixed and certainly could not be moved from room to room. To be able to make a call from another room involved a time-consuming and complex process of adding cables and drilling holes. Now you can literally make calls from almost anywhere using a tiny personal phone.
   e The capitals draw attention to the fact that it was something special, something that people would talk about in tones of awe.
   f All the different ways that we now have of communicating may actually add to the stress that people feel.
   g The point of the story about President Carter is that it is very unusual for people to stop and think before speaking. Many people speak but have nothing really to say.

2. Ask students to discuss the questions with a partner. Take some feedback from each group by asking students to elaborate on the points that you heard them discussing with most interest.

**SPEAK AFTER THE TONE**

# Exam folder 3

## SB pages 44–45

## Paper 3 Part 3
## Word formation

This section is to help students cope with Part 3 of the CAE Use of English test (Paper 3).

1 The parts of speech are provided in brackets below together with the words that were originally in the text. Although it should be possible to identify the required part of speech, it is unlikely that students will identify all the original words, and several alternatives may be equally possible. Accept any likely alternatives.

**Answers**
1 (adverb) viciously  2 (adjective) courteous
3 (noun) team  4 (verb – past tense) ordered
5 (noun) union  6 (adjective) unruly
7 (verb – past participle) saved  8 (noun – plural) pupils

2 Ask students to think back to the work done on prefixes in Unit 4.

**Answers**

| Verbs | Adjectives | Nouns |
|---|---|---|
| unwrap | unsafe | disappearance |
| de-ice | disloyal | insecurity |
| misspell | insane | unease |
| untie | uncomfortable | discomfort |
| disentangle | non-European | immobility |
| misunderstand | irresponsible | imbalance |

3 You may wish to add other words to the list in addition to those suggested.

**Suggested answers**
a law — lawyer, lawful, unlawful, lawless, law-abiding
b hope — hopeful, hopeless, hopelessness, hopefully
c act — action, actor, react, reaction, enact, enactment
d press — pressure, pressing, depress, oppress, repress, oppression, oppressive, oppressor
e centre — central, centrally, centralise, decentralise, centralisation, concentrate, concentration
f head — heading, header, subhead, behead, heady, big-headed, pig-headed
g office — officer, official, officiate, officious, officially
h spoon — spoonful, teaspoon, tablespoon
i place — placing, replace, misplace, displaced
j broad — breadth, broaden, broadly, broad-minded

4 This exercise is similar to the one students will need to do in the exam.

**Answers**
1 inspection  2 violence  3 leadership  4 outrageous
5 uncontrollable / uncontrolled  6 later  7 properly
8 councillors  9 successful  10 unsatisfactory
11 remarkably

5 This provides further practice of the Part 3 exam task.

**Answers**
1 happily  2 skilled  3 recognition  4 unfamiliar
5 injury  6 dislodged  7 safety  8 discharged
9 convulsions  10 psychological  11 limitations / limits
12 marriage  13 fortunately

### Teaching extra

Ask students to find at least one other word based on the same root for each of the root words in either 4 or 5. They could then write sentences with blanks to test their words, e.g. *Harry took a degree in accounting and then became a tax* ............... **(INSPECT)**
Students then test each other with their sentences.

# 7 Running a successful business

| Genre | Reports |
|---|---|
| Topic | The world of work |

| Speaking 1 | Work and business |
| Reading | Young people's success in business |
| Vocabulary | Multiple meanings |
| Grammar | Cause and effect |
| Writing | Reports |
| Speaking 2 | Evaluating jobs |
| Listening | People and their jobs |

**Workbook contents**

| Reading | True/False exercise |
| Writing | A report |
| Grammar | Cause and effect |
| Use of English | Part 1 multiple-choice gap fill |

## SB pages 46–49

**Lesson planning**

SV  Reading 3 and Writing 1 or 2 could be set for homework

LV  See extension activities in the Vocabulary and Speaking 2 sections

## Speaking 1

1 Ask students to discuss these questions in small groups to arouse their interest in the topic.

## Reading

1 Allow students enough time to read the text through quickly without worrying about what words might fill the gaps. Then ask them questions a–d.

> **Teaching extra**
>
> This exercise helps to train students in the skills needed to do Part 2 of the Use of English paper. Questions a–d show that it is possible, indeed necessary, to understand what the text is about before filling in the gaps. Use this procedure whenever you are working with a similar exercise type in class. Encourage students to read the text through first, check their comprehension by asking a few comprehension questions and only then begin to think about how to fill the gaps in the text.

**Answers**
a 10,000 young people aged 12 to 25
b the legacy of the prosperous 1980s, the changing nature of work, the targeting of youth culture, a new work ethic
c Big business needs the kind of young people who are now preferring to set up businesses of their own.
d The words refer to the key factors affecting young people's attitudes to work today.

2 Encourage students to look at the clues in the words on either side of the gap.

**Answers**
1 for  2 whom  3 making  4 what  5 everything
6 were  7 their  8 own  9 in  10 being  11 to
12 best  13 such  14 in  15 else  16 are  17 up
18 at  19 which  20 would

3 Students should do the exercise, then discuss their answers with a partner.

**Answers**
a False. Reasons include a desire for financial independence, to be valued and challenged but not just to get rich.
b True, although it was investigating attitudes not only to work but also to the family and to other aspects of life.
c False. The economy was strong (*buoyant*) and people were encouraged to take risks.
d True.
e False. Many large companies have targeted young people, specifically trying to attract them to buy their products.
f True.
g True.
h False. The article says that established businesses need young people on their staff in order to survive and so should be doing more to attract them.

## Vocabulary

Refer students to the Vocabulary spot and remind them that many words in English have more than one meaning.

1 Students should work on this exercise individually or in pairs. Point out that all the words are to be found in the reading text and are used in the order in which they come in the exercise.

**Answers**
1 setting  2 drives  3 strike  4 decline
5 stage  6 industry

RUNNING A SUCCESSFUL BUSINESS  41

2   Deal with this exercise as a class. Again, all the words are to be found in the reading text and are used in the order in which they come in the exercise.

> **Answers**
> 1 legacy  2 buoyant  3 eroded  4 targeting
> 5 buckling down  6 reap

### Extension activity

If your students are particularly interested in the vocabulary of work, you may wish to focus on this aspect of the language in the text.

1 Ask students to write down all the words and expressions from the text that are directly related to work
  e.g. *setting up a business, long-term employment prospects.*
2 Students then work in pairs. Each pair should write sentences that are true for at least one of them using some of the words and expressions they wrote down in 1
  e.g. *Marco's brother set up his own business last year.*
3 Ask students to head a page in their folder or vocabulary notebook *The language of work* and to note down the relevant expressions from the text there.

The most important expressions that they should note down are given below, but students may, of course, add any others that they feel are personally useful.

| | |
|---|---|
| to set up a business | leisure markets |
| entrepreneurs | work ethic |
| the nature of work | do something productive |
| long-term employment prospects | or beneficial |
| contract work | to exploit others |
| freelance work | to reap the benefits |
| occupational pensions | industry |
| sick pay | field (of work) |
| company cars | an employee |
| work circumstances | to work on their own |

## Cause and effect

The grammar here is covered on pages 193–194 of the Grammar folder.

1   Students read the text and underline any words and expressions connected with the language of cause and effect.

> **Answers**
> the reason for   reasons why   had a profound influence on
> resulted in   be a consequence of   stems from
> have its roots in

2   Ask students to do the exercise individually and then compare their answers with a partner.

> **Answers**
> 1 to  2 towards  3 on  4 about  5 as
> 6 of  7 As  8 why

3   Check that students know all the words in the box. Explain any that they are not sure about.

Play the recording and ask students to tick the expressions that they hear.

> **Answers**
> motive, grounds for, so, accordingly, explanation, objective, outcome, thanks to

### Tapescript

How did I become an actor? Well at school when I was about sixteen or seventeen I was in quite a few plays and once my godfather, who was a television director, came to one of these plays just to see what was going on, not in any professional sense. There wasn't any other sort of motive. He just really came to see me work as his godson. And we, we did the play and afterwards he and I were sitting having a chat and he thought maybe having seen my work there was, had I ever thought of going into the theatre as a profession? He thought there were grounds there for a possible career move. So I wrote to the drama schools and, I don't know, filled in all the forms and did everything that was asked of me and accordingly I was called up to London for an audition and I was late. They wanted an explanation of course – the trains had held me up – but anyway, I got there, I did my audition and waited to hear what was going to happen. The audition's quite interesting. You have a couple of pieces to do and then they give you a scene. They want to know, as an actor, if you can tell what the objective is in the scene, whether you think the outcome of the scene can go one way or another. They're quite interesting moments, they're improvised. And that was that, and then after about two or three months, I heard from the drama school and I'd got in. So it was thanks to my godfather really that I'd managed to go to drama school and I did a two-year course and here we are, I'm speaking to you.

## Writing

1   Students might be expected to write such a report in Part 1 of the CAE Writing test (Paper 2), although at over 500 words, it is longer than any report they would be required to write in the exam. They should, therefore, pay careful attention to all aspects of its structure and language.

2   Ask students to think about questions a and b as they read the report.

With a partner, students should write an answer to question a and discuss their answer to question b.

> **Answers**
> **a**
> **Introduction to the work experience programme**
> - ten students did work experience
> - in supermarket doing range of types of job
>
> **Usefulness of the programme**
> - learnt about life behind scenes of supermarket including learning to respect people who work there
> - learnt a bit about complex international operation of supermarket
> - learnt about importance of being able to deal with people of very different types
> - gained confidence
>
> **Drawbacks to the programme**
> - felt exploited at times
> - do not ever want to work in supermarket again
> - would have preferred experience in possible future area of work
>
> **Conclusion**
> - programme in general a very good thing
> - would prefer to have opportunities to do different types of jobs
>
> **b**
> The headings are appropriate and useful in that they state clearly what each paragraph includes. The report is clear and unambiguous and uses headings to inform and guide the reader. The report therefore follows a fairly standard pattern.

Tasks c and d may be set for homework or done in class. For question c, some students may feel that some other words and expressions also have a linking function in the text, e.g. *there*, *in a number of ways*, etc. Allow anything to be included that they can justify. However, make sure that the answers listed below are highlighted and discussed by all the class. Ask students what the function is of each of the words and phrases in the box.

> **Answers**
> **c**
> *Firstly, Secondly, Thirdly, Finally* – listing points
> *Moreover* – adding a point
> *For example* – giving an example
> *In conclusion* – drawing a conclusion
> *However* – making a point that contrasts in some way with what has gone before

For question d, compare students' ideas for headings and discuss what might be included under the headings suggested.

# Speaking 2

1. Check that the students know what all the jobs in the box are and ask them to discuss which they think are most valuable to society.

2. Students should now work with a partner and choose what they think are the three most valuable and least valuable jobs from those listed in the box.

3. Organise students so that they are now working with a different partner. Students compare the jobs they chose in the previous activity and explain their choices.

4. Ask students to brainstorm other advantages to add to the list.

5. Write on the board all the different ideas that come from the students. Ask each person in the class to select one thing from the board and make a note of the name(s) beside the aspect of work selected.

   Students should now mill around the classroom, conducting a survey in which they interview as many students as they can and keep a note of the answers.

6. Students should give feedback to the rest of the class on the results of their survey. Wherever possible, they should comment on trends and tendencies rather than simply reporting the answers of individual students.

7. When discussing this with the class, remind students of the desirability of having about five headings including an introduction and a conclusion. The information must be presented as clearly and unambiguously as possible. One of the easiest ways of ensuring clarity is to include paragraph or section headings.

### Extension activity

Students write up their reports at home.

## Listening

1. Ask students to listen to the recording and answer questions a–c. The tapescript is on pages 181–182.

> **Answers**
> 1 hairdresser  2 detective  3 stunt woman
> 4 window cleaner  5 fitness instructor  6 journalist
> 7 psychologist  8 sports commentator

2. As a round-up, students should discuss which of the eight jobs appeals to them most and why.

**RUNNING A SUCCESSFUL BUSINESS**

# Writing folder 3

## SB pages 50–51

## Formal letters

You may prefer the letters in question 5 to be prepared in class and written at home. These letters should then be brought to class for the final part of question 5 where students read each other's work.

**1**

> **Answers**
> a F (I: not your name, only your address)  b F  c F,I
> d F,I  e I  f I  g F

**2**

> **Answers**
> a apologise, delay, replying
> b should, grateful, could, further
> c acknowledge, receipt
> d enclose, self, addressed
> e would, appreciate, response
> f forward, hearing, earliest, convenience

**3**

> **Answers**
> a ✔  b ✘  c ✘  d ✔  e ?  f ✔

4 Discuss the tasks in groups in class. Then set the letter for homework.

5 Distribute the letters in class once they have been written and ask people how they would feel about receiving such a letter. Students should note their comments at the end of the letter(s) they look at. When you mark the letters, indicate whether you agree with the comments made by other students.

# 8 Best thing since sliced bread

| Genre | Describing objects |
|---|---|
| Topic | Inventions |

| Speaking 1 | Twentieth century inventions |
| Reading | Curious inventions |
| Vocabulary | Positive and negative adjectives |
| Listening | What we can't live without |
| Grammar | Modals: *must, should, ought to, shall, will, would* |
| Speaking 2 | Exclamations and fillers |

**Workbook contents**

| Use of English | Part 2 open gap fill |
| Grammar | Modals: *used to, would, should, should have, ought to, shall* |
| Reading | Comprehension questions |
| Vocabulary | Positive and negative associations |

## SB pages 52–55

**Lesson planning**
- SV Vocabulary 1–3 could be set for homework
- LV See extension activities in the Vocabulary and Grammar sections

## Speaking 1

1 Students should work with a partner to put the objects in the order in which they were invented.

**Answers**
1 wristwatch (1904)   2 electric dishwasher (1914)
3 sliced bread (1928)   4 pop-up toaster (1937)
5 biro (1945)   6 video recorder (1956)
7 can with ring-pull (1962)   8 personal stereo (1979)
9 computer mouse (1984)   10 MP3 player (1997)

## Reading

1 Ask students to read the text and then discuss the question with a partner. As a class, compare the scores given for the different objects.

2 You may like to point out that all the objects in the text were patented, i.e. their inventors thought that they could become commercially successful.

3 Encourage a class discussion of this question as a round up.

## Vocabulary

1 Students discuss their answers to the questions with a partner, using an English–English dictionary if necessary.

**Answers**
**a**
| courting | having a romantic relationship |
| contours | shape |
| suction pad | piece of rubber that fixes itself to a smooth surface using suction |
| treadmill | wide wheel turned by people climbing on steps around its edge (used in the past to provide power for machines or as punishment) |
| mop | stick with material on one end for washing floors |
| pivotable | can be moved about a fixed point |

**b**
| mini- | small (e.g. *minicab, mini-series, Mini Disc*) |

**c**
| -able | can or able to be (e.g. *disposable, regrettable, comparable*) |
| -less | without (e.g. *hopeless, thoughtless, careless*) |

**d**
| common | separate |
| flexible | inflexible, rigid |
| inner | outer |
| drives | halts, stops |
| mess up | keep tidy |
| stowed | unfolded |

2 Refer students to the Vocabulary spot and ask them to give other examples of adjectives conveying strong positive or negative feelings. Then ask students to work on this exercise with a partner, using a dictionary as required.

**Answers**

| Positive | Negative |
|---|---|
| absorbing | grotesque |
| breathtaking | hackneyed |
| brilliant | hideous |
| delightful | ill-conceived |
| enchanting | impractical |
| engrossing | monstrous |
| ingenious | pointless |
| inspired | repulsive |
| ravishing | ridiculous |
| stunning | trivial |

BEST THING SINCE SLICED BREAD

Encourage students to use some of these words to describe the inventions in the reading texts.

3 This could be set as homework to revise the work done in class.

> **Answers**
> a breathtaking  b ridiculous  c ingenious
> d hackneyed  e stunning  f repulsive
> g ill-conceived, delightful

> **Extension activity**
>
> Put the following adjectives on the board – *absorbing, breathtaking, delightful, enchanting, engrossing, grotesque, hackneyed, hideous, inspired, monstrous, ravishing, repulsive, ridiculous, stunning*. Ask students to suggest a noun that collocates with each of them.

# Listening

Before looking at the pictures, ask students to name some things that they could not live without.

1 Ask students to look at the pictures and listen to the recording to identify which things are mentioned by the speakers. Which other things are mentioned?

> **Answers**
> Speaker 1: car (bike also mentioned)
> Speaker 2: washing machine, hair dryer
> Speaker 3: contact lenses (microwave also mentioned)
> Speaker 4: Swiss army knife (pepper mill also mentioned)

2 Students should then listen again to focus on the positive and negative adjectives used by the speakers.

**Answers**

|  | Positive adjectives | Negative adjectives |
|---|---|---|
| Speaker 1 | brilliant, great | impractical, ridiculous, pointless |
| Speaker 2 | good, eco-friendly, inspired, ingenious, great, breathtaking | repulsive, trivial |
| Speaker 3 | indispensable, brilliant, extraordinary, inspired | vain, ugly, hideous |
| Speaker 4 | brilliant, wonderful | terrible, grotesque, impractical, fastidious, pointless |

## Tapescript

**Speaker 1:** Well, I'm sorry to say it living in London but I couldn't do without my car. I love having my car. I mean it's, it's tiny, it's a soft top, it's completely impractical for most journeys but I love it and driving round in the country, well, it's just brilliant. I have a great time in it. I also, I couldn't do without my bike which is somehow a better idea around London. I can use it a lot more and I can get round all the traffic jams because it's just ridiculous in a car. You just spend your time hanging around waiting all the time. It's pointless.

**Speaker 2:** Well, I've got a little baby and one thing I really couldn't do without is my washing machine, especially – I know it sounds really repulsive – but we actually wash our nappies. It's, it's really good and that might sound trivial but not in these days because, I don't know, it's so eco-friendly to have washable nappies and it's an inspired design, our washing machine, because it's got lots of features like the half-load button for example and yeah, it's very ingenious the way it can do that. And another thing I really couldn't do without is my hair dryer. Oh I love my hair dryer! It's really great. I think that's another piece of breathtaking design because it's really great the way that you can have a cold shot at the end of the dry so it doesn't make your hair too hot really. Yeah, those are the things I really couldn't do without.

**Speaker 3:** Well, my contact lenses are indispensable to me. They are, apart from being a brilliant invention, they – without them I couldn't see. I'm too vain to wear glasses so I really do need them. I mean, I think they're an absolutely extraordinary and inspired invention. But the other thing that I couldn't possibly live without is my microwave and to have that, I mean as ugly and hideous as it is in the corner, is an absolute boon to my life and being able to heat things up at the last minute and cold cups of coffee suddenly become wonderfully hot, so I'm – yes, without those two, with those two things I'm fine. Without them, I'm lost.

**Speaker 4:** Two things that I can't live without? Let me think. One of them goes everywhere with me, is a pepper mill for black pepper. I do a lot of travelling and I always – a terrible old piece of stuff, I mean it's, it's quite grotesque. It's not a normal wooden black pepper mill. It's got, it's made out of, almost looks like a small tree. It's quite impractical, I can't pack it anywhere and when you turn the top not much pepper comes out but I've had it for so long now, it automatically finds its way into my case when I, when I go away. My other thing that I have everywhere, and it sounds a bit, a bit fastidious, is my Swiss army knife. I think it's a brilliant piece of engineering really. There are several things on there that are quite pointless. I'm never going to get a stone out of a horse's hoof and there's a little swirly piece of metal with a funny nodule on the end. I don't know what that's for. It's a wonderful piece of engineering, though, and I take it everywhere with me and I couldn't live without it. I really don't think I could.

## Modals: *must, should, ought to, shall, will, would*

1 The grammar here is covered on page 194 of the Grammar folder. Ask students to identify the modal verbs in the sentences.

> **Answers**
> a ought to   b should   c must   d must have
> e should have   f must   g shouldn't have
> h should   i would   j will   k must, shall

2 Students should do this with a partner and then compare their answers with those of other students.

> **Answers**
> a obligation   b requesting   c advice   d deduction
> e advice   f offering   g deduction   h past habit
> i requesting   j advice

3 Ask students to complete the sentences. It is not necessary to use any of the modals in the box more than once.

> **Answers**
> a must   b should / ought to   c should have, must have
> d would   e mustn't   f should / ought to   g Will
> h shouldn't have

4 Students could discuss this exercise in groups and then write about their invention as revision of the work on modals and inventions.

> **Extension activity**
>
> In a follow-up lesson, students could read out the descriptions of their inventions which they wrote in Modals 4 and the other students could award the inventions a mark out of ten as they did for the curious inventions in Reading 1.

## Speaking 2

Students often do not know quite what to say in English when they need to put in a supportive exclamation or filler. Elicit the exclamations or fillers that they have found useful and draw their attention to the Exam spot.

1 Before students do this, point out that different intonation can give these expressions quite differing meanings. They can all be made to sound ironic or bored, for example. In this exercise the aim is to go for the most usual use.

> **Answers**
> Expressing agreement: a, e, i
> Expressing admiration: b, g
> Expressing surprise or disbelief: c, h, k, l, n
> Expressing sympathy: d, f, j, m

2 Ask students to match the expressions in 1 to the sentences a–h.

> **Suggested answers**
> a Brilliant!   b Poor you!   c How extraordinary!
> d Oh dear!   e Fantastic!   f Surely not!   g Me too!
> h What a shame!

3 Play the recording all the way through to allow students time to think about how they might respond.

Then play the recording again, stopping after each snippet to allow students time to respond. Note that there are several different possible responses to each item.

### Tapescript (suggested answers in brackets)

1 The safety pin was invented in 1849. (Surely not!)
2 I've got dreadful toothache! (Poor you!)
3 When Mrs Lincoln, the wife of President Lincoln, had her photograph taken after her husband had been assassinated, the photograph included a ghostly image of the President. (How extraordinary!)
4 You have been selected to advise the Prime Minister on the problems of education in this country.
(You must be joking!)
5 My grandfather, my mother, my sister and I were all born on the same date – the 6th of June!
(What a coincidence!)
6 There are 400 billion stars in the Milky Way.
(That's incredible!)
7 From 13th June 1948 to 1st June 1949, one person in Los Angeles hiccuped 160 million times! 60,000 suggestions for cures were received before he eventually stopped.
(You must be joking!)
8 King Gustav II of Sweden thought that coffee was poisonous. He once sentenced a man to death by ordering him to drink coffee every day. The condemned man in fact lived to be very old! (How amazing!)
9 The first alarm clock was invented by Leonardo da Vinci. It woke the sleeper by gently rubbing the soles of his feet. (Fantastic!)

10 The common housefly may be the biggest threat to human health. It carries 30 different diseases which can be passed to humans. (Surely not!)

4 Refer students to the Exam spot and then practise saying the fillers *Yes*, *Right* and *Mm* to express enthusiasm, doubt and surprise. If necessary demonstrate yourself with *Yes*.

Students should practise in pairs, using the fillers that have been worked with. Ask students to choose one of the three emotions and demonstrate it using any filler to their partner. Can their partner identify which emotion they had in mind?

5 Allow students a few moments to think of what they are going to tell their partner. As they talk, their partner is only allowed to use the exclamations and fillers worked on in this section.

# Exam folder 4

## SB pages 56–57

## Paper 3, part 4  Gapped sentences

You might like to remind students of the exercises they did on page 47 which focused on this type of task.

1 Do not spend too long on this. The purpose of the exercise is merely to emphasise the point that there is unlikely to be a simple one-to-one translation for any individual word. Meaning often varies considerably with context.

2 Students may prepare this exercise individually at home or in pairs in the classroom before checking through it in class.

| Answers | |
|---|---|
| 1 mean | 15 flat |
| 2 figures | 16 put on |
| 3 Put on | 17 bar |
| 4 flat | 18 figures |
| 5 put on | 19 mean |
| 6 bar | 20 put on |
| 7 Mean | 21 bar |
| 8 bar | 22 flat |
| 9 flat | 23 figures |
| 10 mean | 24 bar |
| 11 bar | 25 put on |
| 12 flat | 26 flat |
| 13 figures | 27 figures |
| 14 mean | 28 put on |

3 Students should prepare their sentences at home. They should use a good dictionary such as the *Cambridge Advanced Learner's Dictionary* to help them. When they read out their sentences to their partners they should make a noise like BEEP or TOOT in place of the blank for the word being focused on. You might like to illustrate this by introducing the activity with an example of your own, e.g.

*Every year publishers from all over the world go to the Frankfurt Book BEEP.* (answer = *fair*)

Going through the sentences in class should not take too long as the students' example sentences may well be quite similar.

4

**Suggested answers**
(Other examples may also be found.)
a palm, hands, sets, common
b strip, pad, top
c belt, drives, collar, panel
d wearing, head, support, frame
e wear, seat, down

5

**Answers**
a bank   b score   c stick   d beat   e eye

# 9 You live and learn

| Genre | Academic texts |
| Topic | Further study |

| Speaking 1 | Studying in English |
| Reading | Academic texts |
| Vocabulary | Word formation |
| Grammar | Participle clauses |
| Speaking 2 | Contrastive stress |

**Workbook contents**

| Reading | Multiple-choice questions |
| Vocabulary | Matching meanings to definitions, word formation |
| Grammar | Participle phrases |
| Writing | A report |

## SB pages 58–61

**Lesson planning**

SV  Vocabulary 1 or 2 could be set for homework
LV  See extension activities in the Reading, Vocabulary and Speaking 2 sections

## Speaking 1

The aim of these questions is simply to arouse interest in the concept of studying in English, something which students may be increasingly likely to do in future as Internet-based courses (which are largely in English) increase in number.

## Reading

1 Encourage students to read the texts through as quickly as possible to match them with the subjects.

**Answers**
1 sociolinguistics  2 history  3 economics
4 law  5 psychology

Students match the texts with the pictures.

**Answers**
1 e  2 b  3 d  4 a  5 c

Now allow time for students to read the texts more fully in order to be able to answer question c. They should decide on a title with a partner and then compare their answers with those suggested by other students.

**Suggested answers**
1 The observation of language change
2 Changes in eighteenth century Russian life
3 Consumerism prevails
4 Minority in law
5 Experiments in extra-sensory perception

2 Point out to students that academic language – whatever the subject – often uses language that is rather different from everyday spoken language. However, text 3 is written in a far less formal style than the others, while text 4 is even more formal and academic than the rest. Encourage students to look at the words in their context and try to work out the meaning before choosing their answers from the options in the box.

**Answers**
a a firm no  b before  c previously  d behind
e spare money  f stage where nothing more is needed
g reaches  h previously  i permission  j get
k the other way round  l make a difference between

3 Set this for homework if time is short and check the answers in a follow-up lesson.

**Answers**
a saturation  b differentiate  c vice versa  d leave
e in arrears  f obtain  g formerly  h spending power

**Extension activity**

Language corpora have drawn attention to the fact that language is often used in fixed chunks. Point out to students that becoming aware of this as they read will also help them to write in a natural way.

Work through one of the extracts with the class highlighting the chunks. Here are some of the key chunks from the first extract (you may wish to include others as well):

recent work in (sociolinguistics)
has raised (once again) a (long-standing) question
the answer to that question
following the example of
all that you can possibly hope to

Divide the students into four groups and assign each group one of the four remaining extracts. Each group should select what they feel are the key chunks from their extract and should then present these to the rest of the group.

> **Suggested answers**
> Text 2 – as a (further) symbol of, an important symbolic change, as it were
> Text 3 – the immediate crisis (of 1968) soon passed, dismissed it as a (fantasy), did their bit to
> Text 4 – fixes the age of majority, holding office as
> Text 5 – experiments have shown that, this is by no means necessary, be taken as evidence of

## Vocabulary

1 Students do as much as they can first and then use dictionaries to complete the table, if necessary.

**Suggested answers**

| Verb | Noun | Adjective |
|---|---|---|
| occur | occurrence | occurring |
| found | founder | founding |
| – | consequence | consequent, consequential |
| oblige | obligation | obligatory |
| disappear | disappearance | disappearing |
| glamorise | glamour | glamorous |
| authorise | authority | authoritative, authorised |
| vary | variety | various |
| presume | presumption | presumptive |
| perceive | perception | perceptive, perceptible |

2 Ask students to try this exercise individually before discussing it with the class as a whole.

> **Suggested answers**
> a It is obligatory for (all) pupils to wear school uniform.
> b There is a wide / large / great variety of animals which are indigenous to Australia.
> c Burglaries are an everyday occurrence in this part of town.
> d The mountaineer is presumed to have died in the blizzard.
> e Giving up work to bring up a child and the consequent loss of income is difficult for many women.
> f How do people in your country perceive the role of the United Nations?
> g Cambridge University Press was founded in 1534.
> h Modern films tend to glamorise violence.

## **E**xtension activity

Suggest that students prepare sentences for each other from the words in the table, using the format of the word formation question in the exam.

Example: Are you going to put in an ............................. for that job? (apply)
Answer: application

When you have checked the sentences, have students give them to other students in the class to do.

## Participle clauses

1 Discuss the examples and the question with the class as a whole. The grammar here is covered on pages 194–195 of the Grammar folder.

> **Suggested answers**
> Most linguists, who have followed the example of two of the founders of the modern discipline, de Saussure (1959) and Bloomfield (1933), maintain that change itself cannot be observed …
>
> The Tsar took scissors and cut off their beards. He also snipped the capacious sleeves of their traditional robes …

## **T**eaching extra

Point out that the differences are between the two perfectly correct alternatives – the version with the participle phrase sounds more sophisticated in style and is, therefore, appropriate for an academic text.

2 While doing this exercise, draw attention to the three basic types of participle phrase – those beginning with an -ing word, those with a past participle and those with having + a past participle. Point out also how It is used in sentence c. You may wish to give students some other examples of how a different subject can be included with a participle clause:
*England having been knocked out in the first round, I decided to support the Irish team.*
*There only being two entries to the competition, the judges decided that they should both share the prize.*

> **Answers**
> a Because they hoped to gain a speedy victory, the army invaded.
> b They killed many people who were living in the border areas.
> c Because it was a Sunday, most of the shops were shut.
> d Charles I was generally considered a weak king and was eventually beheaded.
> e Because he had previously learnt their language, Picton was able to communicate with the tribe.
> f When you have measured the wood carefully, cut it as indicated.

YOU LIVE AND LEARN

3   Students should discuss the sentences with a partner and then present their answers to the rest of the class.

> **Answers**
> a   Walking round the exhibition, I caught sight of an old school friend at the far end of the gallery.
> b   Having made so many mistakes in her homework, Marti had to do it all over again.
> c   Being only a child, she can't fully understand what is happening.
> d   Not knowing anyone / Knowing no one in the town to spend the evening with, Jack decided to have an early night.
> e   Considering all the inequalities of life before the revolution, it is surprising that a revolution did not happen sooner.
> f   Having climbed to the top of the church tower, be sure to walk right round, admiring the view from each of the four sides.
> g   We set off at midnight, hoping to avoid the rest of the holiday traffic heading for the coast. OR Setting off at midnight, we hoped to avoid the rest of the holiday traffic heading for the coast.
> h   Seeing me, he stood up, knocking his glass to the floor.

4   Students could prepare this at home as revision of the grammar covered in this unit and bring their example sentences to share in the next lesson. Refer students to the Exam spot at this point.

> **Possible answers**
> a   Having been a major news item last week, the earthquake has now been completely overshadowed by the latest political scandal.
> b   Having become successful at quite a young age, she grew up believing that things would always be easy for her.
> c   Being one of the largest cities in our country, Birmingham inevitably has major problems with transport.
> d   Not daring to interrupt him, I closed the door and went to listen to music in another room.
> e   Starting this CAE course, I felt I would never be able to manage it but now the work is beginning to feel a bit easier.
> f   Having worked hard all his life, he considers that he has the right just to laze around if he feels like it now that he has retired.

### **T**eaching extra

Although students may well have few difficulties understanding this structure, they are likely to be rather slow at using it in their own written work. When you mark any free writing from your students over the next few weeks, try to suggest ways in which they could have used it in their work. This may help to encourage them to use it themselves in future writing.

## Speaking 2

1   Ask students to discuss which words Speaker B would be likely to stress.

2   Play the recording for students to check their answers. The words which are stressed are underlined in the tapescript.

### Tapescript and answers

1   **A:** Did you go to the cinema last night?
    **B:** No, but I went to the <u>theatre</u>.
2   **A:** Did you go by bike to the theatre last night?
    **B:** No, <u>Marco</u> was using my bike last night.
3   **A:** Did you go to the theatre by bus last night?
    **B:** No, I went to the theatre by <u>taxi</u> last night.
4   **A:** Did you go home by taxi last night?
    **B:** No, I went home by taxi <u>two</u> nights ago.
5   **A:** Anne's wearing a lovely green dress.
    **B:** It's a green <u>blouse</u> and <u>skirt</u>, actually.
6   **A:** Did you have a good time at the party last night?
    **B:** Yes, we had a <u>brilliant</u> time.
7   **A:** Are you hungry yet?
    **B:** I'm not <u>hungry</u>, I'm <u>starving</u>.
8   **A:** Are you hungry yet?
    **B:** <u>I'm</u> not hungry but <u>Tina</u> is.
9   **A:** Are you tired?
    **B:** Yes, I'm <u>exhausted</u>!
10  **A:** Are you feeling a bit cold?
    **B:** Yes, I'm <u>freezing</u>!

3   Students should practise reading the dialogues, with each student having the opportunity to practise as both A and B.

4   Ask students to work with a partner. Have some initial prompts ready to suggest to students who may find this difficult, e.g. *Does Mary love Bobby? Did you have tomato soup for lunch today?*

### **E**xtension activity

Students pass their dialogues to another pair of students who read them out, stressing the important words to the rest of the class. The other students should note down which words they think are being stressed.

5   Refer students to the Exam spot at this point. Practise one or two sentences describing the differences between the pictures with the class as a whole. Then ask students to work with a partner and to take care to stress the important words in an appropriate way. Encourage students to make strong contrastive word stress in English where this is appropriate.

# Writing folder 4

## SB pages 62–63

## Reports and proposals

1 Students should discuss these questions with a partner. Ask for their feedback, making sure the points mentioned in the answers below are covered.

If your students have had little experience of report or proposal writing, it may be helpful if you are prepared to give them an example or two of such types of writing that you have had to do. You could show this to them when they discuss 1b.

Discuss the answers to 1d with the class before reading the information given in the list that follows.

> **Suggested answers**
> **a Types of reports**
>    scientific report, e.g. of experiment
>    business report, e.g. of progress made over last year
>    sports report, e.g. of football match played
>    school report, e.g. of child's progress over a term or year
>    shareholders' annual report, e.g. of company's performance over the year
>    product report, e.g. weighing up the good and bad features of different products of the same type
> **Types of proposals**
>    academic proposal, e.g. about research with a view to getting some money or a place at university
>    work proposal, e.g. with a view to introducing some innovation at the workplace
>    social proposal, e.g. a plan for change that aims to persuade readers of the desirability of such changes
> **c** It will probably have some or all of the following:
>    factual title
>    clear statement of aims at beginning
>    facts presented unambiguously
>    clearly drawn conclusions at the end
>    headings used frequently to help clarify
> **d** An article aims to be interesting and lively as well as clear, whereas the main aim of a report is to be unambiguous and straightforward.
>    An article may be more personal in style and approach. The title of an article aims to be eye-catching rather than factual.

2 Before they choose a writing task, remind students of the work they did on reports in Unit 7 and of the importance of using headings to signpost their writing. Then ask each pair of students to choose a task. Try to ensure that the three tasks are fairly evenly distributed among the pairs.

3 Students should now discuss these questions, bearing in mind the pair of tasks they have chosen.

4 Students mill around the class asking as many people as possible the questions they prepared in 3b. They should keep a note of the answers they get. They then return to their partner to discuss 4b and 4c.

5 Students discuss questions a–c with their partner.

6 Tell students to decide which of them will write the report and which the proposal. Students write the report or proposal in class or at home.

> **Extension activity**
>
> In a later lesson it may be useful to follow this procedure with the reports and proposals that the students write.
>
> 1 Students exchange their work with a partner. They read each other's work thinking carefully about these questions:
>    • Is the information totally clear?
>    • Are the headings informative?
>    • Are the paragraphs well-organised?
>    • Does the language seem accurate?
>    • Is the language varied in terms of both structure and vocabulary?
>    • What do I particularly like about this piece of writing?
>    • What suggestions could I make about how it could perhaps be improved?
>
> 2 Students share their ideas about each other's work.
>
> 3 Students rewrite their work in the light of any helpful suggestions they have received from other students.

# 10 I have a dream

| Genre | Speeches |
|---|---|
| Topic | Social change |

| Speaking 1 | Speeches |
|---|---|
| Reading | Martin Luther King's *I have a dream* speech |
| Listening | Martin Luther King's speech (continued) and other speeches |
| Vocabulary | Metaphors and idioms |
| Grammar | Future forms |
| Speaking 2 | Social change |

**Workbook contents**

| Reading | Multiple-choice questions |
|---|---|
| Grammar | Future forms |
| Vocabulary | Metaphor and idiom |
| Use of English | Part 2 open gap fill |

## SB pages 64–67

### Lesson planning

- **SV** Vocabulary 1 or 2 and Grammar 1 or 2 could be set for homework
- **LV** See extension activities in the Reading, Listening and Grammar sections

## Speaking 1

Discuss the warm-up questions with the class as a whole. Allow for students to interpret *speeches* as widely as they wish in question 1, i.e. any extended piece of speaking to an audience. It could be a speech at a wedding or other family function, for example, or on an academic topic to classmates.

### Background information

The speech was delivered by Martin Luther King, a black American clergyman and civil rights campaigner, on the steps at the Lincoln Memorial in Washington DC on August 28, 1963, as the climax of a civil rights march on Washington. He was advocating a non-violent approach to his campaigners but was himself assassinated five years later.

## Reading

1 Students read the text then choose the sentences which best sum up each paragraph.

### Answers
1 d  2 a  3 e  4 b

Go over any major language difficulties that students may be having with the speech but try to get them to feel the mood of the speech rather than to worry too much about details.

2 Discuss this question with the class as a whole.

### Extension activity

Extra questions for the reading text:
- What is King's purpose in this part of the speech?
- What do you think the dream that he has will be?
- What do you think he might say in the rest of the speech?

### Answers
His purpose in this part of the speech is to rouse his listeners to press for action by pointing out that one hundred years after the freeing of slaves in the USA, black people still do not enjoy freedom.
The last two questions are simply conjecture at this point. Encourage students to give their ideas but do not comment on how accurately they have guessed.

## Listening

1 Before students listen to the next part of the speech, make sure that they understand all the points they are to listen out for. Go through the list with them and elicit an example of each of the points listed. Then play the rest of the speech, while the students listen and tick the relevant items on the list.

### Answers
Techniques that students should tick are listed below with some examples in brackets (other examples may also be found for many of these points).
- repetition (*Go back to, I have a dream ...*)
- mixing short and long sentences (mainly long sentences followed by the final short one)
- addressing the audience directly (*I say to you today, my friends, ...*)

- making use of metaphor (*sweltering with the heat of injustice, an oasis of freedom and justice*)
- quoting famous lines (*We hold these truths to be self-evident: that all men are created equal* – from the American Declaration of Independence)
- making dramatic pauses
- appealing to the audience's emotions (almost all the speech)

## Tapescript

Go back to Mississippi, go back to Alabama, go back to South Carolina, go back to Georgia, go back to Louisiana, go back to the slums and ghettos of our northern cities, knowing that somehow this situation can and will be changed. Let us not wallow in the valley of despair.

I say to you today, my friends, so even though we face the difficulties of today and tomorrow, I still have a dream. It is a dream deeply rooted in the American dream.

I have a dream that one day this nation will rise up and live out the true meaning of its creed: 'We hold these truths to be self-evident: that all men are created equal.'

I have a dream that one day on the red hills of Georgia the sons of former slaves and the sons of former slave owners will be able to sit down together at the table of brotherhood.

I have a dream that one day even the state of Mississippi, a state sweltering with the heat of injustice, sweltering with the heat of oppression, will be transformed into an oasis of freedom and justice.

I have a dream that my four little children will one day live in a nation where they will not be judged by the color of their skin but by the content of their character.

I have a dream today.

### E xtension activity

Ask students to look again at the first part of the speech in Reading 1 and see if any of the techniques that were not ticked in Listening 1 are exemplified.

#### Answers
- drawing attention to the location in which the speech is taking place (*a great American, in whose symbolic shadow we stand*)
- alliteration (*dark and desolate*)
- appealing to the audience's senses (*seared in the flames, a joyous daybreak to end the long night of captivity, cooling off*)

2   Students look at the pictures and try to identify the occasions shown in them. They then listen and match each speaker to a picture as they do so.

**Answers**
1 a   2 d   3 b   4 e   5 c

## Tapescript

**Speaker 1:** I've known Johnny since our first day at school when we were five. We were two scared little boys sitting at the same table hoping that we were going to enjoy this strangely exciting new world. Now Johnny is beginning another new stage of his life. In some ways it may be rather like starting school again! Especially, of course, as Megan, his beautiful bride, is a teacher herself. Johnny as teacher's pet! None of the staff at Morley Primary School would ever have expected that of him!

**Speaker 2:** You may not believe it of an old man like me but it seems no time at all to me since I had a 'shining morning face', as Shakespeare so aptly put it, a face that was amazingly once as young and eager as those of yours that I see before me now. I too was dreaming of a life beyond the inevitably restricted confines of these walls. I promised your headmaster that I would not be either too sentimental or too long-winded. I guess I'd better change track before I fail on the sentimental count, but I promise to do my best to be brief. I hear your sighs of relief from the back of the room, cooling me nicely on this sweltering day!

**Speaker 3:** Maria, you are a beautiful baby. May you grow up to bring your own parents as much joy as they have brought their own parents in so many different ways and most recently, possibly best of all, by producing you! A quick check on the Internet showed me that you share your birthday with the philosopher, Jean-Paul Sartre and the actress, Jane Russell. Brains and beauty. Like mother, like daughter!

**Speaker 4:** This next slide shows the narrow pathway down to Petra, the 'rose-red city half as old as time'. We were there on one of the hottest days of the whole trip but who could not be impressed by the glorious red-sandstone buildings of this city, reputedly the oldest city in the world? Once known as Palmyra, it grew to importance because of its location enabling it to control the trade routes of the ancient world.

**Speaker 5:** Well, Fiona. You've been working here for longer than any of us, including the boss and we're all going to miss you very much. We've clubbed together to get you this little token of our appreciation for all the good – and occasionally not so good – times we've shared together. We hope that whenever you make yourself some coffee you'll think of us and the thousands of coffees we've shared over the years. Remember us all as you drink your favourite cappuccino – with plenty of chocolate, of course. But I'd

I HAVE A DREAM

like everyone now to raise a glass of something a bit stronger than coffee to wish you, Fiona, all the very best for a long, happy and healthy retirement.

3   Give each student one or two of the techniques from the list in Listening 1 to listen out for. They should note down the examples of the techniques which they hear. After listening, go through the speeches one by one and ask students to report back on any examples of points that they found.

> **Answers**
> Students may come up with other suggestions that you find acceptable but some of the main techniques used in these speeches are indicated here in brackets after the relevant places in the tapescripts.
> **Speaker 1:** I've known Johnny since our first day at school when we were five (*presenting interesting or surprising facts*). We were two scared little boys sitting at the same table hoping that we were going to enjoy this strangely exciting new world (*appealing to the audience's emotions*). Now Johnny is beginning another new stage of his life. In some ways it may be rather like starting school again (*making analogies or comparisons*). Especially, of course, as Megan, his beautiful bride (*appealing to the audience's senses*), is a teacher herself. Johnny as teacher's pet! None of the staff at Morley Primary School would ever have expected that of him (*humour*)!
> **Speaker 2:** You may not believe it of an old man like me but it seems no time at all (*exaggeration*) to me since I had a 'shining morning face', as Shakespeare so aptly put it (*quoting famous lines*), a face that was amazingly once as young and eager as those of yours that I see before me now. I too was dreaming of a life beyond the inevitably restricted confines of these walls (*making analogies or comparisons*). I promised your headmaster that I would not be either too sentimental or too long-winded. I guess I'd better change track before I fail on the sentimental count, but I promise to do my best to be brief. I hear your sighs of relief from the back of the room, cooling me nicely on this sweltering day (*humour, appealing to the audience's senses*)!
> **Speaker 3:** Maria, you are a beautiful baby (*appealing to the audience's senses*). May you grow up to bring your own parents as much joy as they have brought their own parents in so many different ways and most recently, possibly best of all, by producing you! A quick check on the Internet showed me that you share your birthday with the philosopher, Jean-Paul Sartre and the actress, Jane Russell (*presenting interesting or surprising facts*). Brains and beauty. Like mother, like daughter (*appealing to the audience's emotions, mixing short and long sentences*)!
> **Speaker 4:** This next slide (*using visual aids*) shows the narrow pathway down to Petra, the 'rose-red city half as old as time' (*quoting famous lines*). We were there on one of the hottest days of the whole trip (*appealing to the audience's senses*) but who could not be impressed by the glorious red-sandstone buildings of this city, reputedly the oldest city in the world? (*asking rhetorical questions*) Once known as Palmyra, it grew to importance because of its location enabling it to control the trade routes of the ancient world (*presenting interesting or surprising facts*).
> **Speaker 5:** Well, Fiona. You've been working here (*drawing attention to the location where the speech is taking place*) for longer than any of us, including the boss and we're all going to miss you very much. We've clubbed together to get you this little token of our appreciation for all the good – and occasionally not so good – times we've shared together (*appealing to the audience's emotions*). We hope that whenever you make yourself some coffee you'll think of us and the thousands of coffees we've shared over the years. Remember us all as you drink your favourite cappuccino – with plenty of chocolate, of course (*appealing to the audience's senses*). But I'd like everyone now to raise a glass of something a bit stronger than coffee (*humour*) to wish you, Fiona, all the very best for a long, happy and healthy retirement.

## Vocabulary

A metaphor is an expression that describes a person, object or something else in a literary way by referring to something that is considered to possess similar characteristics to the person or object that is being described, e.g. *Her words cut into him.* (Here, her obviously sharp or unkind words are compared to a knife in that they hurt him.)

An idiom is a group of words in a fixed order having a different meaning from each word understood on its own, e.g. *to give someone a hand* (to help someone).

NB Many idioms are also metaphors but metaphors can only also be called idioms if they have a fixed format and are in common use.

1   Work through the exercise as a class. As you deal with each item, ask the students to explain what the relevance of the metaphor is in each case. Draw students' attention to the Vocabulary spot at this point.

> **Answers**
> a punishment   b light, punishment   c light
> d economics   e heat   f economics
> g natural environment, light
> h natural environment, heat   i natural environment

2   Ask students to look at the idioms in italics and check the meanings of any that they do not understand. They should then try to complete the exercise. Remind them that they will sometimes need to change the form of the idiom slightly so that it fits the grammar of the sentence. As you check the answers, ask students to

**I HAVE A DREAM**

explain what each idiom means in non-idiomatic English. The meaning is given in brackets after each answer below.

> **Answers**
> a *will foot the bill* (will pay)
> b *went up in smoke* (vanished)
> c *am tied up* (am busy)
> d *feeling all at sea* (not knowing what you should do)
> e *shedding light on* (clarifying)
> f *light dawned* (she realised)
> g *common ground* (points that could be agreed on)
> h *was pilloried* (was strongly criticised)
> i *in debt* (very grateful)
> j *put its money where its mouth is* (be prepared to spend money as well as to talk)
> k *will get your fingers burnt* (will get into trouble)

# Future forms

The grammar here is covered on page 195 of the Grammar folder.

1 Before looking at the section in the book with students, brainstorm as many ways of talking about the future as possible and elicit the point that the choice of form made will depend on the meaning the user wants to convey (e.g. degree of certainty in the user's mind) and grammatical constraints.

Students then discuss the exercise with a partner before checking their answers. Deal with any issues that arise as difficulties for the class as a whole.

> **Answers**
> a 5  b 1  c 6  d 4,6  e 8  f 9  g 7  h 3  i 10  j 2

2 Work through this exercise with the class as a whole.

> **Answers**
> a I'm going  b get  c we'll be lying  d he'd leave
> e to get  f leaves / is leaving  g are, are going to spend
> h gets, she's going to study  i will have set foot

3 Students practise the questions in pairs. Monitor as they do so to check that they are using the correct forms.

> **Extension activity**
>
> Do some quick class practice of the questions in Future forms 1, choosing students at random to answer each of the questions and some variations on them, e.g.
> - What are you doing this weekend?
> - What will you be doing this time next week? etc.

4 Elicit what students remember about the texts in Listening 2.

Assign to students either Johnny and Megan, baby Maria or Fiona and ask them to write about their future using as many different future forms (in appropriate ways) as they can. When they are ready, the students who were assigned Johnny and Megan all read out their sentences to the class. The students who were dealing with baby Maria and Fiona then vote on whose predictions they think are best. Follow the same procedure with the other groups.

# Speaking 2

1 Briefly discuss some of the issues in the bubble with the class before starting this activity. Pick on aspects of these topics that the class are most likely to feel strongly about and to feel that there is a need for change. Point out that they do not have to choose one of the issues from the page – anything that concerns them will be appropriate as long as they all agree that changes are necessary. Encourage them to think of at least three or four specific changes that they would like to make with regard to their chosen subject.

2 Allow plenty of time for students to plan for an effective presentation.

3 Encourage students to think about how to give the presentation.

4 This activity is intended to focus students' attention on the ideas that the groups present. After each presentation, invite a student to present the notes he or she made while listening. The group who made the presentation should then comment on how accurate those notes were.

5 Do not do this until all the group presentations have been made. If possible, organise students so that they are working with someone from a different group.

# UNITS 6-10 Revision

## SB pages 68-69

### Topic review

Follow the standard procedure outlined on page 29 of the Teacher's Book.

### Grammar

1 Students could prepare their answers to the questions at home. Encourage students to write two or three full sentences in answer to each of the questions. Students should work with a partner taking turns to ask each other questions a–f. They should then compare their answers for questions g and h.

### Reading

1 Check that students know what teleworking is (working from home rather than going to work in an office and instead communicating with one's office by phone, email, etc.). Refer students to the Exam spot at this point.

2 When checking the answers together, encourage students to explain how they knew what the right answer was in each case.

**Answers**
Correct paragraph order – C, E, F, B, D, A, G

3 Students do this individually and then compare their answers with a partner.

**Answers**
a fair  b draw  c hit  d set  e bear  f bar

4 Refer students to the Exam spot. Before doing the exercise, look at the words in the box and discuss what other words could be formed from the same roots.

Students then do the exercise and compare their answers.

**Answers**
1 alphabetical  2 obsessive  3 coverage  4 addiction
5 extension  6 editor  7 expensive  8 pride  9 latest
10 survival

# TEST 2

## Paper 1 Part 2

You are going to read an extract from a book. Eight paragraphs have been removed from the extract. Choose from the paragraphs **A–I** the one which fits each gap (**1–7**). There is one extra paragraph which you do not need to use.

### KEEPING UP WITH THE NEW ENGLISH

The internet is destroying the English language. Well, isn't it? The English literature woven by poets such as Tennyson is not the clumsy, mispeld englsh of email communication, in which speed takes precedence over spelling and punctuation. It is not the MANIC SHOUTING!!! in the online chat room, where myriad chatterers rattle away through vast, overlapping conversations in which the fastest typist is king. And it is certainly not the vwls-r-4-wmps desiccation of the txt message, whereby communication is shrunk to a pared-down minimum.

**0** E

"You can't avoid Weblish, for the simple reason that whenever a new variety of language comes along, it inevitably impacts on the language as a whole," says Dr David Crystal, honorary professor of linguistics at the University of Wales in Bangor, whose book *Language and the Internet* has just been published (CUP £13.95). "These things won't be limited to internet nerds, they'll come to all of us."

**1**

However, these days, as Crystal points out: "New technology is going round the world more rapidly than it ever could have done before. In the past, it would take years for a word to become common currency; these days, a word can make it into a dictionary in a few months. So the main impact of the internet lies not in the number of extra words that have come in, but in the speed with which they are spread." In other words, just because a piece of internet jargon is unfamiliar to you today, does not mean that it will not be a part of common speech tomorrow.

**2**

Yet there is more to this new English than a mere expansion of vocabulary, and text messages are essentially a red herring, because they do little more than reduce communication to the smallest number of keystrokes possible, albeit with clever use of soundalike words and numerals, as in U R 2 good 2 B 4gotten (you are too good to be forgotten). It is more useful to look at the language used in email.

**3**

Such symbols and abbreviations placed inside angled brackets are inevitably a common element of keyboard banter in internet chat rooms, where one of the most common solecisms is the misuse of the acronym LOL. This generally stands for Laughing Out Loud to indicate an appreciative reaction, yet newbies (internet novices) tend to assume it means Lots of Love. If you are telling someone how sad you are about the death of their hamster, it would be better not to sign off with LOL. Other popular acronyms in chat rooms are FWIW (for what it's worth), IMHO (in my humble opinion) and WYRN (what's your real name) and, of course, TLA (three-letter acronym).

**4**

The trouble with keeping up with the new English is not just these new words but also that the old words no longer mean what we thought they did. In the past, if someone said they did not have Windows, you would have to assume they lived in a cave. These days, it is probably because they use a Mac (which is a computer, not a raincoat). Spam is as groanworthy as it ever was, but now comes down a net connection rather than in a can. Booting up is something you do to your computer when switching on, not when going for a walk in muddy terrain.

**5**

A further change is that Weblish loves to see nouns happily become verbs ("Please bookmark this site"; "Stop flaming me!"), and verbs become nouns ("Send me the download"). Verbs and prepositions are regularly thrown together to become new nouns or adjectives (dial-up, logon, print out, pull-down, upload), while others are created from simply pairing nouns: ethernet, netspeak.

**6**

In conclusion, should we be worried by all this linguistic evolution? Not if you believe David Crystal. "Every new technology has brought its prophets of doom," he says. "The internet is no exception. Language consists of dozens of different styles; I could speak to you in any one of them. This is not to say that I have lost my identity simply because I can switch into one or another."

**7**

Next year's words are already with us. It is up to us to make sure our voices are in tune.

**A** One of the peculiarities of email is that it often feels closer to a phone call than to a letter. So the opening salutation "Hi" is replacing the standard "Dear" for relatively formal communications. This might sound funky and overfamiliar, but compare it with the Roman greeting "Ave!" ("Hail!") and you see that we are simply back where we were 2,000 years ago. OTOH (on the other hand), email lacks the tonality of spoken language, which led early senders to incorporate "smileys" or "emoticons" – little faces :-) made from punctuation marks – to emphasise or enhance the true sense of their messages.

**B** Spellings are changing as well as meanings. Not only is text-messaging playing hvc wth vrbs, but the conventions of email communication place little premium on perfick speling. Most intriguingly, some words are now intentionally misspelt, such as swear words in online chat rooms. Spell certain four-letter words in their correct Anglo-Saxon form, and the chat-room software will automatically eject you from the forum. Misspell them slightly, and people will still know what you mean but the filters will not detect you.

**C** The change is happening at high speed, and if you do not know the difference between a cookie and a chunky floppy, or between a spider and a Trojan horse, the chances are that you are being left behind. Technology has always been the main source of new vocabulary entering the English language, whether from the industrial revolution or developments in medicine.

**D** Willingness to adapt – this is the key. The internet has not destroyed the English language, nor is it likely to. If we are to stay on top of our language, however, rather than watch it slowly being pulled like a rug from beneath us, it makes sense to try to keep abreast of developments rather than run them down. As the poet T S Eliot declared, many decades ago: "For last year's words belong to last year's language / And next year's words await another voice."

**E** No, the English language is changing, and fast, thanks to the frenetic progress of technology. We all have a choice: either to bury our heads in the sand and spend the rest of our lives wishing Shakespeare were alive and well, hoping that these sinister linguistic developments fade away. Or we can embrace the new English, enter into the spirit of the internet age and call it Weblish, concede that the growth of the language is inescapable and become willing masters, rather than sulky victims, of its 21st-century possibilities.

**F** Accordingly, Oxford University Press published its first *Dictionary of the Internet* (OUP £16.99) last week, explaining the meaning of words such as "adhocracy", "facemail" and "spamhaus". And as if to stamp an imprimatur on the literary value of text messages, the BBC and TransWorld this year joined forces to publish a book called *The Joy of Text*, reflecting the mainstream popularity of this phenomenon, which sees one billion messages being sent between UK mobile phones every month. It is no wonder that text-messaging is making its impact felt upon the English language.

**G** Today's quickfire communication by internet, email and mobile phone is changing the language at an unprecedented pace. Unfortunately, this means in part that standards in written and spoken English are declining very rapidly too. However, in some ways the changes can be looked on more positively as adding a certain curious richness to the ways in which people express themselves.

**H** While it is always acceptable (and even encouraged) to invent your own words as part of the new English, certain coinages are to be avoided at all costs. Cyber-anything (as in cyberbabe, cybergranny, cyberpizza) is now exceptionally clichéd, as is incorporating the @ symbol to suggest webfangledness (Ethel's C@fe). True geeks would not be heard dead talking about "surfing" the internet, which to them sounds as old-fashioned as "motoring" down to Hastings for tea.

**I** It is worth saying that computer acronyms have yet to be accepted in common speech, with the possible exception of Wysiwyg (pronounced wizzywig, and short for "what you see is what you get"), which you may occasionally hear being applied to people as well as operating systems ("Jim is just so Wysiwyg; he couldn't tell a lie if he tried").

# Paper 2 Part 2

Write an answer to **one** of the questions **1–4** in this part. Write your answer in 220–260 words in an appropriate style.

1  Health experts claim that people are changing how they exercise. You have been asked to write an article for an international magazine, commenting on the situation in your country. Your article must address the following questions:

   - Do people exercise more than previously in your country?
   - What are the effects of taking exercise on people's health?

   Write your **article**.

2  You see the following competition in an international magazine.

> WHO BOTHERS TO READ THESE DAYS?
> People no longer read books for pleasure or for information. They watch TV or videos or use the Internet.
> What can books offer us nowadays?
> Write an entry for the competition, giving your views on this topic. The best entry will win a set of four novels by leading authors.

   Write your **competition entry**.

3  You have been asked by your local Tourist Office to write an information sheet in English giving information about accommodation for visitors to your city. Your information sheet must:

   - compare and contrast different types of accommodation
   - suggest which type of accommodation might suit different visitors: families, people of different ages and people on different budgets
   - give practical advice on how to find and book accommodation before arriving in the city.

   Write the **information sheet**.

4  Write a **review** for your college magazine of the set text you have read. Briefly outline the story and try to persuade other students to read it too.

> Note: In the final exam, the question on set texts will have two options – one on each of the set texts. You will be asked to choose one of these options.

# Paper 3 Part 3

Read the text below. Use the word given in capitals at the end of some of the lines to form a word that fits in the gap in the same line. There is an example at the beginning (0).

**Example: 0**  *feminism*

## MEN AND WOMEN IN THE HOUSE

Those men who fear that three decades of (0) .................. has produced a generation of (1) .................., house-trained husbands will be comforted by a survey showing that women regard their men as being as (2) .................. useless as they ever were. Nearly 60% of women questioned doubted that the male had capacity for self reliance, agreeing with the (3) .................. that "men don't shop, even for their own underpants". Those women with husbands or boyfriends, aged 30–44, were most likely to be in (4) .................. with this. The aim of the survey was to (5) .................. the attitude of women towards their lives in the light of decades of feminist struggle. Some 500 women across the country were asked if they agreed with various views once felt to be (6) .................. female. In the (7) .................. of reponses it was found that, while their partners regarded weekends as a time of (8) .................. , 60% of women considered them a time to catch up on housework. However, the (9) .................. that "every woman knows that, (10) .................. of all her other achievements, she is a failure if she is not beautiful" was disputed by 68% of those polled.

FEMININE

OBEY

DOMESTIC

STATE

AGREE

VALUE

TYPE

ANALYSE

RELAX

CONTEND

REGARD

# Paper 4 Part 2

You will hear a journalist talking about alphabetism, which he calls a new type of discrimination.
For questions **1–11**, complete the notes.

Types of discrimination mentioned:   racism

sexism

[_____ **1** ]

alphabetism

Alphabetism = discrimination against those whose surnames begin with a letter in the [_____ **2** ] of the alphabet.

Number of US Presidents before George W Bush whose names began:

with a letter in the first half of the alphabet   [_____ **3** ]

with a letter in the second half of the alphabet   [_____ **4** ]

Other groups of people who illustrate the same phenomenon include

the world's top three [_____ **5** ] and

the five [_____ **6** ] men in the world.

Children whose names are at the beginning of the alphabet are made to sit at the

[_____ **7** ] of the class in infant school and so get

[_____ **8** ] attention from the teacher.

Lists of people at graduation ceremonies, for job interviews etc. are usually drawn up in alphabetic order and by the end the audience, interviewers, etc. have [_____ **9** ]

What can women do to change their situation? [_____ **10** ]

One consolation for those whose names begin with a letter in the 'wrong' half of the alphabet is that such people are better at [_____ **11** ]

# TEST 2 Key

## Paper 1 Part 2

1 C  2 F  3 A  4 I  5 B  6 H  7 D

## Paper 3 Part 3

1 obedient  2 domestically  3 statement  4 agreement
5 evaluate  6 typically  7 analysis  8 relaxation
9 contention  10 regardless

## Paper 4 Part 2

1 ageism  2 second half  3 26  4 16  5 central bankers
6 richest  7 front  8 more  9 lost interest
10 marry  11 running a big business

## Tapescript

Over the past century all kinds of unfairness and discrimination have been denounced or made illegal. We've fought and are still fighting against racism, sexism, ageism … But yet another has recently been highlighted: alphabetism. This, for those of you who, like me, were unaware of such a sad affliction, refers to discrimination against those whose name begins with a letter in the second half of the alphabet.

It has long been known that a firm called AAA Cars has a big advantage over Zodiac Cars when customers thumb through their phone books. Less well-known is the advantage which Adam Abbott has in life over Zoe Zysman. English names are apparently fairly evenly spread between the halves of the alphabet. Yet a suspiciously large number of top people have surnames beginning with the letters between A and K.

Thus the current American President and Vice President have names beginning with B and C respectively and twenty-six of George Bush's predecessors, including his father, of course, had surnames in the first half of the alphabet with just sixteen in the second half. Even more striking, six of the seven current heads of the G7 rich countries are alphabetically advantaged. The world's three top central bankers have names beginning with letters close to the top of the alphabet, even if one of them really uses Japanese characters. As do the world's five richest men – Gates, Buffet, Allen, Ellison and Albrecht.

Can this merely be a coincidence? One theory, dreamt up in all their spare time by the alphabetically disadvantaged, is that the rot sets in early. At the start of the first year in infant school, teachers seat pupils alphabetically from the front, to make it easier to remember their names. So short-sighted Zysman junior gets stuck in the back row and is largely ignored by the teacher. At the time the alphabetically disadvantaged juniors may think they've had a lucky escape. Yet the result may be worse qualifications because they get less individual attention as well as acquiring less confidence in speaking publicly.

The humiliation continues. At university graduation ceremonies, the ABCs proudly get their awards first; by the time they reach the Zs, most of the audience are asleep. Shortlists for job interviews, election ballot papers, conference speakers and the like all tend to be drawn up alphabetically and their recipients gradually lose interest as they plough their way through the list.

What is to be done? Awkward though it may be for the independent-minded, women can at least achieve alphabetic advancement by marrying up. Thus Ms Zysman could become Mrs Abbott.

However, do not give up hope, all you Ps, Qs and Ws. The alphabetically disadvantaged may not become presidents, central bankers or rich but do seem to thrive at running firms. Nine of the world's ten biggest companies (by revenues) are run by bosses with names that begin in the second half of the alphabet. An old theory is thus supported – only those who have battled against the odds will really make it in business.

# 11 Read all about it

| Genre | Magazine and newspaper articles |
|---|---|
| Topic | Fashion |

| Speaking 1 | Newspapers and magazines |
| Reading | Clothes sizing |
| Vocabulary | Collocation |
| Listening | Company dress codes |
| Grammar | Direct and reported speech |
| Speaking 2 | Discussing fashions |

**Workbook contents**

| Reading | Putting missing sentences into gaps |
| Vocabulary | Gap fill from reading exercise |
| Grammar | Direct and reported speech |
| Use of English | Part 3 word formation |

## SB pages 70–73

### Lesson planning
- **SV** Vocabulary 1 and Grammar 3 or 4 could be set for homework
- **LV** See the extension activity in the Listening section

## Speaking 1

Introduce the unit by asking students to discuss questions a–d with a partner.

a This question might provide more ideas about the types of articles your students are interested in.

b This question might well stimulate debate on whether people read more than before because we use the Internet more or whether people read less because more they get their news and information from television.

c Students might discuss the feel of real paper in the hands as opposed to reading a screen. Can reading a newspaper at a pavement café or over the breakfast table be replaced by a newspaper on a computer?

d If possible, have some examples of English language newspapers to bring to class or if you have access to the Internet, look up some newspaper sites. Elicit the distinction between broadsheets (quality newspapers) and tabloids (popular newspapers).

## Reading

1 In preparation for the article, ask students to discuss their likes and dislikes about shopping. You could develop the discussion by asking if there is a difference between men's and women's attitudes to shopping and whether it is better to go shopping for clothes on your own or with a friend.

2 Ask the students to read the base text first. Then they should read paragraphs A–G and fit them into the gaps 1–6. Remind students to look for reasons for their choices based on meaning and grammar.

**Answers**
1 C   2 F   3 A   4 G   5 D   6 E

3 Go through the base text and paragraphs helping students to find reasons for their answers.

## Vocabulary

1 This exercise could be set for homework. It deals with vocabulary related to fashion. Make sure students read the whole text first to get the general meaning.

**Answers**
1 browsing   2 tailored   3 sleeveless   4 pencil
5 aubergine   6 wear   7 slim   8 suede   9 fake
10 look

## Listening

1 Refer students to the Exam spot at this point. Then use question 1 to introduce the topic of dress code.

### Extension activity
Ask students what they would expect the following people to wear (male and female versions): a lawyer, a doctor, an architect, a teacher, a shop assistant in a clothes shop, a bus driver, an air steward.

2   This prediction exercise will prepare students for the listening. If your students need help, lead the discussion with the following questions:
    *In which jobs is appearance important?*
    *What do you think dress-down Friday is?*
    *What is body jewellery?*
    *Why might some people object to a dress code?*

3   Explain that students will hear the information they need to fill the gaps on the tape.

> **Answers**
> a reception   b a tie and a dark suit   c accountants
> d dress-down Friday,   e smart-casual
> f (a) training day(s)   g a nose ring   h civil liberties
> i Human Resources

## Tapescript

Now, it's been brought to my attention that certain members of staff have been flouting the dress code. So I want to make it crystal clear to everyone just exactly what's expected in terms of attire. Those of you who work in reception must be, how shall I put it, business-like at all times. You are the first person visitors see when they enter the building. Whether they then go on to the Managing Director or the canteen is irrelevant. You create the first impression of the company; and as we all know, first and last impressions count. Now, for men that means a tie and a dark suit – accepted business practice. For women, a suit, er, that can be a trouser suit, or a smart dress or skirt and jacket. It goes without saying that hair and so on needs to be neat and tidy.

The accountants. You never know when a client may come in to see you. You may think you're not in the public relations business but in a way, you are. And I know most of the time people make appointments but there are odd occasions when someone just happens to be in the area and decides to come in. In this case you are the embodiment of your profession. This is a firm with a good reputation. Clients expect their accountant to reflect this, not only in their work but also in the way they present themselves. Don't forget, in many people's eyes sloppy clothes means sloppy work, and I must say, I tend to agree.

The only possible exception to this is the so-called dress-down Friday. This new idea. And of course that only applies if you have no appointments with clients in your diary. Now, this doesn't mean that you can turn up wearing whatever you like. It's got to be 'smart-casual'. That's what it says here. And that still means a tie, but you can wear smart jeans and a jacket or even a sweater.

Now, something's come to my attention that I'm not at all happy about and that is training days. It seems as though some of you have got the idea into your head that when you're on a training day that means you can dress like a student. It does not. You're still a representative of this company. When you go out to management college, you are judged there too. I've heard remarks about a certain man who turned up wearing a nose ring. This is not acceptable; it's all in the company's dress code, which you've all had a copy of. What I want to emphasise is that it's a matter of professional pride, the way you dress.

I know some people start murmuring about civil liberties and all that, but I'm sorry, as I see it, we're all here to do a job of work. We are employees of a company and as such we have to toe the line and not only in what we do and how we do our job, but also the way we dress.

If anyone feels particularly aggrieved by any of this, all I can suggest is that you take it up with the Human Resources department. Go up to the fifth floor, you know, next to the UK department.

But really, I hope I won't have to refer to this again and I expect to see a dramatic improvement in personal presentation.

4   Ask this question as a round up.

## Direct and reported speech

The grammar here is covered on page 196 of the Grammar folder.

1   Ask students to work with a partner, then talk through the 'rules' as necessary. The aim here is to consolidate and extend students' range of reporting verbs and to point out that we do not always change the verb tense.

> **Answers**
> a exactly what was/is expected in terms of attire.
> b those of us who work/worked in reception must/had to be businesslike at all times.
> c us that in many people's eyes sloppy clothes meant/means sloppy work.
> d she was/is not at all happy about the way some people dressed/dress for training days.
> e it seemed/seems as though some of us had/have got the idea into our head that when we were/are on a training day we could/can dress like a student.
> f who had turned up to a management college wearing a nose ring.
> g it was/is a matter of professional pride, the way we dress.
> h we had/have to toe the line.
> i if anyone felt/feels particularly aggrieved by any of that/this, all she could suggest was/is that we take/took it up with the Human Resources department.
> j she wouldn't have to refer to this/that again.

2   This gives students practice of reported questions. Ask them to read through the questions on their own and then to add two more questions. Students interview each other and note the replies to questions. They then write a summary of the interview using reported speech. The summary could be set for homework.

3   The structures which follow certain reporting verbs can be problematic for students. The aim of this activity is to raise students' awareness of the various structures and to provide practice of them.

> **Answers**
> a 2   b 1,4   c 2,4   d 3   e 2,3   f 2   g 1,3   h 1,4
> i 1   j 3   k 3   l 4   m 2   n 1

4   This exercise could be set for homework to consolidate the work done in direct and reported speech.

> **Answers**
> a buying   b another style to us   c promised myself
> d that she would refund   e to be   f her name was
> g I was   h recommended   i that you pay
> j to help me   k the Isa Hotel to you

# Speaking 2

Go through the information in the Exam spot which is about Part 2 of the CAE Speaking test (Paper 5). You will be able to find examples of Part 2 tasks in Practice Test Books and the CAE Handbook.

1   Explain that comparing means looking for similarities whereas contrasting means looking for differences. Using appropriate linking devices will help students structure their response to this part of the Speaking test.

> **Suggested answers**
>
> | Comparing | Contrasting |
> |---|---|
> | is similar to the other picture in/in that … | however |
> | shows the same kind of … | although |
> | like the second picture, … | on the one hand |
> | is much the same as | on the other hand |
> |  | while |

2   Ask students to look at the pictures while they discuss which plan or part of a plan they think they will use. All these plans are good. It may depend on the pictures and the task as to which one is most suitable. You could ask students which plan they would use in the exam.

3   Ask students to look at the pictures. They should answer the questions as they listen to the recording.

> **Answers**
> a C   b but, and, then, in contrast   c 2   d 3

## Tapescript

**Examiner:** In this part of the test, I'm going to give each of you the chance to talk for about a minute and to comment briefly after your partner has spoken. First, you will each have the same set of pictures to look at. They show people wearing different types of clothes.

Angela, it's your turn first. I'd like you to compare and contrast these pictures, saying what the clothes might tell us about the wearer. Don't forget, you have about a minute for this, all right? So, Angela, would you start please?

**Angela:** I, I'd like to talk about pictures a and b as they are both pictures of men but they are wearing very different clothes. In picture a, we can see a man wearing a pin-striped suit and in fact the stripe is quite prominent; it's not a subtle sort of stripe that the typical businessman wears. And there's another interesting thing about the suit; it's got pink lining – that's quite flamboyant. Then this man is wearing a tie – pale pink with dots of a deeper pink. Again, that's outrageous, some might say.

This leads me to think that perhaps he's not a businessman who works in a bank or insurance company but perhaps he's something to do with the arts or in advertising. It's got to be a profession which allows him to express his slightly extrovert personality.

In contrast, in picture b there's a man wearing casual clothes. He's wearing some sort of brown top with a zip and then over that he's got another blue jacket which is undone. It looks as if it's made of that fleece material. He's got a scarf tucked into his top. His trousers have got large pockets on the sides of the legs – quite fashionable, I think. I'm not absolutely sure but perhaps they might be made of corduroy. And then he's wearing walking boots.

Looking at this picture, I would say this man is enjoying some time at the weekend, out in the country – he's a man who loves being out in nature and he's quite a free thinker. I can't imagine him working in a bank either – look at his hair. He could be a teacher.

**Examiner:** Thank you. Now, Luciano, which picture shows the clothes that you would be most comfortable wearing?

**Luciano:** Oh, definitely picture b. I feel much better when I'm wearing casual clothes and I would certainly never wear a suit like that!

**Examiner:** Thank you.

> **Teaching extra**
>
> The candidate who comments on the other candidate's long turn often has a tendency to want to talk for too long. There are only about 30 seconds allowed for this comment.

4 Go through the notes and then brainstorm other phrases Angela could have used in her talk.

> **Suggested answers**
> I'd like to choose pictures a and b. Although they are both pictures of men, they show very different types of people, mainly because of the clothes they are wearing and the setting.
>
> Pictures a and b look interesting because although they are both pictures of men, the different characters come across in the clothes they are wearing.

5 Divide students into groups of three. One student is the Examiner, one is Student A and one is Student B. Give A and B five minutes to prepare for their long turn. They should plan an opening line, consider some of the comparisons/contrasts they want to make and think about linking devices to use. During this time the Examiner should also think about the questions. The group should then go through the whole speaking task. At the end, the Examiner comments on how effective A and B's answers were.

# Exam folder 5

## SB pages 74–75

## Paper 3 Part 5
## Key word transformations

Read through the introduction to Part 5 of the Use of English test and draw attention to the example.

1 Make sure students go back over the list of key points before you check the answers.

> **Answers**
> 1 The essay *made a great impression on* me.
> 2 Sarah *insisted on speaking (only)* English with the visitors.
> 3 There was a *sharp increase in* the price of petrol last month.
> 4 I *caught sight of* the postman for a minute as he passed my window.

2 Ask students to work in pairs.

> **Answers**
> 1 The phrasal verb is *to hand something down to someone* – *to* is missing.
> The secret recipe *is handed down to* each new generation
> 2 The given word is in the past tense and cannot be changed.
> The present *came as a complete surprise* to me.
> 3 The spelling of *emotion* is wrong.
> The child's mother *was overcome with emotion* when he was found.
> 4 The idiom for *to help someone* is *to give someone a hand*.
> Could you possibly *give me a hand* with this suitcase?

3 Go through the introduction to fixed phrases. Ask students to work in pairs.

> **Answers**
> 1 c   2 e   3 b   4 f   5 a   6 d

4 As examples, elicit the prepositions that are needed after *to be good* (at), *depend* (on), *a prejudice* (against).

> **Answers**
> 1 in   2 of   3 from   4 in   5 with   6 in

5 Elicit examples of sentences containing the passive form, conditional forms, reported speech.

> **Answers**
> 1 If we don't get the 8 am train, *it will mean* missing lunch.
> 2 Italian football players are *said to earn the highest* salaries.
> 3 The tour operator *apologised for not* emailing the details earlier.
> 4 Your accountant *should have given you* better advice.

6 This could be set as homework as it is exam practice.

> **Answers**
> 1 A medical certificate *wasn't required for* my USA visa.
> 2 The island *is rich in* natural resources.
> 3 Gina *does nothing but* complain.
> 4 The candidate *gave honest answers to* the questions.
> 5 If the tennis court *hadn't been so wet*, the match wouldn't have been cancelled.
> 6 I'd *be on your side* even if you weren't my friend.
> 7 He *flatly refused to* help me.
> 8 Could you get some fruit *on your way* home?

# 12 In a nutshell

| Genre | Short stories |
|---|---|
| Topic | Dreaming |

| Speaking 1 | Dreaming |
|---|---|
| Reading 1 and 2 | *The Dream* |
| Listening 1 and 2 | *The Dream* |
| Grammar | Past tenses and the present perfect |
| Vocabulary | Adjectival order |
| Speaking 2 | Pronunciation of *-ed* |

**Workbook contents**

| Use of English | Part 2 open gap fill |
|---|---|
| Reading | Matching extracts to genres, putting jumbled paragraphs into the correct order |
| Pronunciation | /t/, /d/ and /ɪd/ |
| Grammar | Past tenses and the present perfect |
| Vocabulary | Completing sentences with appropriate words |

## SB pages 76–79

**Lesson planning**
- SV  Grammar 2 could be set for homework
- LV  See the extension activity in the Reading 2 section

## Speaking 1

The aim of questions 1–4 is to introduce the topic of dreams. Ask students to work in small groups to discuss the questions. Allow time for class feedback on any interesting points which come up in the discussion.

Suggested answers for 2 are as follows, but students may well come to other conclusions. Ask them to justify their choices.

**Suggested answers**
a 4  b 1  c 5  d 6  e 3  f 2

## Reading 1

1  Ask the students to read the extract and then answer the questions with a partner.

**Suggested answers**
a He had been advised to travel from New York to Petrograd via Vladivostok as this way would be safer.
b As the station restaurant was crowded, they were sharing a table at dinner time.
c He was tall and very fat and he did not look after his clothes.
  He was well-educated, he spoke English well and he could discuss literature.
d He says he is a journalist, but it is inferred that he wants to keep his real profession secret. He could be a secret agent, a criminal, an undercover police officer or a politician.

2  All the words in this exercise are in the order in which they appear in the text. Check whether students would like any other vocabulary explained.

**Answers**
a stout  b paunch  c sallow  d shabby
e tiresome  f dissimulation

## Listening 1

1  This question is open for students to imagine how the story will continue.

2  Ask the students to listen and get a general impression in answer to questions a–c.

**Answers**
a He drank vodka, he was talkative, he was of noble birth, a lawyer by profession. He had been in trouble with the 'authorities' so he had had to be abroad a lot. He had been doing business in Vladivostok. He would be in Moscow in a week. He was a widower.
b She was Swiss, and spoke English, German, French and Italian perfectly and good Russian. She had taught languages at one of the best schools in Petrograd.
c The narrator seems to have found it unusual that the Russian told him so much about himself unasked. He felt the Russian's question about whether he was married was a little too personal. The narrator was wondering, while the Russian was telling his story, whether he would have time to eat before his train left. The narrator found it laughable that anyone could love the Russian to distraction as he found him very ugly.

3  The significant words are *jealous* and *unfortunately*. They may imply that the Russian had to do something drastic about his wife's jealousy.

4  Ask students to work in small groups to speculate about how the story will continue.

## Tapescript

By this time we had persuaded the waiter to bring us some cabbage soup, and my acquaintance pulled a small bottle of vodka from his pocket which he invited me to share. I do not know whether it was the vodka or the natural loquaciousness of his race that made him communicative, but presently he told me, unasked, a good deal about himself. He was of noble birth, it appeared, a lawyer by profession, and a radical. Some trouble with the authorities had made it necessary for him to be much abroad, but now he was on his way home. Business had detained him at Vladivostok, but he expected to start for Moscow in a week and if I went there, he would be charmed to see me.

'Are you married?' he asked me.

I did not see what business it was of his, but I told him that I was. He sighed a little.

'I am a widower,' he said. 'My wife was a Swiss, a native of Geneva. She was a very cultured woman. She spoke English, German and Italian perfectly. French, of course, was her native tongue. Her Russian was much above the average for a foreigner. She had scarcely the trace of an accent.'

He called a waiter who was passing with a tray full of dishes and asked him, I suppose – for then I knew hardly any Russian – how much longer we were going to wait for the next course. The waiter, with a rapid but presumably reassuring exclamation, hurried on, and my friend sighed.

'Since the revolution the waiting in restaurants has become abominable.'

He lighted his twentieth cigarette and I, looking at my watch, wondered whether I should get a square meal before it was time for me to start.

'My wife was a very remarkable woman,' he continued. 'She taught languages at one of the best schools for the daughters of noblemen in Petrograd. For a good many years we lived together on perfectly friendly terms. She was, however, of a jealous temperament and unfortunately she loved me to distraction.'

It was difficult for me to keep a straight face. He was one of the ugliest men I had ever seen. There is sometimes a certain charm in the rubicund and jovial fat, but this saturnine obesity was repulsive.

## Reading 2

1 Students read on and answer questions a–d.

> **Answers**
> a She was quite old, not attractive and she said unpleasant things.
> b It was stormy. She threw out a coat of his that he loved. He found her boring. They had rows which he tried to ignore as he tried to lead his own life. He accepted the way she was as much as possible. He wondered whether she loved or hated him.
> c The dream could be a kind of omen.
> d This question is open to interpretation but students may suggest that the Russian will kill his wife as in her dream.

### Extension activity

Students could write the ending to the story in any way they choose before listening to the rest of the recording.

## Listening 2

1 Ask students to read the questions before they listen, then play the recording.

> **Answers**
> a The Russian began to think about the dream too. He realised his wife thought he hated her and could be capable of murdering her. When he walked up the stairs it was impossible not to imagine the scene his wife had described in her dream and think about how easy it would be.
> b No. He had wished to be free of her, that she might leave him or die a natural death, but not that he could murder her.
> c For a short time she became less bitter and more tolerant.
> d The second dream was the same as the first.
> e Perhaps because the memory of the situation was so vivid. Perhaps because he had murdered his wife.
> f She fell over the baluster and was found dead at the bottom of the stairs by a lodger.
> g He seemed nervous, he had a malicious, cunning look and his eyes sparkled.
> h Did the Russian murder her or was it an accident? We do not know for sure but this is the narrator's suspicion or nagging doubt.

## Tapescript

'She was much shaken. I did my best to soothe her. But next morning, and for two or three days after, she referred to the subject again and, notwithstanding my laughter, I saw that it dwelt in her mind. I could not help thinking of it either, for this dream showed me something that I had never suspected. She thought I hated her, she thought I would gladly be rid of her, she knew of course that she was insufferable, and at some time or other the idea had evidently occurred to her that I was capable of murdering her. The thoughts of men are incalculable and ideas enter our minds that we should be ashamed to confess. Sometimes I had wished she might run away with a lover, sometimes that a painless and sudden death might give me my freedom, but never had the idea come to me that I might deliberately rid myself of an intolerable burden.

'The dream made an extraordinary impression upon both of us. It frightened my wife, and she became for a while a little less bitter and more tolerant. But when I walked up the stairs to our apartment it was impossible for me not to look over the balusters and reflect how easy it would be to do what she had dreamt. The balusters were dangerously low. A quick gesture and the thing was done. It was hard to put the thought out of my mind. Then some months later my wife awakened me one night. I was very tired and I was exasperated. She was white and trembling. She had had the dream again. She burst into tears and asked me if I hated her. I swore by all the saints of the Russian calendar that I loved her. At last she went to sleep again. It was more than I could do. I lay awake. I seemed to see her falling down the well of the stairs, and I heard a shriek and the thud as she struck the stone floor. I could not help shivering.'

The Russian stopped and beads of sweat stood on his forehead. He had told the story well and fluently so that I had listened with attention. There was still some vodka in the bottle, he poured it out and swallowed it at a gulp.

'And how did your wife eventually die?' I asked after a pause.

He took out a dirty handkerchief and wiped his forehead.

'By an extraordinary coincidence she was found late one night at the bottom of the stairs with her neck broken.'

'Who found her?'

'She was found by one of the lodgers who came in shortly after the catastrophe.'

'And where were you?'

I cannot describe the look he gave me of malicious cunning. His little black eyes sparkled.

'I was spending the evening with a friend of mine. I did not come in till an hour later.'

At that moment the waiter brought us the dish of meat that we had ordered, and the Russian fell upon it with good appetite. He shovelled the food into his mouth in enormous mouthfuls.

I was taken aback. Had he really been telling me in this hardly veiled manner that he had murdered his wife? That obese and sluggish man did not look like a murderer, I could not believe that he would have had the courage. Or was he making a sardonic joke at my expense?

In a few minutes it was time for me to go and catch my train. I left him and have not seen him since. But I have never been able to make up my mind whether he was serious or jesting.

2   If your class is small enough, this will make a good class discussion activity.

# Past tenses and the present perfect

The grammar here is covered on pages 196–198 of the Grammar folder.

1   The aim is to revise and extend students' knowledge and use of the past tenses and the present perfect.

**Answers**
called   was passing   asked   knew   were going to wait
hurried   sighed

2   This exercise could be set for homework if time is short.

**Answers**
a   I had read many other stories by this author before I read *The Dream*.
b   correct
c   The short story was made into a TV drama last year.
d   The author owned an interesting collection of antiquarian books.
e   correct
f   correct
g   correct
h   In the story the villain almost got away with it but the body was discovered.
i   correct
j   correct
k   The first page of the book seemed very boring, that's why I didn't read it.
l   He had been writing for magazines for years before he was discovered by Hollywood.
m  It's the first time I've written a story.
n   correct
o   Are you sure the Russian committed the murder? I thought it was the lodger.

3   Students should use the present perfect simple or continuous in response to the pictures.

# Vocabulary

Go through the Exam spot and then establish the usual order of adjectives.

1   Ask students to put the adjectives in the most usual order.

**Answers**
a small wooden table
an exciting, extensive new menu
a beautiful red silk dress
a shabby black suit
a huge sallow face

2   Accept any appropriate answers from students. Encourage them to use a variety of adjectives.

## Speaking 2

1 Go through the introduction to this section, then ask students to put the words under the correct heading.

| Answers | | |
|---|---|---|
| walked /t/ | loved /d/ | started /ɪd/ |
| chanced | engaged | instructed |
| passed | obliged | landed |
| | dined | crowded |
| | shared | |
| | entertained | |
| | buried | |

2 Play the recording for students to check their answers.

3 Ask students to form rules based on the work they did in the previous exercise.

**Answers**
a /t/   b /d/   c /ɪd/

### Teaching extra

A good way for students to feel the difference between unvoiced and voiced sounds is to ask the students to put the palm of their hand over their throat and produce a sound, e.g. /f/. If they can feel a vibration in their throat the sound is voiced. If there is no vibration the sound is unvoiced.

4 This could be set for homework.

| Answers | | |
|---|---|---|
| /t/ | /d/ | /ɪd/ |
| asked | called | invited |
| helped | discovered | needed |
| jumped | enjoyed | rented |
| looked | lived | visited |
| missed | rained | |
| reached | saved | |
| worked | travelled | |

# Writing folder 5

## SB pages 80–81

## Reviews

1 Discuss this question with the class as a whole. There is no right answer to the question as the purpose of a review may well vary with its context.

2 Establish if any students have seen the film reviewed. Ask them to read the review and complete the lists.

**Answers**
**Facts about the film**
sequel to *Mission: Impossible* (directed by Brian de Palma), directed by John Woo, mammoth hit in the US, hero is Ethan Hunt (played by Tom Cruise), has to cut holiday short to save Australia and the world from a lethal virus that has fallen into the hands of villains, they ask £37 million to surrender their half of the virus

**Phrases that convey the writer's opinion**
a story line that makes sense, klunky, goofy, despite its faults it's quite an engaging film, not nearly as good as the original, it isn't a dud, it's a little unclear, it's a great relief when the tangled threads of the plot finally coalesce

**Things included to interest and entertain**
has holes big enough to drive the entire United States Marine Corps through, there are seven of us globally (intelligent self-respecting critics), (the way the plot is described in the third and fourth paragraphs), it's almost a shame that Woo had to even bother with a plot

3 Students may feel that the title is a good one in that it resembles the title of the film and much of the review is about how implausible the plot is.

4 The language of the review is used to poke fun at the clichés in the film, e.g. *fiendish villains, very, very cruel, unspeakable forces of pure unadulterated evil,* etc.

5 Collocations include: *run a story, highly anticipated, unbelievably complicated, hugely entertaining, finished product, make sense, small mercies.*

6 This exercise provides further examples of strong collocations. The answers give the most likely collocations although others are possible (*intensely* and *deeply* are more or less interchangeable, for example).

**Answers**
a 2,4   b 5,12   c 3,8   d 7,9   e 1,6   f 10,11

7 Point out that this task takes the form of the tasks used in the CAE Writing test (Paper 2). Emphasise that all four bullet points must be addressed in some way or the answer will not pass.

# 13 Leaf through a leaflet

| Genre | Information pages |
|---|---|
| Topic | Leaving home |

| Speaking 1 | Types of information pages |
| Reading | The Titanic Trail |
| Listening | Visiting the Titanic Heritage Centre |
| Grammar | -ing forms |
| Speaking 2 | Pronunciation: linking |

**Workbook contents**

| Grammar | -ing forms |
| Vocabulary | Completing sentences with words from a list |
| Speaking | Linking devices: /j/, /w/ |
| Reading | General comprehension questions |

## SB pages 82–85

### Lesson planning
- **SV** Grammar 2 and 3 could be set for homework
- **LV** See extension activities in the Speaking and Listening sections

## Speaking 1

### Extension activity
If you can arrange for your students to watch some of the film *Titanic*, it would tie in nicely with this unit.

1 Refer to the title of the unit and elicit the meaning of *to leaf through*. You leaf through a book or a magazine by turning the pages quickly and reading only a little of it, e.g. *The passengers were leafing through magazines in the airport shop.*

Then ask students to work in pairs and discuss the questions in 1.

**Answers**
a a brochure  b a prospectus  c a leaflet  d a flier
b A leaflet is a piece of paper, or sometimes several pieces of paper folded or fixed together like a book, which gives you information or advertises something, e.g.

*A leaflet about the new bus services came today.*
*They were handing out advertising leaflets outside the supermarket.*
*The leaflets about the concert were delivered with the local papers.*
The main purpose of a leaflet is to inform and/or advertise.
c It could be said that leaflets are an effective means of communication because they are usually compact, are clearly written, have a good layout and give essential information.

2 The latest version of *Titanic* was made in 1997 and starred Leonardo DiCaprio and Kate Winslet. It was a great hit at the time. If any students have seen *Titanic*, ask them to retell the story. Basically, it is the story of a young man from a poor background who takes the voyage on the *Titanic* by chance. He meets a young lady from a much higher social class and they fall in love. When the *Titanic* sinks, he tries to save her. She survives but he loses his life.

At the beginning of the 20th century, the USA was a land of golden opportunity for many Europeans who wanted to start a new life because of either poverty or persecution. Most of the passengers on board the *Titanic* were going there to live.

## Reading

1 Ask students to look on the map to find Cobh (pronounced /kəʊv/) in the Republic of Ireland. Get students to discuss the questions in a way that varies the pairing. Alternatively, you could discuss the questions as a class. Encourage students to scan the leaflet quickly to find the answers to the questions.

**Answers**
a true  b false  c true  d false  e false

2 The aim is to draw students' attention to the important features of a leaflet.

**Answers**
a There is information about the different types of tours on the Titanic Trail and about the times and content of the tours. There is additional information about activities in and around Cobh.

- **b** It is a typical tourist attraction leaflet which describes activities in a way that will attract visitors and give essential information.
- **c** The layout of a leaflet is very important. Headings must catch the reader's eye and here the headings are in different fonts and sizes. Headings relating to practical information are in capital letters. Bullet points make lists easy to see and more attractive. Visuals (in the form of the illustration and the map) also catch the reader's eye.
- **d** The writer tells visitors to *experience for yourself* and *experience first hand* which appeals directly to the reader.
- **e** The style is a mixture of descriptive prose and facts with bullet points.

3 If your class consists of people from the same town or region, you could discuss this as a class. If you have a multinational group, you could ask students to work in pairs consisting of people from different towns or countries. Students could exchange information about the possible content of a leaflet for tourists. This can be followed up in Writing folder 6 so ask students to keep their notes.

## Listening

Refer students to the Exam spot. Explain that in Part 2 of the CAE Listening test (Paper 4), students are required to listen to a text for specific information. Reading the questions before listening is essential so that students can listen out for the relevant information.

1 The focus on vocabulary lightens the listening load for students and deals with some of the less frequent vocabulary of the text. Ask students to tick the words they think they will hear, then play the recording for students to check their answers.

**Answers**
Words heard on the recording: embarked, crew, berthed, iceberg, quay, setting out, on board, struck

### Teaching extra

Encourage a 'find out' approach to vocabulary by asking students to tick the words they know, put a question mark next to words they are not sure about and a cross next to words they do not know. Then they circulate and try to find other students who know the words they do not know.

### Extension activity

Extend students' vocabulary by asking them to make posters for the classroom which illustrate vocabulary on the theme of travel. Headings could be *Means of travel*, *Verbs associated with travel* or *Pictures of different places* with descriptive texts under them.

2 Students should listen to the recording again to complete the sentences.

**Answers**
a an/the American wake   b railway   c over 1,000
d medical check   e lace and souvenirs   f 2,297

## Tapescript

On April 10th, 1912, the pride of The White Star Line, the *Titanic*, embarked on her maiden voyage from Southampton, via Cherbourg and Queenstown to New York. As was the case with the majority of west-bound liners, Queenstown was scheduled as the last port of call before crossing the Atlantic. One of the last family rituals, performed in the house of the family, was the American wake, which grew out of the tradition of waking or watching the dead. The emigrants were unlikely to return home and so were 'dead' to those who were left behind. For the elderly in particular, parting was a painful experience. The wake was the last opportunity for family and friends to be joined with their loved ones before they departed on their journey.

The railway came to Queenstown in 1862, providing emigrants with a convenient means of travelling to the emigration port. The fond goodbyes usually culminated at the railway station, where tearful partings were sometimes eased by the excitement of setting out on a new adventure to a new land. Passengers on the *Titanic* were no doubt looking forward to travelling on the brand new luxury liner.

Over the previous fifty years, Queenstown had become established as the most important emigration port of the southern part of Ireland. In ten years over one thousand emigrants left Queenstown every week over the busy spring and summer months. Most were bound for North America in search of a better life.

A total of 123 passengers embarked at Queenstown on April 11th. Three travelled first class, seven in second class, while the remainder were berthed in third class or steerage accommodation. With steamships plying the Atlantic on a regular basis, Queenstown was a bustling place in 1912. To satisfy American immigration regulations, intending passengers had to pass a medical check. Trachoma, a disease of the eyes, was of particular importance and was sufficient to deny an emigrant the right to travel. Waiting for the ship to arrive, passengers would sometimes be entertained with music. For some, the last chance to buy some trinket as a reminder of home had to be resisted; money had to be prudently managed. Emigrants at Queenstown sometimes could not board a liner because it had its full complement of passengers and then they had to wait until the next ship arrived in port. The pride of the White Star Line arrived at Roche's point, the outer anchorage of Cork harbour, at 11.30 am. Meanwhile, the intending passengers went to the White Star Line quay to board the paddle steamer tenders, *Ireland* and *America*, which would ferry them to the liner. After boarding the tenders, they proceeded to the deep-water quay located beside the railway station to load mail bags from the train. The two tenders then travelled out to the *Titanic* along with a number of smaller vessels carrying vendors who hoped to sell local specialities such as lace and souvenirs to the wealthy passengers on board.

At 1.30 pm an exchange of whistle indicated that the tenders' business was complete and the *Titanic* weighed anchor to the strains of *Eirin's Lament* and *The Nation Once Again*. A total of 1,308 passengers were on board when *Titanic* left Queenstown together with 989 crew, making a total of 2,297 people. Shortly before midnight on the 14th April 1912, *Titanic* struck an iceberg and sank with the loss of over 1,500 lives. Of the 123 passengers who boarded at Queenstown, only 44 survived.

3  As a round up, ask students to discuss question 3.

## *-ing* forms

The grammar here is covered on page 198 of the Grammar folder.

1  Ask students to work with a partner to match sentences a–g with explanations 1–7.

> **Answers**
> a 3  b 5  c 6  d 1  e 4  f 5 and 7  g 2 and 5

2  Ask students to put the sentences in the correct order, then underline all the *-ing* forms.

> **Answers**
> 2 e  3 c  4 f  5 d  6 b
> *-ing* forms: **b** tending, encouraging  **c** travelling
> **d** taking, making  **e** setting out  **f** feeling

3  Ask students to correct the sentences if necessary.

> **Answers**
> a correct
> b Since he started his new job, he's got used to *getting* up very early.
> c *Having* time to spend talking with friends is very important.
> d I'm looking forward to *seeing* you soon.
> e correct
> f It's no use *telling* me now that you can't finish the report. You should have told me last week.
> g What I miss is not *being* able to have lunch with all my family every Sunday.
> h correct
> i I'm fed up with not *having* all the facilities I need to do the job properly.
> j correct

## Speaking 2

Go through the notes about linking spoken English. Write the example of Type 1 on the board (*get up*) and show this with a curved line between the letters *t* and *u* (*get⌣up*). Elicit more examples from the students to make sure they have understood, e.g. *set out*, *Ben ate*, *have it*. Stress that we are talking about sounds, not letters, so the final sound of *have* is /v/.

Write up the examples of Type 2 on the board, linking with the insertion of /j/ in *he is* and the insertion of /w/ in *do it*. Ask students to repeat these two examples and exaggerate the position of the mouth so that students can see and feel the difference.

Give more examples and ask the students to say if /j/ or /w/ should be inserted, e.g.

| /j/ | /w/ |
|---|---|
| we⌣are | to⌣it |
| I⌣am | through⌣Italy |
| see⌣it | are you⌣interested? |

1  Encourage students to say the words several times as they decide how they would be linked.

> **Answers**
> a Type 1  b Type 2: insert /j/  c Type 2: insert /w/
> d Type 1  e Type 2: insert /j/ between *we are* and *quay at*

Play the recording for students to check their answers.

2  Ask students to identify where /j/ or /w/ could be inserted in the sentences in natural, connected speech. Then play the recording for students to check their answers.

LEAF THROUGH A LEAFLET

**Answers and tapescript**
a If you /w/ are part of a group, it's much more fun.
b So /w/ I'm going to start off by telling you /w/ about the conditions on board.
c You'll see /j/ it in the film.
d When I'm asked about that, it's difficult to /w/ answer.
e You can do /w/ it too.
f Book through /w/ our agency which is open from 9 am to 6 pm.

> **Extension activity**
>
> Students could write their own sentences which illustrate the two types of linking devices and do similar exercises with those sentences.

# Exam folder 6

## SB pages 86–87

## Paper 1 Part 1 Themed texts

Go through the introduction to this folder and the Advice box.

1 Ask students to read the first text task (questions 1 and 2).

**Answers**
1 There was something in the stance or movement of the accompanist and the woman that strongly suggested that they were about to kiss.
2 A musical event, because the word *accompanist* suggests a musician accompanying a singer.

2

**Answers**
1 D   2 A

3

**Answers**
3 C   4 A

4 Make the point that students should always justify their choices by identifying exactly where the answer is in the text.

**Answers**
3 Alastair Marriott, whose new work *Kiss* was created for her, understands that it is in her expansiveness that Bussell's dance is at its most appealing. Her limbs have a gorgeous plush, her legs especially seem to unfold in a swelling *legato*, her back melts at the very touch of air – Bussell is big, her dance is big and Marriott has offered her choreography which is undoubtedly big in gesture.
4 Yet somehow it seems to be at odds with the conceit (and the length) of the work which is inspired by the quiet and intimate love of the sculptor Auguste Rodin and his muse Camille Claudel:

5 Ask students to check all the points in the Advice box on page 86 before you confirm the correct answers.

**Answers**
5 C   6 A

# 14 Views from the platform

| Genre | Lectures |
|---|---|
| Topic | Language development |

| Listening and Reading | Types of speeches |
|---|---|
| Listening | A lecture |
| Reading | A lecture (continued) |
| Grammar | The passive; *to have/get something done* |
| Vocabulary | Word formation |
| Speaking | Giving a talk |

**Workbook contents**

| Vocabulary | Exercises with the word *talk* |
|---|---|
| Reading | Multiple-choice questions |
| Grammar | The passive |
| Reading | A ranking exercise |
| Writing | An informal letter |

## SB pages 88–91

**Lesson planning**

SV  Listening 1 could be set for homework
LV  See the extension activity in the Reading section

## Listening and Reading

1  Ask students to look at the photos and say what the situation is, who is giving the speech and what type of speech is being given.

**Answers**
1 c   2 d   3 b   4 a

## Tapescript

**Speaker 1:** Now we have, over the last four days, heard that the goods were taken from the warehouse on the night of February 14th. The theft was discovered by Mr White when he arrived on the morning of February 15th. There is overwhelming forensic evidence which puts Geoff Warren in the frame. His fingerprints were found on the window along with fibres from his jacket. Later, police officers found some of the goods at his home address in Germaine Street.

**Speaker 2:** It was announced by the Prime Minister this morning that the General Election will be held on May 3rd. The election campaign is to start with immediate effect with the three main parties having air time on both TV and radio over the coming weeks.

**Speaker 3:** Jill Davies will be remembered both as devoted mother and wife and also for her work at St Thomas's hospital where she worked as a paediatrician for many years. She will remain in the hearts of all those who knew her even though her body may have departed this world. Her pioneering work with neo-natal babies at the hospital has meant that many more families have had the joy of taking home their newborn. The procedures she introduced are now an established part of hospital life.

**Speaker 4:** We can see in our communities many who are in need and the parable of the Good Samaritan teaches us that we should not pass by those in need. Those who, for whatever reason, cross our path in our daily life, and are less fortunate than ourselves, should be shown true compassion. Even the smallest gesture, such as listening for an extra few minutes to someone who has a problem, can make all the difference.

2  Students should work with a partner to match the words to the definitions.

**Answers**
a 2   b 5   c 4   d 3   e 1

## Listening

Go through the Exam spot so that students can appreciate the relevance of the class work in relation to the exam.

1  The aim of the pre-listening and pre-reading questions is to make students aware of the issues through discussion and so make the exercises more accessible. Do not go through the answers until students have listened to and read the lecture. Were their predictions correct?

**Answers**
1 a or b   2 b   3 b   4 c

2  Encourage students to look at the questions before you play the recording.

VIEWS FROM THE PLATFORM

> **Answers**
> a 6,000  b 9,000, 1.3 million  c 1.5 million years
> d 300,000  e gestures  f primitive, basic, natural
> g tools, at night (time)

## Tapescript

In this lecture on the evolutionary factors of language, I'm going to begin by looking at early language in humans.

Writing began about 6,000 years ago, so it is fair to say that speech preceded that, although estimates of when humans began to speak range from 9,000 years ago to 1.3 million years ago. Primitive tools have been found that date back to 1.5 million years BC – the tools show that our ancestors had at least low level spatial thinking. Later tools, about 300,000 years old, are more advanced, revealing that cognition was on a level that was similar or equal to modern intelligence – tools had been planned in three dimensions, allowing for abstract thought – the cognitive capacity for language was present.

Krantz (1980) argues that language emerged 50,000 years ago because then the fossil records show that significant changes took place. Tools became more sophisticated and specialised, projectiles appeared along with fire and there was a large spread and expansion of the population. According to Krantz, the cause may have been to do with the emergence of full language and a new cognitive competence in humans.

Presumably, initially, people used gestures to communicate, then gestures with vocal communication. Both provided an evolutionary push towards a higher level of cognition, fuelled by a need to communicate effectively and the frustration at not being able to do so. Pettito and Marentette (1991) examined deaf infants, and found that they start to babble, and then because there is no auditory feedback they stop. Deaf children use manual babbling (an early form of sign language equivalent to the vocalisations of hearing infants) but this manual babbling stage starts earlier than in hearing children and ends sooner. Pettito and Marentette suggest that manual language is therefore more primitive, basic and natural than spoken language, a clue that the first languages were iconic, not spoken.

The emergence of tool use with spoken language is particularly interesting. Possibly, hands were needed to manipulate tools, and humans found it difficult to communicate with sign language and use tools at the same time. Vocal communication, if possible, would allow the hands to do other things. Also, a vocal language would allow humans to communicate at night time, and without having to look at each other.

## Reading

1 Allow students time to read the text on their own. Tell students not to worry about unknown vocabulary at this stage. Then ask them to work with a partner and answer the questions.

> **Answers**
> 1 B  2 C  3 A

> **Extension activity**
>
> Make a matching exercise for the vocabulary your students might like to explore. Write definitions of the unknown words and get students to match them.

2 Allow time for a discussion to round off the Listening and Reading sections.

## The passive

The grammar here is covered on pages 198–199 of the Grammar folder.

1 Refer students back to the lecture by pointing out that the passive is often used in this situation. If you consider it necessary, ask your students how the passive is formed (*to be + past participle*).

2 Ask students to do this exercise which serves as revision and expansion of the use of the passive.

> **Answers**
> 1 e  2 h  3 b  4 i  5 g  6 d  7 c  8 a  9 f

3 The continuous text will make students think about whether it is suitable to turn a sentence into the passive. Obviously, not every sentence would be in the passive in normal continuous text.

> **Suggested answers**
> Three important areas have been revealed recently in the study of the evolutionary factors of language.
> The second is that humans' hands were freed (you may argue that it is better to keep this in the active voice) in order to make and use tools, which meant a method of communication other than sign language had to be found.
> It is said that chimps can be taught to speak.
> It should be noted that the form of the human teeth, lips, tongue and larynx are all important when it comes to speech.

4 The aim is to revise and expand students' understanding of this form.

**Suggested answers**
The vase has been stolen.
The TV and video have been stolen.
The chair has been moved nearer to the fireplace.
The mat has been disturbed.
The camera has been moved.
The sofa cushion has been moved.
The photo has been dropped on the floor.
A light has been broken.
The fireplace grate has been moved.
The windows have been closed.
A blind has been pulled down on one window.

## *To have/get something done*

1 Go through the example with students. Their answers will vary here according to how they interpret the pictures.

**Suggested answers**
He's going to have his hair cut.
She's going to have her tooth filled / taken out.
They've had the room painted.

2 Refer to the Grammar folder on page 199 for the explanations to these questions.

## Vocabulary

> **Teaching extra**
>
> Whenever possible, elicit or give the different forms of words when students meet new vocabulary. Develop this habit in the students.

1 Refer students to the Vocabulary spot. Ask students to read the whole text first before they begin to write the words. It is important to understand the meaning of the texts. Remind students to check which part of speech is required in the sentence. Ask students to work on their own first and then to compare their answers with another student.

Elicit the correct answers from the class and ask students to write the words up on the board so that the spelling can be checked.

**Answers**
1 overlooked  2 underpractised  3 introductory
4 reference  5 excellent  6 scientific  7 relatively
8 memorable

## Speaking

1 This activity will help students with the CAE Speaking test (Paper 5) and allow them to gain confidence in speaking.

Go through the instructions. Ask students to get into groups of three. Give out the role cards (in the Photocopiable activities section on page 185 of the Teacher's Book) – all students in Group A should read role card A, all students in Group B should read role card B and all students in Group C should read role card C. At this point, students should not say aloud which piece of information is correct.

2 Regroup students so that each group of three has one student with card A, one with card B and one with card C. Ask students to give their talk based on the notes on the card while the other two students listen out for the piece of information they think is incorrect.

3 Ask students to tell each other which piece of information was incorrect. Did they guess correctly?

# Writing folder 6

## SB pages 92–93

## Information sheets

1 Ask students to read through the extracts from information sheets and to discuss the questions with a partner.

**Suggested answers**
a Parents and children are the intended readers. Strong colours attract the attention, especially of the young. The different fonts make different information stand out. The colour photo is also eye-catching.
b Bank customers are the intended readers. The heading with *you* in a box attempts to make customers think that they are important to the bank. The picture of the man on a deckchair is to make the customer think that his life will be leisurely if he uses

> the telephone banking service. The tone of the text is also very soothing. The use of a direct question to the customer makes him feel this new type of banking applies to him.
> c The intended readers are tourists as the first piece of information is followed by directions on how to get there by road. The leaflet seems to be aimed at those interested in history and uses bullet points to list places of interest.

2   Ask students to choose two or three features they do not expect to find in information sheets.

> **Answers**
> jargon, very formal language, long sentences

3   This activity, together with activity 4, guides students through the preparation and planning for writing a contribution to an information sheet.

> **Suggested answers**
> A tourists; a contribution to the brochure; what can be done on a countryside holiday, kinds of accommodation, weather conditions
> B visitors to your company; a brief history of the company; main activities, plans for the future, any other points that you think are important
> C a London museum; items of great interest from your country; a contibution to the guide; history of the items, their importance within and outside your country

4   This question provides preparation for writing a contribution to an information sheet. If students have kept their notes from Unit 13, they could make use of them here.

> **Suggested answers**
> Key parts of the question: Your town, visitors, Tourist Board, activities or visits for the young people and older people, balance of fun activities and more intellectual activities for the different age ranges
> Content: Examples of country activities, e.g. sports, parks, walks, wildlife parks, historical places to visit
> Style: welcoming, using lots of adjectives to describe places. Informal or neutral language would be suitable.
> Headings:
> **Country activities/places**
> Possible subheading: What to do in the countryside or (name of region)
> **Information about accommodation**
> Possible subheading: Where to stay
> **Information about the weather**
> Possible subheading: Weather reminder (this will depend on the place and its local climatic conditions)

## Extension activity

If your students would like to choose one of the other writing tasks, you could develop the following:

Task B
This question is easier to answer if you can base your contribution on a real company you know.
Decide on a company you know or a type of company that you could write about. Make sure you have enough information to answer all parts of the question.
The style should be neutral. The main purpose of the information sheet is to give information.
Heading: A description of the origins and past of the company.
Possible subheading: A brief history of X (name of company)
Heading: A description of the business of the company.
Possible subheading: Our product/services

Task C
Include details of historical/cultural items from your country. Remember they must be suitable for a museum in London, so they must be transportable and of interest to museum visitors.
The style should be neutral or formal to reflect the importance of the items.
The introduction should give background to items.
Possible heading: Our legacy
Historical details of the items. The origins of X (name of items)
The significance of the items in our country and abroad.
Possible heading: True treasures

5   Students can write their contributions either in pairs or on their own. Students then exchange their first draft with another student/pair of students.

Encourage students to use the Advice box as they check each other's writing.

The final draft could be written for homework.

# 15 If you want to know what I think ...

| Genre | Expressing opinions |
| Topic | Family life |

| Speaking 1 | Family life |
| Reading | Bringing up children |
| Speaking 2 | Agreeing and disagreeing |
| Grammar | The infinitive |
| Listening | TV programmes |

**Workbook contents**

| Reading | Putting paragraphs into gaps, matching words to definitions |
| Grammar | The infinitive |

## SB pages 94–97

**Lesson planning**

- **SV** Grammar 2 could be set for homework
- **LV** See extension activities in the Reading section

## Speaking 1

Establish that the theme of the unit is expressing opinions by asking when the phrase in the title could be used.

1 Ask students to match the photographs to the speakers.

**Answers**
a 1   b 3   c 4   d 2

2 Personalise the context of the language by asking students this question.

3 Raise awareness of the language we use when we want to be forceful (or tactful/kind/sensitive).

## Reading

To introduce the reading section you could elicit from students ways that are commonly used for people to air their opinions. (Newspaper articles, speeches, letters to magazines/newspapers, radio phone-in programmes, Internet forums and weblogs are some of the common ones in the UK.)

1 Encourage students to look at the title and speculate about what might be included in the article. Possible suggestions could be issues to do with manners, behaviour, staying out late, spending too much money, doing homework, helping in the house, etc. You could also elicit what sort of sanctions parents impose on children when the children have done something wrong.

2 Ask students to read the whole text, then read the questions and choose the best answer, A, B, C or D.

**Answers**
1 B   2 D   3 C   4 A   5 C

### Extension activity

Ask students to go through the article and underline Jonathan's opinions. Then ask students to go through each one and discuss whether they agree or disagree with them.
Jonathan's opinions
- I think children want to feel proud of their parents because it makes them feel secure in a Darwinian sense.
- I have inherited from my father a strong sense of the importance of doing the right thing.
- I believe strongly in proper bedtimes, that chores have to be done and that certain times of the day are reserved for adults.
- I want to make my children into the sort of children I want them to be.
- We live in a terribly liberal age when people feel they should take a back seat in making moral decisions.
- I don't believe in reasoning with my children.
- I can't stand all those Saturday morning programmes.
- I think it's a parent's job to preserve childhood as long as possible.
- I am strict about homework and achievement. Our children will work hard until they finish university and I think they will thank me for the rest of their lives.
- I don't like the attitudes in football.

3 Students rank the items and support their views with reasons.

4 Round up this section by personalising this question for students.

## Speaking 2

1 Ask students to think back to the article and then state their opinions. Omit this activity if you have done the Reading extension activity.

Go through the Exam spot. It is important that students work well together in Part 3 of the CAE Speaking test (Paper 5). They will be expected to contribute fully to the task and to develop the interaction. They should also be sensitive to turn-taking and should neither dominate nor give only minimal responses.

2 Go through the selection of phrases for starting off the CAE Speaking test Part 3 and decide which ones are appropriate.

> **Answers**
> 1 A appropriate B inappropriate
> 2 A inappropriate B appropriate
> 3 A appropriate B inappropriate
> 4 A inappropriate B appropriate

> **Extension activity**
>
> Make posters of different functions, e.g.
> **Inviting opinions**
> What do you think?
> Do you agree?
> And you?
> What about you?
>
> **Giving an opinion**          **Justifying an opinion**
> I think ...                    because
> As far as I know ...           so
> Well, in my opinion ...        since

3 Encourage students to practise giving their opinions, using some of the language worked on in this unit.

4 This serves as a reminder that students should use the phrases they have just worked on to practise for Part 3 of the CAE Speaking test (Paper 5).

## The infinitive

The grammar here is covered on pages 199–200 of the Grammar folder. Go through the introduction to this section, making sure students understand the terminology.

1 Ask students to look for some examples of the infinitive with and without *to* in the reading text.

> **Answers**
> Infinitive with *to*: decide to, want to, used to, be going to, know how to, allow (children) to, have to, would like to, need to, persuade (people) to, ask to, try to, be prepared to
>
> Infinitive without *to*: should live (up to), make (them) feel, might call, will agree, let (them) watch

2 This could be set for homework. Point out that some of the sentences need no corrections.

> **Answers**
> a I don't want *you to* think I'm doing this as a punishment.
> b correct
> c I must *go* home before I miss the last bus.
> d In my opinion parents should not let their daughters *wear* make-up until they are over 16.
> e correct
> f correct
> g correct
> h It was fantastic *to see* so many young people enter the competition.
> i correct

3 This activity provides practice in giving opinions, agreeing and disagreeing and the use of infinitives.

## Listening

1 Students should work with a partner or in small groups to discuss these pre-listening questions.

2 Go through the instructions for the listening task. This is the same task type as in the CAE Listening test (Paper 4) Part 4. As they listen, students match the speakers to the programmes.

> **Answers**
> 1 H  2 E  3 B  4 C  5 G

3 Play the recording again and ask students to complete the second part of the task. Point out that in the exam, they will hear the recording twice but will need to complete both tasks simultaneously.

> **Answers**
> 1 F  2 G  3 C  4 D  5 A

### Tapescript

**Speaker 1:** Well, this is already my favourite series of the year. They're slices of TV heaven. I watched *I Love the Seventies* and enjoyed it thoroughly but as a thirty something who was on the brink of those troubled teenage years at the start of the eighties, this new series was always going to bring back the best and the worst memories! I admit to having a sort of emotional vested interest in this period but when it's executed as well as this, I feel absolutely no shame!

**Speaker 2:** Well, the only thing I can compare this with really is the equally brilliant *Predators*, which was a fascinating and amazing nature documentary. I guess what makes these prehistoric times really come to life is the use of computer imagery, it's just so impressive. And added to that, there's a kind of tongue-in-cheek commentary, it just makes it one of the most enjoyable evenings I've had for a long while.

**Speaker 3:** Mm, I sat down to watch this period piece with great interest. Now, yeah, I basically approve of employing composers to write new music, but the Tudor period boasts some of England's greatest composers and finest music, so why couldn't some of it have found its way into this programme? After all, we know what music was performed at the great state occasions described in the narrative and yeah, there are plenty of performers who could have done it justice.

**Speaker 4:** Yeah, it was, it was great to see that this programme was coming back on TV, I mean it's been off our screens for far too long, but what has happened to the format? I mean the programme seemed to be more about the presenter than anything else. The recipes looked delicious but why on earth can't we have normal shots of him preparing the dishes? There seemed to be something obscuring every shot, completely distracting the viewer from what was going on. If it wasn't a vase of tulips, it was a bowl of lemons or, more often than not, some floaty greenery.

**Speaker 5:** Well, what an absolute delight and a perfect presenter, and no, I am not the presenter's grandmother, just your average music addict who, well, I want to tell as many people as possible about this lovely late-night programme. And for anyone who finds music an endless adventure, full of familiar delights and new experiences, this programme is without gush, without formality, without advertising, well, it's the one for us!

4   A discussion in small groups will round off the unit.

# UNITS 11–15 Revision

## SB pages 98–99

## Topic review

Follow the standard procedure outlined on page 29 of the Teacher's Book.

## Reading

1 Go through the extract with the students.

> **Answers**
> a He says he has left a present inside which he wanted his wife to take to Ellen.
> b She is frantic as she does not want to be late.
> c The main clue as to their relationship is in the part about the combs. Mrs Foster criticises her husband and he reacts angrily. We can imagine that she has to be a dutiful wife, letting him get his own way.
> d The use of direct speech and short sentences adds to the sense of urgency.

## Grammar

1 This tests students' knowledge of the use of the infinitive with and without *to*.

> **Answers**
> 1 to be  2 to fetch  3 lying  4 to remain
> 5 to say  6 flocking  7 to find  8 to stand up to
> 9 to secure  10 complaining

## Speaking

1 Although one aim of this exercise is for students to practise the grammar points listed in the rubric, be flexible about this as the other aim, allowing students to take stock of their progress and study skills, is equally important.

2 Encourage students to change places in the room and interview each other. After they have interviewed each other, allow time for discussion of anything the students want to bring up regarding their course.

## Vocabulary

1 Ask students first to identify the missing part of speech and then to work on their own to fill the gaps.

> **Answers**
> 1 possibly  2 foolishness  3 misery  4 unnecessarily
> 5 timing  6 purposely (also accept purposefully)
> 7 unhappy

# TEST 3

## Paper 1 Part 3

You are going to read a newspaper article. For questions **1–5**, choose the answer (**A**, **B**, **C** or **D**) which you think fits best according to the text.

### THE WORLD OF PACKAGING

Each week, container ships leave British ports bound for China, India and the Far East. Their giant 40-tonne metal boxes are not full of new manufactured goods but with plastic waste from the British food packaging industry: British food containers, bags, bottles and trays are now big in Shanghai.

In a few years we can bet these same ships will be exporting millions of old plastic 'pouches', – the flexi, collapsible milk containers that have taken over from the glass bottle or cardboard container in parts of mainland Europe and North America and are now being tried out in southern Britain by Britain's largest milk products company.

The dairy industry loves its low-density polyethylene pouches, which are widely expected to take over from the ubiquitous rigid plastic and cardboard containers that milk usually comes in. The industry claims the pouches use just over half as much plastic as an equivalent rigid 'jug', about a third as much 'material' as a carton and 70 times less than a glass bottle. They argue that they are greener, cheaper and easier for the consumer.

Well, up to a point. Food packaging today is really about marketing, and few people want to think too much about what happens to their food and drink containers after they have been binned. Never mind the impact arising from the energy use, toxins and pollutants released at every stage in their production and transport, they can be disposed of at expensive landfill sites, where they will take 300-odd years to biodegrade, or be incinerated, and ultimately there may be little option but to export them, because their chemical composition makes them economically practically unrecyclable in rich countries.

So, because the 'pouches' cannot be reused or refilled, they could end up travelling half way round the world (some of them ending up as damp proof courses or drain pipes) and then sent back to undercut our own recycling and building industries.

But this is the wacky world of the global food packaging industry which, like world trade, has been on a roll for 50 years. From being worth almost nothing, it is now a $100 billion-a-year monster, growing 10%–15% a year. Every extra deal brokered by the World Trade Organisation, every extra food shipment, every new line of processed food means more packaging.

We have become obsessed with food packaging, to the amusement of the rest of the world, where the idea of an inferior tea being sold inside an envelope itself protected by cardboard and in turn covered in Cellophane to be served in a polystyrene cup is unimaginable.

'In my country, a cup of tea at the railway station comes in a clay cup which will hold liquid for just 10 minutes. You throw it on the lines, where it dissolves within weeks,' says an Indian friend. 'But your plastic disposable cups, also designed to hold tea for 10 minutes, may take 500 years to decompose.'

1   What changes does the writer foresee in the export of waste from Britain?
    A   The size of the containers will increase.
    B   The type of waste will change.
    C   China will become the chief recipient.
    D   The waste will weigh less.

2   How does the writer think people will react to the new pouches?
    A   They will find the pouches more convenient.
    B   They will recognise that the pouches are greener.
    C   They will be concerned about the pouches' disposal.
    D   They will continue to be unconcerned about packaging.

3   What does the writer claim to be the greatest drawback of the use of the pouches?
    A   They are not biodegradable.
    B   A great deal of energy is needed for their production.
    C   They are costly to dispose of.
    D   A great deal of land will be given over to their disposal.

4   What irony does the writer draw the reader's attention to when referring to the export of pouches?
    A   They will ultimately have a detrimental effect on British businesses.
    B   They will add to the needless transportation of waste.
    C   They will help boost global trade.
    D   They will be obsolete in 50 years' time.

5   What point does the writer make by including his Indian friend's comments?
    A   Packaging hides inferior products.
    B   It strengthens his case against packaging.
    C   Packaging adds to the cost of the product.
    D   We should return to former values.

# Paper 2 Part 1

You **must** answer this question. Write your answer in **180–220** words in an appropriate style.

1. You recently saw an advertisement for job opportunities in Australia. You are very interested and have made some notes on the advertisement. Read the advertisement below with your notes written on it and write a letter to *Sydney Opportunities* saying why you are interested in working in Australia and raising the questions referred to in your notes.

# Sydney Opportunities

## Job opportunities in Australia

Have you ever thought of working in an English-speaking country?

Would you like the opportunity of learning some new skills? *possible to request a job where I can use my IT skills?*

Are you interested in improving your English? *international company - so I can use my mother tongue and English?*

## Then you should write to us.

We at **Sydney Opportunities** find part-time work placements in large companies.

Your salary covers your living expenses. *any help with finding accommodation?*

We are unable to offer accommodation.

## Write and tell us:

- what qualifications and experience you already have
- when you would like to start
- your reasons for applying for a placement

Now write your **letter** to *Sydney Opportunities*.
You do not need to include postal addresses.

# Paper 3 Part 3

For questions **1–8**, read the text below. Use the word given in capitals at the end of some of the lines to form a word that fits in the gap in the same line. There is an example at the beginning (**0**).

## Low water

The world is getting drier. Climate change and irrigation have reduced Lake Chad, the African freshwater lake, to a (**0**) ...*twentieth*... of its size. For the **TWENTY**
world's water experts there is no doubt as to the (**1**) .................. of the issue. **GRAVE**
The main reason for the global (**2**) .................. of water is increased demand. **SCARCE**
Growing the crops needed to feed the world's expanding population
accounts for about 70% of all water (**3**) .................. . But increases in population **DRAW**
are also taking their toll. In many parts of the world, rivers and lakes are so
polluted that their water is (**4**) .................. even for industrial use. In some **FIT**
countries, problems are likely to be exacerbated by future climate change.
However, not everyone is so pessimistic. Other experts believe that the
issue is water (**5**) .................. ; that there is a water crisis but it is not about **MANAGE**
too little water to satisfy our needs but rather that we do not manage it
well enough. There is enough water to satisfy people's personal needs
almost everywhere, but agriculture is a different story. (**6**) .................. **GROW**
food for an individual requires a thousand times as much water as it
takes to meet that person's need for (**7**) .................. water. Water-deficient **DRINK**
economies balance their water budgets by importing 'virtual water' in the
form of grain and other staple foods. There are also concerns about the
(**8**) .................. costs of irrigation for food production. **ENVIRONMENT**

# Paper 3 Part 5

For questions **1–8**, complete the second sentence so that it has a similar meaning to the first sentence, using the word given. **Do not change the word given**. You must use between **three** and **six** words, including the word given. Here is an example (**0**).

**0** I don't feel like walking all the way into town.
**mood**
I'm <u>not in the mood for</u> walking all the way into town.

**1** The island was completely uninhabited.
**sign**
There was ............................................. on the island.

**2** James ignored the 'Danger' sign.
**notice**
James ............................................. the 'Danger' sign.

**3** Without a new tennis coach, Olga would never have won the tournament.
**had**
If ............................................. a new tennis coach, she would never have won the tournament.

**4** The teacher made all the students do presentations last week.
**had**
All the students ............................................. presentations last week.

**5** You can't smoke in here.
**allowed**
You're ............................................. in here.

**6** We haven't got any milk left.
**run**
We've ............................................. milk.

**7** If Sophie worked as hard as everyone else, we'd be finished in no time.
**weight**
If Sophie ............................................., we'd be finished in no time.

**8** I don't know why my neighbour thinks she's so superior to everyone else.
**down**
I don't know why my neighbour ............................................. everyone else.

# Paper 4 Part 3

You will hear part of a radio interview with a writer of crime fiction. For questions **1–6**, choose the answer (**A, B, C** or **D**) which fits best according to what you hear.

1 According to Caroline, what do her books offer the readers?
   A   a social issue to think about
   B   a complicated mystery to solve
   C   a shock which will thrill them
   D   a record of contemporary society

2 Caroline deals with the brutality of crime in her novels by
   A   concentrating on the psychological aspects of the crime.
   B   describing the research which produces the evidence.
   C   writing mainly about what happens after the crime.
   D   referring to it in a light, almost humorous way.

3 How does Caroline account for the personality of her main character?
   A   It has evolved from her observations of real life.
   B   It reflects the dark side of the criminal world.
   C   It offers an alternative to the usual serious detective.
   D   It allows Caroline to analyse a secretive lifestyle.

4 What is Caroline's attitude to the suggestion that she could write a different type of book?
   A   She wishes she had written different books.
   B   It is irrelevant which type of book she writes.
   C   Only detective novels offer scope for deep feelings.
   D   Detective novels allow her to write about areas which interest her.

5 How does Caroline feel about receiving a writer's award?
   A   proud
   B   flattered
   C   dismissive
   D   embarrassed

6 How does Caroline feel about writing a novel with a new main character?
   A   She refuses to talk about her plans.
   B   She is seriously tempted to do so.
   C   She recognises the commercial value of her current work.
   D   She would feel lost if she abandoned her chief inspector.

# TEST 3 Key

## Paper 1 Part 3

1 B  2 D  3 A  4 A  5 B

## Paper 3 Part 3

1 gravity  2 scarcity  3 withdrawals  4 unfit
5 management  6 Growing  7 drinking  8 environmental

## Paper 3 Part 5

1 no sign of habitation / life / anyone living
2 took no notice of  3 Olga hadn't had
4 had to do  5 not allowed to smoke
6 run out of  7 pulled / would pull her weight
8 looks down on

## Paper 4 Part 3

1 B  2 C  3 A  4 D  5 A  6 C

## Tapescript

**Interviewer:** We're very pleased to have with us in the studio today Caroline Stevenson, whose famous detective novels have just been shown as a very successful series on TV. Now, Caroline, a lot of people seem to be getting concerned about crime fiction writing, like a lot of TV programmes, just making an entertainment of crime. What's your view on that?

**Caroline:** Well, I know the actuality and reality of crime is far from entertaining, but when you look at crime writing you can see all sorts of motives if you like. It can be seen as documenting and articulating the times that we live in and engaging society in a larger debate. Then there are those who want to shock the reader and that in itself is really a form of entertainment. Being a crossword addict, I present the readers with a puzzle which they have to try to unravel. And that's a far cry from any sort of need to communicate a moral message or say anything of true significance.

**Interviewer:** But we can't get away from the fact that a crime has to be committed and that's usually something quite brutal in crime writing, isn't it?

**Caroline:** I suppose that's one type of crime fiction but I never have brains bespattering the walls in my books. I get over all the horror in the first few chapters and then make things a little bit lighter. And there's quite a fashion among crime writers at the moment to focus on the psychological profile of the criminal which can be another way of avoiding the gore. And of course the new TV drama series, *Westwood*, focuses on the clinical analysis of the whole business, seen through the eyes of the forensic scientist.

**Interviewer:** Mm. Now, your main character, the chief inspector, many people find him an unfathomable character. He seems to have many sides to his character.

**Caroline:** Over the years I've worked with a lot of the professionals whose jobs revolve around crime. Now, I do realise what a grim life many people lead but there is a bit of humour for undertakers and pathologists. In fact, in those jobs there needs to be a counterbalance to the seriousness of the situation. And my chief inspector reflects this aspect of what I've witnessed. Some readers think there's a subplot going on because he's single but that's purely in their imagination, I can assure you.

**Interviewer:** And have you ever thought of writing about something else?

**Caroline:** Well, I suppose I could have turned my hand to other genres but there would always have to be characters who showed a depth of passion and I'm quite interested in what motivates people's behaviour. With any good complex plot you can work in all those elements, but quite honestly, the whodunit offers all that, so I haven't really felt the need to explore.

**Interviewer:** And you are at the top of your profession which has been once again recognised in the form of your latest crime writer's award.

**Caroline:** Yes, I know it's quite fashionable to play down awards like this, you know, you get all these suggestions that it's rigged and so on, but it does make you feel good when you've been judged worthy by your peers. Mind you, for me, the greatest thrill is when I meet someone who says, 'I just couldn't put the book down, I had to find out what happened next'. So it's almost these personal encounters that count just as much if not more than the glamorous awards.

**Interviewer:** Mm. And what does the future hold? Rumour has it that you're going to kill off your famous chief inspector. What then?

**Caroline:** Have you heard that from me? Although sometimes it appeals to me because it's become so expected of me, that every year I'll churn out another one in the series, I sometimes wonder if I shouldn't be trying something new. But on the other hand I know my chief inspector so well. It's almost as though I've lived with him for all these years. And when it comes down to it, it's proved an extremely lucrative business.

# 16 Raving and panning

| Genre | Reviews |
| --- | --- |
| Topic | The arts |

| Speaking 1 | Raving and panning |
| Reading | Reviews |
| Speaking 2 | Giving opinions |
| Grammar | Articles and determiners |
| Listening | Films |
| Vocabulary | Collocation |

**Workbook contents**

| Reading | General comprehension questions |
| Vocabulary | Collocations |
| Grammar | Articles |
| Writing | A review |

## SB pages 100–103

**Lesson planning**

- **SV** Listening 4 could be omitted
- **LV** See extension activities in the Speaking 2, Grammar and Listening sections

## Speaking 1

1 Before opening the book, write the headlines on the board and elicit from students that they all come from reviews pages.

2 Students work with a partner to answer questions a–d.

## Reading

1 Set a time limit for students to scan the texts to answer this question. They should establish what is being reviewed and whether the review is favourable or not.

**Answers**

| Text | What is being reviewed | Critic's opinion |
| --- | --- | --- |
| A | hotel | favourable |
| B | novel | favourable |
| C | computer game | favourable |
| D | music album | neutral |
| E | website | favourable |

2 This exercise contains three statements about each of the reviews.

Ask students to read each review in turn and decide whether each statement is true, false or if the information is not given in the extracts.

**Answers**

1. a false (he stumbled on it, i.e. he found it by chance)
   b true
   c the answer is not given in the extract
2. a true
   b false (it is a romance that reads more like a thriller)
   c true
3. a true
   b false (they have pea-sized brains, i.e. are stupid)
   c the answer is not given in the extract
4. a true
   b the answer is not given in the extract
   c false
5. a true
   b the answer is not given in the extract
   c true

3 This exercise explores the texts in more detail.

**Answers**

| Text | Words identifying the topic | Positive words and expressions | Negative words and expressions |
| --- | --- | --- | --- |
| B | Howard examines – subtle romance – reads more like a thriller – parallels with the author's own life | the trap is gently laid – we sit back, transfixed – subtle – added piquancy – prepare to be seduced | callous con man – predator and prey – to watch the kill (NB These are describing aspects of the story rather than being negative opinions of the novel.) |
| C | veteran gamers – arcade classic – proceed across the screen – platforms – iMac | hours of light-hearted entertainment | won't stretch your iMac to the limits (slightly but not very negative in tone) |

**RAVING AND PANNING** 91

| | | | |
|---|---|---|---|
| D | rock's gothic underworld – noise-mongering – quiet piano balladry – songs – record | finest (positive opinion of the previous record) – maintain the contemplative style | morose noise-mongering (negative opinion of pre-1997 records) – takes half a pace backwards towards his anguished past |
| E | Speechtips.com – was still under construction | sweat no more – concise guide – in easy steps – common-sense advice should be compulsory reading | unfortunately |

4 Students discuss this in pairs.

## Speaking 2

This section deals with the language of opinion and suggestion. Refer students to the Exam spot.

1 Students could discuss the exercise with a partner before checking their answers with the class as a whole.

> **Answers**
> a don't   b giving   c well   d right   e words
> f matter   g convinced   h whole, take

2 This exercise focuses students' attention on the fact that there are fixed collocations which should be learnt as chunks.

3 Divide students into groups of three to five. Encourage them to use some of the expressions from the previous two exercises.

> **Extension activity**
> Students work in groups of three. They are going to prepare and record a radio review.
> • They discuss what they are going to review. It could be a CD, a DVD, a computer game, a school concert, a local café or a sports event, for example. They should be advised to choose something that all three are familiar with.
> • They share their opinions about what they are going to review. What do they each like and dislike about it?
> • They discuss how best to present their review for the other students in the class. How much information do they need to include about the subject? How can they make the review more interesting for the listeners?
> • Record the review, then play it for other students to listen to.

## Articles and determiners

The grammar here is covered on page 200 of the Grammar folder.

1 The questions here serve to highlight some of the key points about the use of articles and determiners in English.

> **Answers**
> **Review A**
> a It is the name of a hotel and these usually take a definite article – *The Holiday Inn, The Ritz, The Red Lion*, etc.
> b It is the first time the loch has been mentioned.
> c It is talking in general rather than about a specific group, in which case *the Americans* or *some Americans* might be used.
> **Review B**
> a It is asking a general question about any intelligent woman and any con man. The same idea could be expressed by using the words in the plural: *Have you ever wondered how intelligent women could fall for callous con men?*
> b The process of a con man tricking a woman.
> c Because it is referring to the specific author of the novel that is being reviewed.
> **Review C**
> a Because possessive adjectives are usually used when referring to parts of our bodies in English, e.g. *I've hurt my leg*, not *I've hurt the leg*.
> b Because it is referring to a specific, named game.
> **Review D**
> a Because the phrase 'quiet piano balladry' is modified by a following expression, 'of 1997's *The Boatman's Call*'.
> b Because these refer to unique aspects of our environment.
> **Review E**
> a *Few* without *a* would suggest that the objective is to say as little as possible, which clearly does not make sense in the context.
> b *The* is used in the first two sets of brackets because it is referring to a specific situation whereas *notes* and *memory* are being considered more generally.

2 Discuss these sentences with students. First correct the sentences, then deal with the rules. Point out to students that these sentences exemplify the most common mistakes with articles made by students at CAE level.

> **Answers**
> a Life is hard! (No article used in general statements.)
> b The life of the poor in a country with no welfare state is very hard. (The article is used in general statements where the noun has a post-modifying phrase.)
> c My brother is a biochemist in London. (The indefinite article is used when saying what people's jobs are.)
> d Jack broke his leg skiing. (A possessive adjective is usually used before parts of the body.)

e He's only 18 but he already has his own business. (A possessive adjective is usually used before *own*.)
f Maria's on a business trip to the People's Republic of China. (*The* is not used with most countries but it is used with plural names for countries or with places whose name contains a common noun like *Republic* or *Federation* or *Kingdom*.)
g Do they sell fruit in the USA by the kilo or the pound? (*The* is used in measuring expressions with *by*.)
h Since they built the tunnel, fewer people are using the ferry. (*The* is often used with means of transport to refer to the type of transport being used, rather than a specific bus, car or boat, e.g. *I take the bus to work*.)

## Extension activity

Ask students to prepare their own examples to illustrate each of the rules worked on in Articles and determiners.

# Listening

1 Students should look at the pictures and speculate about the kinds of films or shows they might be from.

2 Personalise the topic by asking students to talk about their own preferences.

3 Play the recording once and ask students to think about questions a–c.

**Answers**
a The people are discussing two films – *Billy Elliott* and *Moulin Rouge*.
b *Billy Elliott*
Has little boy in it who dances but was not a trained dancer
Julie Walters acted in it
Has scene where the boy and his dad are sitting laughing on a wall and they fall off
*Moulin Rouge*
Has Nicole Kidman and Ewan MacGregor in it and they both sing as well as act
Baz Luhrmann is the director
c loved   great   lovely   a bit unconvincing
have reservations about   couldn't believe that
over-romanticised   what I did really like
I was blown away by   in your face and brash and brave
unrelenting   just pow pow pow   dodgy
remarkably well   really went for it   looked fantastic
most amazing   something different   stunning
wonderfully brave   brilliant

## Tapescript

**Man:** Did you see that film, *Billy Elliott*? Did you like that?
**Woman:** I did, I really – I loved the little boy in it, I thought he was great, yeah.
**Man:** Did you? Were you convinced by his dancing, did you …
**Woman:** I wondered whether he was a trained dancer.
**Man:** Yeah, I can tell you he isn't, because I worked with him.
**Woman:** Oh, really, did you? Was he nice?
**Man:** He was lovely, he's a lovely young kid, yeah.
**Woman:** I'll tell you what I didn't really like, I thought that Julie Walters was a bit unconvincing, actually.
**Man:** Oh, did you?
**Woman:** Yeah.
**Man:** Isn't that funny! I mean I have reservations about some of the things. I couldn't believe that his, his dad – I don't know if you remember the scene where they suddenly fall back laughing off the, they're on a fence or a wall somewhere.
**Woman:** That stile or a wall, yeah.
**Man:** And suddenly they all, it's all loving happy families and until then he's been bashing around the house.
**Woman:** It's a bit over-romanticised.
**Man:** Yeah.
**Woman:** I'll tell you what I did really like, though, was *Moulin Rouge*. Have you seen that?
**Man:** Did you? Yeah, I was blown away by the first ten minutes, the first quarter of an hour. It just, it's so in your face and brash and brave and – I just needed a couple of breathing spaces in it afterwards because I just, it just seemed unrelenting, do you know what I mean?
**Woman:** Yes, I know what you mean.
**Man:** Just pow pow pow!
**Woman:** I thought Nicole Kidman's singing was a bit dodgy sometimes.
**Man:** Yeah. I thought they both did remarkably well. I, I mean, you know …
**Woman:** I heard that Ewan McGregor really went for it with the singing. He just absolutely – had a great time.
**Man:** I can believe that because it just looked fantastic. I mean he's, I think Baz Luhrmann is an amazing director.
**Woman:** So do I – the audience …
**Man:** He always does something different.
**Woman:** Visuals are stunning I always think.
**Man:** Yes, it's wonderfully brave, I just think it's a brilliant film.

4 Allow students time to think about what to choose and how to describe it. They should then explain their choices to their partner.

**RAVING AND PANNING**

> **Extension activity**
>
> Students could get into groups with each group focusing on one of the categories that the students are interested in. For example, you might be able to have a restaurant group, a web-site group and a film group. Allow students to join the groups dealing with the topics that they are most interested in. Within these groups, students choose one thing that they would definitely recommend and one that they would definitely not recommend. They list as many reasons as possible for their selections. When they are ready they present their recommendations to the rest of the class.

## Vocabulary

Remind students of work that they have previously done on collocations in Unit 6. Point out that these collocations all come from the texts they have read or listened to in this unit.

1  Ask students to match the collocations in this exercise.

> **Answers**
> a 11  b 12  c 1  d 9  e 6  f 2  g 3  h 7
> i 4  j 8  k 10  l 5

2  This exercise could be set for homework as revision of the collocations worked with in Vocabulary 1.

> **Answers**
> a compulsory reading  b family tree  c love letters
> d middle age  e light-hearted entertainment

3  Allow students to use an English–English dictionary to complete this exercise. Put the different collocations that students come up with on the board and elicit which collocations students think are the strongest.

> **Suggested answers**
> a family: entertainment, connections, holiday
> b to drive someone: crazy, round the bend, potty
> c love: affair, story, nest
> d middle: school, ages, ground
> e to lay: open, the table, to rest

# Exam folder 7

## SB pages 104–105

### Paper 1 Part 2 Gapped text

Read through the Advice box and ask students to discuss why each point is a sensible piece of advice.

1  Students do this exercise either in class or at home if time is short.

> **Answers**
> 1 C  2 D  3 F  4 E  5 G  6 A

2  Encourage students to identify the words and phrases which help them fit the paragraphs into the gaps.

# 17 Do it for my sake

| Genre | Proposals |
| Topic | Persuasion |

| Speaking 1 | Proposals and applicants |
| Reading | Preparing a proposal |
| Listening | Persuading people |
| Grammar | Language of persuasion |
| Vocabulary | Multiple meanings |
| Speaking 2 | The perfect holiday |

**Workbook contents**

| Use of English | Part 2 open gap fill |
| Use of English | Part 4 multiple meanings |
| Grammar | Language of persuasion |
| Use of English | Part 5 keyword transformations |

## SB pages 106–109

**Lesson planning**

SV  Grammar 1 and 2 and Vocabulary 1 and 2 could be set for homework
LV  See the extension activity in the Vocabulary section

Point out to students that the language in this unit is useful for the CAE exam because it deals not only with proposals and persuasion, but also with some of the most important exam topics, i.e. work, study and travel. Although these themes are dealt with elsewhere in the book, they are reviewed here as they are such frequent themes in the exam and are also topics that candidates are likely to find useful in 'real life'.

## Speaking 1

1 Ask students to describe the people in the photos and to use their imagination to suggest what their lives might be like.

   Students should then read the adverts and decide who might apply for each one. In general, there is no right or wrong answer, although d is most likely to appeal to an older person and a to a younger person. Any answer that the students can justify is acceptable, however.

2 The point of this question is to encourage students to put themselves in the situation of someone who might actually be replying to one of the adverts. This should help them to include the kind of information that is appropriate for the task.

3 This question helps to personalise the situation for students.

## Reading

1 If students are more interested in adverts b–d, you could ask them to discuss question 1 in relation to them.

2 If another advert was focused on in question 1, then this text should also be read in the light of that advert. The points which students tick here will depend on which advert they chose.

## Listening

1 Refer students to the Exam spot at this point. Students then discuss questions a–d with a partner.

2 Play the recording once and ask students to complete as much of the table as they can. Then they should compare their answers with a partner.

| Answers | | |
|---|---|---|
| | What speaker wants others to do | How speaker tries to persuade them |
| 1 | mother wants toddler to eat his vegetables | encourages, plays games, eats some too, praises |
| 2 | schoolboy wants friend to play truant from school in order to watch a football match | reassures that they won't be found out, taunts by calling him a coward, exhibits great confidence in own plans |
| 3 | boss wants workers to do some overtime | explains why it's necessary, shows sympathy with how workers must be feeling, threatens |
| 4 | girl wants friend to lend her a special dress to wear to a party | promises to be careful, explains why she wants it so much, praises the dress, promises to do various favours for friend in return |
| 5 | sales person is trying to sell a fitted kitchen | uses very positive language about the offer, emphasises throughout what a bargain it is, says it will all be very easy for the customer |

| | | |
|---|---|---|
| 6 | teenager wants to persuade mother to let her stay out late | reminds mum that there is no school next day, uses moral blackmail, tries to reassure mum, says all friends are going to be allowed, reminds mum how good she's been |
| 7 | wife wants to persuade husband that they should move to a house in the country | emphasises benefits to children, says husband could use commuting time productively and so would be freer when home |
| 8 | sales assistant in clothes shop wants to persuade woman to buy a dress | flatters, goes into detail about why the dress is good for the specific customer, points out how versatile it is |

## Tapescript

**Speaker 1:** Now look, fish fingers and peas and carrots and broccoli. Oh, you like broccoli, don't you? Let me just put that on the fork. There, you have that. Go on, open your mouth. That's a good boy. You chew, that's it. And now a carrot. There you go, in it goes. You take that carrot, that's a good boy. Can I have some, can mummy have some? Oh, that's lovely, thank you. Now you have some, go on. You have that spoon. One for you, one for me. Good boy.

**Speaker 2:** Hey, Rog, it's Jim, hey, how are you doing? Listen, tomorrow afternoon, you know we're playing QPR? Yeah yeah, well it kicks off at 3, you up for it? Yeah? No, don't worry, don't worry. No, he won't, he won't, they won't know. They'll never know, I mean it's PE tomorrow afternoon. They're never going to know. There's forty of us all in white shorts. How are they going to know there's two of them missing, you know what I mean? Now come on, yeah, come on. No, don't be such a coward. Yeah, yeah, 3 o'clock, yeah, we'll bunk off around lunch time and then we'll go down and come back. It'll be all over by, what, half-five? We'll be back, yeah, it'll be brilliant.

**Speaker 3:** Now, I think you all know why we've had to meet today. I've got the monthly figures back from head office and for the third month running, sales are down and we all know the margins are getting tighter so we've got to try and get a march on the competition. I'm going to have to ask some of you to put in more overtime. No, no, I know, I know that's not going to be very popular and there's not going to be a great deal of money in it for people but we really have to get ahead of the opposition here, OK? I mean if you don't want to do it, maybe you'd be better off finding a job with them.

**Speaker 4:** Oh, go on, oh, look. I don't want that, I don't want the red one. I actually just want to borrow the blue one. Oh, it's beautiful, go on, you know it suits me, please! I wouldn't ask unless it was for this party. I mean I've been, I just think he's going to be there and I'd just like to look nice and that dress is the most beautiful thing I've ever seen. Look, I won't spill anything on it, I promise, I – I won't even drink anything all night. I won't eat anything either. There'll be no crumbs, nothing, I promise. Look, I'll wash up for a month or take your bike in. I'll do all your washing. Oh, please let me?

**Speaker 5:** Good morning, I wonder if I could just take a few seconds of your time just to tell you about a special offer we're doing at the moment. We're in your area and we're doing free quotations on brand new kitchen units. Now these units are made to measure, they're marvellous, they're handmade by our craftsmen up in Yorkshire. Therefore it's very much cheaper making them directly from our workshop than going to the shops and also you don't have to pay at all for anything this year so basically we'll install the kitchen for you and you don't have to pay anything till next year. Now that's a fantastic offer, I'm sure you'll agree.

**Speaker 6:** Oh, go on, mum, please let me stay out. Look, all the others are going to be there and there's no school the next day. Oh, go on, please let me! Do you remember you said that if I started doing better in French you'd let me stay out? Well, I got good marks, didn't I? Oh, go on, mum. And I'll get a taxi home and I'll pay for it. Look, everyone else is going to be there, please let me go, oh, go on, mum. I know you want me to be happy, don't you?

**Speaker 7:** Look darling, I know you love the city but, well, we don't often go out and use it, do we? So I was thinking perhaps if we moved to the country? I mean we'd get more for our money out there. Think of the children. They could actually walk to school, mm? Not take that horrible tube. I do hate them using the tube. It'd be cheaper, wouldn't it? And well, the air is much much cleaner and therefore much more relaxing. They could play. Wouldn't all the time have to be on their backs worrying. And think of you, you wouldn't have to drive into work. You could get the train and do some work on the train so therefore you can play with the children in the evening. Oh, think about it, please?

**Speaker 8:** Yeah, the mirror's right over here, yeah. Oh, it really looks lovely. Yeah, oh, it's gorgeous on you though, you've got such a lovely figure. What size is that one? Oh, it's a size ten, yeah well there you are, you see. I can only get into size twelve/fourteen. You are lucky. Well, I'll tell you what, though. That dress really looks nice because the way it's cut over your hips, you see if you just turn round there, look, look in the mirror there. It's ever so nice. And the colour's good on you as well because, like, green, green really goes with red hair. Yeah, oh, I think it's really nice, yeah. You could do with getting that one and it's quite good because you can use that dress for all sorts of things, couldn't you? You could go to parties in it and wear it out anywhere really.

3   With a partner, students should take it in turns to try to persuade each other to do some of the things on the list. Tell the students that when they are being persuaded to do things, they should not give in too easily but should agree to do what their partner wants if they feel that their partner has made effective use of the language of persuasion.

## Language of persuasion

The grammar here is covered on page 201 of the Grammar folder. Students read the introductory notes to this section.

1   Students discuss which would be the better alternative with a partner before comparing answers with those of the rest of the class.

**Answers**
1 a   2 b   3 a   4 a   5 a   6 b   7 b

2   Students should complete the table in any appropriate way.

3   For Part a, students should first decide what the teenager and parent are discussing. This will, of course, affect how the teenager tries to persuade the parent. If they are trying to persuade the parent to let them have driving lessons, for example, the language used will be rather different from that used if they want the parent to let them drop out of college.

Monitor the dialogues as they are being written, then ask some of the students to read out their completed dialogues to the rest of the class. Encourage them to put as much feeling into their reading as possible, as intonation is also important when trying to persuade people to do things. After listening to each of the dialogues, students comment on how effective they were.

Repeat this process for the dialogue between a manager and a member of staff in Part b.

## Vocabulary

1   Go through the examples with students, then ask them to do the exercise individually.

**Answers**
1 grant   2 terms   3 stick   4 sense   5 current

2   Ask students in pairs to think of at least two senses for each word and to illustrate each through a typical sentence. Encourage them to use an English–English dictionary if they wish.

**Suggested answers**
call: phone, name, shout to
course: track, stage of a meal, naturally (*of course*)
direction: way, guidance, instruction
fit: be the right size, short attack, in a good state of health
order: request, sequence, state of tidiness
own: possess, admit, alone (*on your own*)
step: stand, stage, related through a re-marriage
sum: mathematics problem, amount of money, come to a conclusion (*sum up*)

### Extension activity

Students could work with a partner and make up at least three sets of sentences like those in Vocabulary 1. They should then work with another pair, testing each other on their sets of sentences.

## Speaking 2

1   Divide students into groups of about four or five. Each group should choose a type of holiday from those illustrated in photos a–e. As far as possible, ensure that each group chooses a different photo to focus on.

a   Ask students to stay in their groups and to think of as many reasons as possible which they could use to persuade other groups to go on that particular kind of holiday. How will they counter any possible objections?

b   Now regroup students so that those who chose the holiday in photo a are sitting with students who chose holidays b–e, and so on.

c   When each student has presented the case for their choice of holiday, students should stay in their new groups and vote on which holiday all the group would like to go on. Students may not vote for their own suggestion!

d   Students should then feed back to the class as a whole, saying which holiday was selected and why.

# Writing folder 7

## SB pages 110–111

## Set texts

Introduce the topic by asking students to look at the pictures and comment on:
- whether they read/watch DVDS in similar situations
- where their own preferred places for reading/watching DVDS are, and why.

As it is impossible to provide work for the specific set texts, this Writing folder looks at general aspects of working with set texts for CAE. Make sure your students are clear that they are not expected to write answers with an academic literary focus. It is not a literature test. Candidates are encouraged to read for pleasure and because it will improve their knowledge of English, not because they are expected to develop literary appreciation skills.

Questions 1–3 depend on the specific texts and so answers cannot be provided here. If you do not know what the set texts are for the current exam, you will be able to find out from the Cambridge ESOL website.

Make sure your students have the skills to use an Internet search engine such as Google to find information about the texts that they might decide to study. The Wikipedia website may be a useful source of information and links to other information.

4   The answers below give some common topics for a question on a set text. However, there are many other equally valid topics that the students may come up with.

> **Possible answers**
> - most interesting character
> - key moment in the plot
> - relationship between two main characters and how this develops during the story
> - the way the writer interests the reader in reading more
> - the importance of the place where the story is set
> - the importance of the period when the story is set
> - the significance of the title of the story
> - whether the story makes / would make a good film
> - whether the story resonates with anything in the students' own lives
> - anything unsuccessful about the story
> - how appropriate the story is for someone learning English

5   The answers below give some characteristics of these four genres, which students should be aware of.

> **Suggested answers**
> **Article:** is written for a large audience, about whom the writer knows little beyond the fact that they read a magazine of a particular type; benefits from a title and an opening sentence that will intrigue readers and encourage them to read on; aim is to interest
>
> **Report:** is mainly concerned with facts; has to be clearly organised and expressed; headings may be a useful way of guiding both the reader and writer through the text; it is often necessary to finish with a recommendation and if so the reasons for the recommendation should be clearly and unambiguously stated; aim is to inform
>
> **Review:** the reader wants to get a general impression of what is being reviewed but does not want a detailed description of the plot; aim is to help the reader decide whether to read the book / watch the film for themselves
>
> **Essay:** written for a teacher and so is likely to be in a neutral to formal style; should be clearly structured and logically argued; aim is to impress in terms of both content and style

6   This activity may be done in pairs or small groups. Allow plenty of time for discussion as it may encourage students to read or watch the books or films they talk about with other students. It would also be possible to follow up by asking students to write a review of their film or book.

7   In the light of your class discussions of task 5, you may wish to add some further topics to those listed here

# 18 May I introduce ... ?

| Genre | Small talk |
| --- | --- |
| Topic | White lies |
| Speaking 1 | Telling lies |
| Reading | Lying |
| Vocabulary | Collocations and longer chunks of language |
| Grammar | Cleft sentences and other ways of emphasising |
| Listening | Answering the examiner's questions |
| Speaking 2 | The truth game |
| **Workbook contents** | |
| Reading | Putting paragraphs in gaps |
| Vocabulary | Chunks |
| Grammar | Cleft sentences |

## SB pages 112–115

> **Lesson planning**
>
> **SV** Any of the Vocabulary section could be set for homework
>
> **LV** See the extension activity in the Listening section

## Speaking 1

1 Identify the jobs represented in the pictures with the class as a whole. Students should then discuss questions a–e with a partner.

## Reading

1 Focus students' attention on reading for gist as they read the text for the first time.

> **Answers**
> a He is at a party.
> b He is telling a lot of lies, pretending that he hears people, pretending that he knows people and so on.
> c Perhaps because he wants to make the other person feel good or because he wants to make himself look good.

2 Students should read the list and then read the text again, ticking points as they read.

> **Answer**
> He mentions lying about b, c and f. With g, he pretends to like a joke that he didn't hear rather than pretending to like a joke that he didn't find amusing.

3–6 Deal with these questions with the class as a whole.

> **Answers**
> 3 a The writer can't hear what 'Mr ... er ... er' is saying to him.
> 3 b The writer is misled by the homophones, *reign* and *rain*.
> 4 no
> 5 He comes to the conclusion that it is sometimes a good idea not to be too honest. The reason is that being pointlessly honest can lead to long, tedious conversations which are of no interest to anyone and may be embarrassing for both participants.
> 6 a 3   b 2   c 1

7 Use this question to personalise students' reactions to the reading text.

## Vocabulary

1 Students do this individually and then compare what they underlined with a partner. They then each choose one collocation to present to the class, explaining why they chose the one they did.

2 Students do this individually, seeing who can complete the collocations first.

> **Answers**
> a 8   b 3   c 6   d 11   e 1   f 7   g 12   h 4
> i 9   j 10   k 5   l 2

3 This exercise allows students to put some of the collocations in Vocabulary 2 into context.

> **Answers**
> a catch your name   b hopelessly mixed up
> c on second thoughts   d home town
> e a year's free supply   f are twisting my arm
> g with one or two obvious exceptions
> h no conceivable purpose   i field of research

# Cleft sentences and other ways of emphasising

The grammar here is covered on pages 201–202 of the Grammar folder.

1 Students do these sentences with a partner. Discuss their suggestions with the class as a whole.

> **Suggested answers**
> a The girl (who) / The only person Paolo loves is Maria.
> b What happened was that Katherine had an accident.
> c What Rolf won / The amount that Rolf won was a million dollars.

2 This exercise makes students aware of other ways of emphasising.

> **Tapescript and answers**
> 1 I *do* believe what you're saying. (Emphasis given to auxiliary verb *do*.)
> 2 He's *such* a nice man and has been *so* kind to us. (Use of *so* and *such*.)
> 3 I'm boiling! (Use of exaggerated lexis.)
> 4 He's *intensely* jealous of his sister. (Use of intensifying adverb.)
> 5 That joke is as old as the hills! (Use of simile.)
> 6 Little did he imagine what was going to happen next. (Use of inversion after a restricting adverbial.)
> 7 Never was so much owed by so many to so few! (Use of inversion after a negative adverbial.)
> 8 What on earth is that man doing? (Use of *on earth*, only used after a question word.)
> 9 I *really* like this exercise very much indeed! (Use of intensifying adverbials such as *really*, etc.)

3 Note that this kind of emphasis is often used when correcting a statement that someone else has just made. Practise saying the sentences with the class as a whole with a very strong stress on the auxiliary verb.

> **Answers**
> a Jake *does* admire her work.
> b I *do* love you.
> c Mary *did* do her very best.
> d I *did* use to be able to dive quite well.
> e They *have* agreed to help us.

4 Students work with a partner and prepare two-line dialogues. They then read them out to the class, making the stressed auxiliary verb more emphatic.

5 Ask students to write in an appropriate response using a stressed auxiliary verb.

> **Answers**
> a No, I *am* right.
> b I *did* give you the right information.
> c I *do* help you with the housework.
> d He *didn't* cheat.
> e I *shall/will* be able to!
> f I *haven't* forgotten it!
> g Yes, she *is* going this year.

# Listening

1 Explain that students will listen to some questions similar to the ones they might be asked in the CAE Speaking test (Paper 5).

2 Play Part One of the recording and ask students to take down the examiner's questions as dictation.

## Tapescript

1 What have you enjoyed most about studying English?
2 What interesting things have you done recently?
3 How would you feel about living abroad permanently?
4 What kind of parties do you enjoy?
5 What are your plans for the future?
6 Have you always lived in the same place?
7 What would you say has been the most memorable event in your life so far?
8 How would you describe your best friend?

Now play Part Two. Students should listen and complete the table. When checking the answers, ask students what makes the better answer (it's either fuller or it answers the question that was asked).

> **Answers**
> Better answers are given by:
> 1 woman  2 man  3 woman  4 man
> 5 man    6 woman 7 man   8 woman

3 Play the recording again and ask students to note the main points made by the speaker who gives the better answer. These points are underlined in the tapescript below.

## Tapescript

**Examiner:** What have you enjoyed most about studying English?
**Man:** Well, actually I found it quite hard. I think first of all the pronunciation of many words is very very different in English, something to do with the spelling maybe. There are very many words, so it's difficult to learn them all and the main thing I think is the verbs, I'm used to putting at the end of a sentence, not at the beginning or the middle so that's difficult.

**Woman:** I've really enjoyed now that I can speak English so much better going to see films and understanding exactly what is going on. I also like being able to find my way around, understanding street signs and of course listening to English pop songs and knowing what they are singing about. And I also really enjoy English people. They are very friendly and of great interest to me.

**Examiner:** What interesting things have you done recently?

**Man:** Well, funnily enough last Saturday I went to a football match in England which I've never been to before and that was a great experience, very very exciting and it's good to be amongst so many people. I enjoyed that very very much.

**Woman:** I have been shopping in a supermarket. I have taken a bus around town, I have visited some friends and also read a book.

**Examiner:** How would you feel about living abroad permanently?

**Woman:** Oh, that's something I would really like to do. I think you get a very interesting sense of yourself when you live abroad and you can meet very interesting people.

**Man:** I have a friend who, a school friend, who went to live in France for a few months and he said that for the first two months it was very good, very exciting but after that he said that he started to miss his friends and his family, and he wanted to get home and it wasn't so good after that.

**Examiner:** What kind of parties do you enjoy?

**Woman:** Well, I don't really enjoy going to parties at all.

**Man:** For me it depends what kind of mood I'm in. Often I like going to parties where you can dance a lot and there's loud music playing and other times I like going to parties where you can talk to people and get to know them, get to meet them and I think most of all I like going to parties that last a long time, you know? They go on all over the weekend maybe, or – not just one evening.

**Examiner:** What are your plans for the future?

**Man:** Well my course here lasts another three and a half months and as soon as that finishes, I'm going to stay with a family and get a job I hope, earn a little bit of money and travel around England because I haven't seen much of England, and then after another four months I am going back home to see my family and go back to my studies there.

**Woman:** Well, I don't know really. I haven't made any definite plans at the moment.

**Examiner:** Have you always lived in the same place?

**Man:** Oh, no, no, I've lived in a lot of different places.

**Woman:** Yes, I've always lived in just one place and for me I really enjoy this. It's a great sense of community life and I've known people in my village who have known me all my life and I've known them for as long as I can remember. Whenever I go out, I meet someone that I know. For example, all my friends from school still live in the same village and I, it's something I really really like.

**Examiner:** What would you say has been the most memorable event in your life so far?

**Man:** Er, I think probably when I was eighteen I was given my birthday present which was a weekend course in how to, how to jump with a parachute. And a few weeks later I went up in a plane and I actually jumped out of the plane with the parachute, and that was something I will remember for ever, for sure.

**Woman:** I think my earliest ever memory was when I first started going to nursery. I remember the first day and I had to say goodbye to my mother and I was very upset but as soon as I went inside, there were so many things to look at and play with. It was, you know, something I can remember very clearly.

**Examiner:** How would you describe your best friend?

**Woman:** My best friend is Silke and she has a brilliant sense of humour. She is also a very good gymnast. She is eighteen years old and she has short brown hair and I have known her since we were very young and she is very intelligent as well.

**Man:** Gerhard is my best friend. I've known him a long time from school, from early school and he's, he's good, you know.

4  Draw students' attention to the Exam spot. Then ask students to look back at the questions they took as dictation in Listening 2. They should ask each other these questions.

5  Refer students back to the reading text as they discuss this question.

6  Play the recording when students have read through questions 1 and 2.

## Tapescript

**First man:** Oh, Jason, can I introduce Sophie? This is Sophie, she works in our Cologne office. Sophie, this is Jason.

**Sophie:** Hi, Jason.

**First man:** Jason's the manager of our – sorry. He's the manager of the branch in New York.

**Sophie:** Yeah, pleased to meet you.

**Jason:** And you. You're in Cologne, right?

**Sophie:** Yeah, that's right, yeah.

**Jason:** Yeah, did we meet before because I was in Cologne a couple of years ago? I don't think we met then, did we?

**Sophie:** No, I don't think so. I can't remember your face but I've only worked for the company for a couple of months you see, so …

**Jason:** Oh, right, OK, so who did you work for before?

**Sophie:** Oh, well I was with Smith & Goldberg in Philadelphia.

**Jason:** Oh, really, in Philly? Excellent! I know it well, I grew up there actually.

**Sophie:** Oh, really?

**First man:** I spent a year at graduate school there. Great place, isn't it, great place?

**Jason:** Yeah, yeah, it's great.

**Sophie:** Amazing coincidence. Absolutely yeah, oh I loved my time there. I'd have been really happy to stay actually but …

**First man:** Did you have to come back?

**Sophie:** Yeah, well the thing is my husband's German so …

**Jason:** Oh, right.

**Sophie:** Yeah, we wanted to come home and then we'd be closer to the family because when our little boy was born, we thought it would be nice for him, you know.

**First man:** How many children have you got?

**Sophie:** Well, now we've got a little boy, Adam, and we've got a girl as well called Maisie. Little girl, yeah, she's just two.

**First man:** Have you got children, Jason? I can't remember.

**Jason:** No, no, I don't have any kids right now but you know – never too late! So you know, of course I have to get a wife first but – you know, that could be arranged I guess!

> **Answers**
> 1 b  2 b

Now play the recording again and ask students to take notes as they listen.

> **Answers**
> Second man: name is Jason, manager of branch in New York, was in Cologne a couple of years ago, grew up in Philadelphia, unmarried, no children

> Woman: name is Sophie, works in Cologne office, has only worked for company for a couple of months, worked previously for Smith and Goldberg in Philadelphia, loved Philadelphia, husband is German, wanted to be closer to home when first child, son called Adam, was born. Also has little girl called Maisie.

> **Extension activity**
>
> Divide students into groups of three. They should role play the scene they have just listened to. They do not need to use the exact words from the recording but should act out a similar situation. They should then continue the conversation in any way that seems appropriate. Groups then compare the different ways in which they completed the situation.

## Speaking 2

1 Point out to the students that they may either tell the truth or invent a story (but if they invent something they should make it sound convincing). Ask them to work with a partner.

2 Students now work alone to think of two more questions for their partner.

3 As they listen to each other's answers, students note down whether they think their partner is telling the truth or not.

4 After they have asked each other all the questions, students should check whether they guessed correctly or not.

# Exam folder 8

## SB pages 116–117

## Paper 1 Parts 1, 3 and 4 Multiple choice and multiple matching

Go carefully through both Advice boxes in this folder and point out that they are based on examiners' reports and on what candidates lose marks for in the CAE exam.

1 Refer students to the Advice box and ask them to bear in mind the points raised as they answer the questions.

> **Answers**
> 1 B  2 B

2 Remind students to follow the points raised in the Advice box as they answer these questions.

> **Answers**
> a 1  b 3  c 2  d 3,5  e 4  f 1  g 5  h 3  i 2,5  j 2

> **Extension activity**
>
> Each student thinks of two more questions. Their questions may relate to any of the films mentioned.
> They then give their questions to other students who have to answer the questions as quickly as possible.

# 19 Feeding the mind

| Genre | Talks |
|---|---|
| Topic | Food, pictures and science |

| | |
|---|---|
| Speaking 1 | Food, pictures and science |
| Reading | Eating out, freezing food, a famous painting |
| Vocabulary | Word formation |
| Grammar | Emphasis |
| Listening | A good talk |
| Speaking 2 | A practice interview |

**Workbook contents**

| | |
|---|---|
| Reading | Part 3 multiple choice |
| Vocabulary | Word formation |
| Grammar | Emphasising |
| Speaking | Giving a talk |

## SB pages 118–121

**Lesson planning**

SV  Reading 5 and Grammar 3 could be set for homework

LV  See extension activities in the Reading and Vocabulary sections

## Speaking 1

1  Students work with a partner to discuss questions a–c.

## Reading

1  Remind students that being able to talk about pictures is an important skill for the CAE Speaking test (Paper 5).

2  Students skim the three texts and answer the questions as quickly as they can.

**Answers**
a 1   b 3   c 2

3  This time, allow students as long as they need to read the texts and answer the questions.

**Answers**
a 1   b 3   c 2

4  Students work with a partner to write a sentence summarising each text. They should then compare their answers with another pair and decide on what they think would be the best sentence.

**Suggested answers**
1  There is a strong correlation between people's social background and the extent to which they go to restaurants or entertain people other than family for dinner.
2  Although the idea of freezing food to preserve it had occurred to Francis Bacon in the seventeenth century, the process was only developed commercially in the twentieth century when Clarence Birdseye was inspired by native practices of freezing food in northern Canada.
3  Gainsborough's picture, *The Painter's Daughters Chasing a Butterfly*, is not only a portrait but also says a great deal about the passing of time.

5  Discuss these questions with the class as a whole.

**Answers**
**Text 1**
a  Younger, single, highly educated people who earn more money.
b  Again, younger, single, highly educated people who earn more money.
c  People of all social groups.

**Text 2**
d  They were both interested in the idea of preserving food by freezing it.
e  Bacon died and was not able to carry his experiment through.
f  Because the process of freezing prevents food from going off and it can be done so quickly that ice crystals do not form and thus spoil the cellular structure of the foodstuff.

**Text 3**
g  Margaret is younger than her sister and looks less thoughtful and more instinctive.
h  That life is short perhaps, and childhood quickly passes.
i  This will depend on personal opinion but there are both happy elements (carefree scene, father's pride in his daughters) and sad elements (the fragility of life, the rapid passing of happy moments) in the painting.

FEEDING THE MIND

**6** Discuss this question briefly with the students. If at least one student expresses a preference for each of the different texts, ask them briefly to explain why they liked that text best.

> **Extension activity**
>
> Ask students to identify the sources of the three texts. You may give them these alternatives to choose from.
> - a magazine supplement from a serious newspaper (3)
> - a sociological research report (1)
> - a lay person's history of scientific breakthroughs (2)

## Vocabulary

**1** The aim of the exercise is to focus attention on what part of speech is needed for each gap.

> **Answers**
> 1 noun   2 adverb   3 adjective (comparative)
> 4 noun   5 noun   6 adjective

**2** Students should do the exercise without looking back at the text. They should then check their own answers from the text.

> **Answers**
> 1 Painter   2 faintly   3 deeper   4 childhood
> 5 precision   6 attentive

**3** Identify the parts of speech required with the class as a whole. Students then go back and complete the exercise with a partner, filling the gaps with an appropriate word formed from the word in brackets at the end of each sentence.

> **Answers**
> a adverb: scientifically   b noun: breadth
> c adjective: inconclusive   d adjective: leisurely
> e verb: clarify   f adjective: argumentative
> g noun: helping   h adjective: unhygienic
> i adjective: invigorating   j verb: defrost

> **Extension activity**
>
> For further practice, ask students to fill the gaps with an appropriate word formed from the word in brackets at the end of each sentence.
> a Phrasal verbs are used quite ............................. in spoken English. (extend)
> b There isn't a lot of ............................. at that holiday resort. (entertain)
> c Unfortunately, buses here run quite ............................. . (frequent)
> d The weather there in winter is quite ............................. . (chill)
> e He hasn't studied English for a long time so he's planning to do a ............................. course before going to work in Australia. (fresh)
> f Your description is very ............................. . You must rewrite it. (precise)

> **Answers**
> a adverb: extensively   b noun: entertainment
> c adverb: infrequently   d adjective: chilly
> e adjective: refresher   f adjective: imprecise

## Emphasising

The grammar here is covered on page 202 of the Grammar folder. Discuss the example sentences with students. Elicit the point that the verb is inverted (or put into a question form) when the sentence begins with a negative or restricting adverbial.

**1** Students complete the sentences in any appropriate way.

> **Suggested answers**
> a Little did I imagine that I was soon to have a big surprise!
> b Never in my life have I seen such an enormous butterfly.
> c Not until I got to the airport did I remember that my passport and tickets were still on the kitchen table.
> d No sooner had I got in the bath than the phone rang.
> e So engrossed was I in my book that I did not notice the lamp post in front of me.

**2** This exercise provides further practice of inversion and can be done with the class as a whole.

> **Answers**
> a Never in my whole life have I tasted anything so awful!
> b Under no circumstances are credit cards accepted.
> c Not until much later did we find out about his research.
> d Only when we arrived back at the lab did we realise what had happened.
> e Not only did we lose our passports but also all our money.
> f Hardly had we got there when the fire alarm went off.
> g Little does he know what's in store for him.
> h Only after her death did I learn her secret.

**3** This exercise provides further practice of inversion in a more personalised way.

# Listening

1 Students listen to the recording on which two speakers describe their favourite pictures.

2 As they listen, students should note the main points made by the speakers.

> **Suggested answers**
> **Talk 1**
> a description of the picture
> b how it made him feel at first
> c what he imagines might have happened next to the two men
> d reflections on work conditions and on the broader feelings that the photo conveys
>
> **Talk 2**
> a experience of first finding the picture
> b description of the picture and why she bought it
> c the picture in her room
> d what is special about the style of the picture

## Tapescript

**Speaker 1:** I think my favourite photograph is the one I've got on my kitchen wall at home. It's – you've probably seen it, it's quite a common one. It's, it's a black and white photograph taken from, I'm going to guess something like the 1930s, and it's a few workers in New York high up, building a skyscraper or something, and they're taking a lunch break and they're all sitting on, on a girder or whatever it is and they've got their packed lunches and they're way way high up, and when I first saw this picture I, I couldn't look at it originally because, well I don't have a great head for heights and so it just made me feel a bit funny about the whole thing because you can see, in the background you can see Central Park and the rest of Manhattan. And it's quite eerie but it's also extraordinary that they don't have any kind of safety gear on, and if you look at the left of the picture, there's, there's two guys, one of them is offering the other one a light for his, for his cigarette and every time I look at it, I keep imagining he's going to pull his hand forward as the guy reaches to try and light his cigarette and fall off. Maybe that just says something about me. But it's just, it's just such an evocative picture. It just makes me think of what conditions must have been like, the work conditions and there's something quite romantic about it, I suppose. We live in a sort of sanitised age and that kind of thing wouldn't happen any more but it's just, it's just a wonderful picture and they all look tired but just so contented so high up above the ground. It's quite extraordinary.

**Speaker 2:** The picture that actually comes to mind is something that I bought about a year and a half ago from Spitalfield Market. It was just staring at me. You know when you're sort of looking around and every time you turn round you keep seeing this picture. Didn't really have any money on me, shouldn't have been spending but I just fell in love with it. It's a huge black and white print in charcoal on Japanese very textured paper. It's very sort of feely-touchy, you want to sort of get hold of it, picture of a bull. At the time I was going out with a Taurean so it seemed very right to go and buy it. I've just got it over my fireplace and it just seems to watch me wherever I am in the room. It's got a beautiful thick black frame as well. It's really an armful of a picture, it's huge but I absolutely love it. I just really like the, the naive quality of the picture. It's very sort of childlike the way it's been drawn, as I as a child would obviously draw the face of a bull, and also having met the artist – she'd only done a couple of them – it was nice to meet the person who'd actually drawn the picture. It's just very special to me. Some people love it, some people hate it but I'm really glad I made that impulse buy and got it.

3 Students discuss the talks, which both convey the speakers' feelings in a very articulate way. They are not formal, prepared talks, but the listener gets a clear impression of each picture and why it is special.

4 Students choose one of the topics to talk about and prepare their talk, bearing in mind content, delivery and use of language.

5 Students could then volunteer to give their talk to the rest of the students in the class.

# Speaking 2

1 Divide students into groups of four. Two students will be Examiners and two will be Candidates. Give the Examiners the set of instructions in the Photocopiable activities section on page 186 at the back of the Teacher's Book and make sure that they are clear about what they have to do. Point out that in Part 3 there is a list of topics for Candidates to discuss – this is a bit different from Part 3 of the CAE Speaking test, where they will be prompted by a collection of pictures.

After the students have done one set of interviews, ask the student who just listened in the Examiner role to give feedback on how well he or she thought the Candidates performed.

Then give students as much feedback as possible on how they performed both as Examiners and as Candidates. Make specific suggestions as to how their performance could be improved.

Now regroup so that Candidates become Examiners and vice versa. Ask students to do the same tasks, but point out that they should now be able to do them better.

# Writing folder 8

## SB pages 122–123

## Articles

1 Students discuss the differences between articles and reports and complete the table with a partner.

| Suggested answers | | |
|---|---|---|
| | Article | Report |
| Who it is usually written for | a wide audience who you don't know and who will only read it if it catches their interest | a boss or some other person in authority |
| What its aims usually are | to interest, entertain or inform the readers | to inform |
| Any special characteristics of its layout | will usually have an eye-catching title and subheadings | informative title and subheadings; may use bullet points or numbered points in order to make its structure even clearer |
| Any special characteristics of its register | may be any register – it depends on the readership of the magazine or newspaper | unmarked or formal |
| Any other special characteristics of its style | the writer will try to be interesting, amusing or original, in order to catch and hold the readers' interest and attention | must be absolutely clear and unambiguous in what it says; usually has clear introduction presenting what it is going to say and usually comes to some distinct conclusion at the end |

2 Students discuss both where the sentences come from and which parts of the sentences lead them to make this decision.

**Answers**
a report (topic, phrases like *In conclusion*, fairly formal, very clear language)
b article (topic, rather literary vocabulary like *balmy*, *chugged*)
c article (informal style, e.g. *never in a million years*, use of suspense)
d report (topic, formal vocabulary, e.g. *ascertain*)
e article (topic, rather informal style)

3 Discuss the task fully with students before asking them to write their article. Make the point that students must read the task extremely carefully and highlight all the key points to deal with before beginning their article.

It should be emphasised that the CAE Writing test (Paper 2) is a test of reading as well as of writing. Having discussed the task fully in class, students write their article at home. When marking, penalise candidates if they miss out any of the elements of the task.

# 20 Answers on a postcard

| Genre | Competition entries |
|---|---|
| Topic | Mini sagas |

| Speaking | Talking about competitions |
|---|---|
| Reading | Mini sagas |
| Vocabulary | Idioms |
| Grammar | Hypothesising |
| Listening | Speculating about mini sagas |

**Workbook contents**

| Grammar | Hypothesising |
|---|---|
| Vocabulary | Idioms of the body |
| Use of English | Part 2 open gap fill |
| Writing | A composition describing a picture |

## SB pages 124–127

**Lesson planning**

- **SV** Reading 2 and Vocabulary 3 could be set for homework
- **LV** See extension activities in the Grammar and Listening sections

## Speaking

When introducing this unit, point out to students that the CAE Writing test (Paper 2) often asks students to write a competition entry. Elicit from students that a competition entry tries particularly hard to be interesting and original and to engage the reader.

1  Students discuss questions a–c with a partner. They should then feed back to the class about any competitions they themselves have entered.

2  Students look at the pictures and put them in order of preference. Take feedback on each student's favourite and least favourite prizes.

3  Discuss the competitions and ask students which ones they would be interested in. The pictures show a crossword (you have to identify words from clues), a 'spot the ball' (you have to guess where the missing ball is) and a chess puzzle (you have to decide what is the next move that a chess expert would make).

## Reading

Students are not asked to read or write a mini saga in the CAE exam but these are focused on here as they offer very interesting use of language.

1  Students should read the mini sagas and match the titles with the sagas.

**Answers**
1 D  2 C  3 A  4 B  5 E

2  The words and expressions in this exercise are in the order in which they occur in the mini sagas. Ask students to match them to the meanings given as quickly as possible.

**Answers**
| Text A | a outstanding | b witty | c a masterpiece |
|---|---|---|---|
| Text B | a plot | b bug | |
| Text C | a bully | b chin up | |
| Text D | a enhance | b bust | |
| Text E | a shaping | b distracted | |

3  Students discuss this question with a partner. There are no precise answers to this question but discussing it should help students to focus on the meaning of what each saga is about.

**Possible answers**
B Don't make up your mind until you know the whole story.
C Treat your children well as it will affect how they treat you in your old age.
D Don't put your trust in modern management techniques.
E Pay attention to what is important.

4  Divide the students into small groups to discuss this question. It may be of interest to them to know that the winner of the competition was *Like Mother, Like Son*.

## Vocabulary

As a lead in, ask the students if they can name any more idioms that are based on parts of the body.

1 Students do the exercise with a partner. Ask them also to be prepared to explain what each of the idioms means. They may use an English–English dictionary if necessary.

> **Answers**
> a 4 (finger)  b 8 (toes)  c 3 (heart)  d 2 (hand)
> e 7 (ears)  f 1 (head)  g 6 (feet)  h 5 (eye)

2 Students do this exercise in pairs. They may use an English–English dictionary if necessary.

> **Answers**
> a 5  b 7  c 4  d 1  e 8  f 2  g 3  h 6

3 This exercise helps students to contextualise some of the idioms they have been working on.

> **Answers**
> 1 fell head over heels in love  2 to give her a hand
> 3 has her head in the clouds  4 has set her heart
> 5 keeps her on her toes  6 was all ears
> 7 bite his tongue  8 was down in the mouth
> 9 is breaking my heart  10 racked my brains
> 11 put his mind at rest
> 12 to keep my fingers crossed

# Hypothesising

The grammar here is covered on pages 202–203 of the Grammar folder. Refer students to the Exam spot before drawing their attention to the examples.

> **Extension activity**
>
> Ask students to make up sentences using each of the examples in the lists to talk about the following situations:
> • what they would do if they won a large amount of money
> • what they would do if a friend suggested that they should both give up their jobs and travel round the world together
> • what they would do if they could have three wishes come true.

1 Play the recording. Students listen and tick any of the expressions from box A that they hear.

## Tapescript

**Speaker 1:** It's great to see you again. It's a pity we haven't kept in touch with any of the other classmates, isn't it? Do you think we're the only ones who ended up as teachers?
**Speaker 2:** Maybe. I often wonder whether Bill managed to get a job in politics, don't you?
**Speaker 1:** Well, I do know that he stood as a candidate in the last election but didn't get in.
**Speaker 2:** Perhaps he will this time round. Just imagine having a friend in parliament!
**Speaker 1:** Mm. Suppose he became a minister one day!
**Speaker 2:** Yes, if only he was Minister of Education! We could write to him asking him to put up teachers' salaries!
**Speaker 1:** Or what if he were Prime Minister! That'd be even better. I'd love to see the inside of Number 10. Yeah, perhaps we should try and get back in touch with him just in case!

> **Answers**
> These expressions are all the ones in the first group. All the expressions in box A are used. These are the ones which are most likely to be used when hypothesising in relatively informal situations.

2 Students prepare these sentences, then listen to check their answers.

> **Answers**
> 1a If we were to appoint a new deputy head, that would allow me to spend a lot more time in the classroom.
> 1b Were we to appoint a new deputy head, that would allow me to spend a lot more time in the classroom.
> 2a If I had more time in the classroom, it would give me more of a finger on the pulse of school life.
> 2b Had I more time in the classroom, it would give me more of a finger on the pulse of school life.
> 3a Let us imagine how a deputy would use his or her time.
> 3b Let us consider how a deputy would use his or her time.
> 4a Let us suppose that a deputy would take over a lot of the day-to-day running of the school.
> 4b Let us assume that a deputy would take over a lot of the day-to-day running of the school.

3 Students listen to the speech once and discuss the questions with a partner.

> **Answers**
> The speaker is arguing that class sizes at primary school should be no larger than 20 pupils. The points are:
> • it will become easier to attract good quality teachers
> • pupils will enjoy school more and there will be fewer discipline problems
> • children will learn more quickly, which will benefit society
> • if enough teachers can be found, the policy can be implemented within five years
> • building budgets for schools will have to be increased
> • the fact that the birth rate has fallen will make it easier to implement the policy than it might otherwise have been.

## Tapescript

I am proposing that class sizes at primary school be reduced to a maximum of twenty pupils.

If I may speculate for a moment, I believe that it will be much easier to attract good quality graduates into the teaching profession if they're guaranteed an environment in which they can truly teach each individual child. Speculating further for a moment, children will enjoy school far more and there will be fewer problems of alienation and truancy among young people.

Let us take a hypothetical case: a rather shy child starts school at four and a half. He is in a class with 36 other children. The teacher never seems to notice when he has trouble understanding the lesson and he gets into the habit of not bothering about being able to keep up with the work. He often soon learns that the one way to get attention is to be disruptive.

On the assumption that children learn more, faster and with greater enjoyment if they are in smaller groups with more individual attention, I have every reason to suppose that the implementation of this proposal would have far-reaching benefits for the future of our society.

Provided that we are able to find enough appropriately talented and suitably qualified primary school teachers, I think that there is no reason why the proposal should not be implemented throughout the country within the next five years. Allowing for the fact that more classrooms will be required if class sizes are to be reduced, we shall have to increase schools' building budgets for the next couple of years. Given that the birth rate has fallen over recent years, it should be more straightforward to implement this proposal now than it would have been ten years ago.

4   Students now complete the sentences in any way they like, about a law of their own choosing. Decide which pair got closest to the original story in each case.

## Listening

1   Students should discuss the titles and speculate with a partner about what the sagas might be about.

2   Play the recording and ask students to match the titles and pictures to the three mini sagas.

> **Answers**
> 1  a  (How Success Can Go to One's Head)
> 2  b  (A Moment in Venice)
> 3  c  (August When the Statue in Her Garden Gives Her Most Pleasure)

## Tapescript

**Speaker 1:** An Aboriginal spent years carving and shaping pieces of wood, missiles to bring down the birds that flew above.
Finally, one day his perfected Bu-Mrang turned in the air and winged its way back to him, silent and swift, straight towards the head.
'Yaroo!' he exclaimed. 'I've just invented the …'

**Speaker 2:** They collided in St Mark's Square.
As they apologised in their different languages, he sensed that something had passed between them.
His heart had been touched.
In that moment something magical had occurred.
He watched her vanish among the gathering of people and pigeons.
She had stolen his wallet.

**Speaker 3:** In the summer of the rain and batik skies, he came by moonlight once again and stood outside, barefoot and soaking wet, the rain dripping opals down his ivory cheeks. Only in August would he come and the marble stand, whereupon he stood, would remain empty for one blissful night.

### Extension activity

After listening to the recording, students could work with a partner to choose any one of the stories. They should then try to recreate it in fifty words. After writing their stories, they could listen again and compare their version with the original.

# UNITS 16-20 Revision

## SB pages 128–129

### Topic review

Follow the standard procedure outlined on page 29 of the Teacher's Book.

### Writing

1 Point out that it is necessary to understand the meaning of the text as a whole to do the exercise. There may be occasional variations from the answer given below that are acceptable (e.g. in the use of commas).

### Reading

1 Students should prepare individually, either in class or at home. Where there is any disagreement or doubt as to what the correct answers are, spend some time looking at the clues that can lead students to select the correct paragraphs to fill the gaps.

**Answers**
1 B  2 G  3 A  4 E  5 F  6 D

**Answers**
1 Now, be honest! Most of us, in the course of our working day, tell the odd little fib.
2 We may pretend we've nearly finished something when we've barely started it or say
3 someone is in a meeting when they don't want to take the call. But it's very easy for
4 white lies to turn into something more serious and the assumption that little
5 porkies are a necessary part of a secretary's role is a dangerous one. 'Most
6 secretaries and PAs are used to telling white lies for the boss,' says Ros Taylor,
7 business psychologist and author of *The Key to the Boardroom*. 'If he asks you to
8 do something that is slightly more dishonest, the easy thing is to assume that it's
9 OK, that he wouldn't ask you to do something illegal. Unfortunately, that isn't always
10 the case.' Last month, a PA to a chief executive who was being tried for fraud
11 admitted in court that she had faked documents to smooth the passage of a huge
12 deal. She argued that lying was standard practice in the city and that she was
13 simply trying to protect her boss. But must secretaries sign up to a culture of
14 dishonesty? What happens if you want to tell the truth? 'I've done things that I know
15 are dishonest,' says Kate Matheson, PA to the director of a large property company.
16 'It's easy to feign ignorance. I've shredded things that, deep down, I know should be
17 kept, and been asked to change figures on documents that, if I really thought
18 about it, I'd know shouldn't be changed, but my boss is top dog in a huge
19 organisation and I'm not about to say no to him. I've always assumed that since I'm
20 doing what I'm asked, it couldn't get me into trouble.'
21 This is a common misconception. The fact is that any untruth, even a seemingly
22 harmless white lie, can lead to trouble, and the best policy is to try to avoid
23 dishonesty from the start. 'Because I've done the odd thing that is a bit
24 questionable in the past, it's even more difficult to say no now,' says Kate Matheson.
25 'My boss can say, "Oh well, you did it last time!" What can I say to that?'

### Grammar

1 Students prepare this individually either in class or at home and then compare their answers with a partner.

**Answers**
1 not  2 what  3 one  4 to  5 the  6 (a)round
7 only  8 most  9 was  10 at  11 long  12 a

# TEST 4

## Paper 1 Part 4

Answer questions **1–16** by referring to the texts **A–G** about seven novels by the same writer.

For questions **1–16**, choose your answers from the list of novels **A–G**. Some of the choices may be required more than once.

Note: When more than one answer is required, these may be given **in any order**.

**Which novel or novels**

| | |
|---|---|
| was the writer's first? | 1 .............. |
| share the same main character? | 2 .............. |
| | 3 .............. |
| | 4 .............. |
| deals with one family over a number of generations? | 5 .............. |
| begins with a reunion of old friends? | 6 .............. |
| focuses on a wedding? | 7 .............. |
| takes its title from a song? | 8 .............. |
| has a journalist as its main character? | 9 .............. |
| deal with the heroine's contacts with a friend in trouble abroad? | 10 .............. |
| | 11 .............. |
| deal with the theme of how going to university can liberate women from the drab domestic lives that were their mothers' only option? | 12 .............. |
| | 13 .............. |
| explores the theme of genetics? | 14 .............. |
| were published at least five years after the writer's previous novel? | 15 .............. |
| | 16 .............. |

**A** *The Peppered Moth*
**B** *A Natural Curiosity*
**C** *The Middle Ground*
**D** *The Radiant Way*
**E** *A Summer Birdcage*
**F** *Jerusalem the Golden*
**G** *The Gates of Ivory*

## MARGARET DRABBLE'S NOVELS
### We look at seven novels by the popular author.

**A  THE PEPPERED MOTH**

It is 1912 and Bessie Bawtry is a small child living in Breaseborough, a South Yorkshire mining town. Unusually gifted, she sits quietly and studies hard, waiting for the day when she can sit the Cambridge university entrance exam and escape the kind of life her ancestors have never even thought to question. Her parents are in awe of her – who is this swan-child, is she a freak? (Where *did* she get her notions? Who *did* she think she was?)

Nearly a century later, Bessie's granddaughter, Faro Gaulden, is listening to a lecture on genetic inheritance. She has returned to the depressed little town where Bessie grew up and all around her she sees the families who have stayed there for longer than anyone can remember. Faro's father was a desperate, wild, drinking man, the scion of part-Jewish, part-Polish, part-German refugees. But for all her exotic ancestry and glamour, has Faro really travelled any further than her Breaseborough kin?

Margaret Drabble's new novel, her first in five years, is a wonderfully absorbing, multi-layered portrait of four generations of one family, with origins similar to her own. It explores themes of relationships between the generations, environmental and genetic inheritance and adaptation, DNA, and the individual's place in history.

**B  A NATURAL CURIOSITY**

"What I *do* suffer from is curiosity," remarks the successful psycho-therapist Liz Headland to her friend the gossip columnist Ivan Warner. "I want to know *what really happened*." This insatiable passion to know drives virtually all the characters in Margaret Drabble's brilliant, engrossing, and wise new novel: there is Liz herself, divorced from her TV producer husband, Charles, but united with him in an effort to find out what has happened to their friend Dirk David, now a hostage in a Middle Eastern country. There is Liz's sister Shirley Harper, who with Liz learns the truth about their mother's life and death – but only after a mad escapade reveals parts of herself she never knew existed. There is Alix Bowen, Liz's friend from university days, now living in a small city in the north of England, where she visits regularly with an imprisoned murderer, bringing him books about the ancient Britons and trying to track down his long-vanished mother – Alix, who learns things she didn't want to know.

**C  THE MIDDLE GROUND**

In her first novel since *The Ice Age*, Margaret Drabble gives us a vibrant woman in her forties, a successful journalist named Kate Armstrong, portrayed at a moment of profound pause in her life – her career realised, the emotional tumults of her young womanhood at an end, her children grown.

She has had a spectacular career as a writer for women's magazines; she began writing "new wave" women's pieces before there was a term for them, sharing her pregnancies, exhaustions, indignations, and adventures with a shocked and enthralled public which is now devoted to her. She has wonderful friends – theatre people who are exotic and nutty and kind, academics, scientists – intelligent, fulfilled, devoted men and women. She was married to a would-be painter, compulsively impractical, with a remarkable capacity for ruining his own chances. She had a long affair with the husband of a friend, but it didn't damage any of those involved, and it's over. She has run through the expected phases of life – intensely, passionately, in the most worthy way – but what now?

**D  THE RADIANT WAY**

Returning to fiction after seven years, Margaret Drabble gives us a novel of extraordinary depth and feeling – an acute and passionate chronicle of our time – a beguiling combination of the contemplative and the concrete, the humorous and the dire. Tracing the lives of three Englishwomen, *The Radiant Way* is not only a story of individuals, but a vivid and penetrating portrait of an entire society.

It begins on December 31, 1979. Liz Headland, Alix Bowen, and Esther Breuer – "the oldest of old friends," part of one another's lives since their Cambridge days twenty-five years earlier – have gathered at Liz's home, where a sprawling New Year's Eve party is about to begin …

Three friends with good lives – not extravagant, not without problems, but full and fulfilling, lived with intelligence and ardour, and studded with pleasures. Yet, as the seventies give way to the eighties, what each has assumed for herself, what each has grown accustomed to, gives way to the unexpected and to upheaval. As we follow them through the next five years, we see their world changing around them and we see each woman confronted with difficult, often painful, truths – about this new world and, more profoundly, about herself within it. *The Radiant Way* is Margaret Drabble's most compelling novel – stimulating and sobering by turns – and, by far, her finest.

**E  A SUMMER BIRDCAGE**

Sarah had come home from Paris to be a bridesmaid for her sister Louise. When a child, Sarah had adored her elder sister, but Louise had grown up to be an arrogant, selfish, cold and extravagant woman. She was also breathtakingly beautiful. The man she was to marry, Stephen Halifax, was a successful novelist, very rich and snobbishly unpleasant. From Sarah's first night at home she began to question Louise's motives in this loveless match.

*A Summer Birdcage* is the story of Louise's marriage as seen through Sarah's eyes. It is also the story of a year in Sarah's own life. She is a young woman, intelligent and attractive, just down from Oxford, but completely at a loose end without close friends or a lover. What she discovers about herself is as fascinating as what she discovers about love, infidelity and her sister Louise.

Literary critic Walter Allen, writing in *The New York Times*, said, "This novel seems to me extremely close to the grain of English life at the present moment. We shall do well if we get another first novel as good this year."

**F  JERUSALEM THE GOLDEN**

From a tender age, Clara Maugham had loved the old hymn which began:

*Jerusalem the Golden*
*With milk and honey blest …*

although what she pictured was not the pearly gates of some heavenly city, but a terrestrial paradise where beautiful people lived in beautiful houses and spoke of beautiful things.

It was the winning of a state scholarship that transported her, incredibly, mercifully, from a drab, restrictive life in the north of England and a mother who seemed the epitome of crushed hopes and limited horizons, to London – Clara's golden Jerusalem.

From her vantage point of age twenty-two, it seemed fortunate to Clara that she did not meet the Denhams until her third year at the university. At first, all people not from home seemed equally brilliant and charming, and although the Denhams had more than their share of both brilliance and charm, they had also a very special faculty for enjoying life.

Under their auspices, Clara discovers that there is indeed a colourful and heterogeneous world available for the asking, and she enters it with single-minded purpose, heedless of the chaos she creates around her …

**G  THE GATES OF IVORY**

In *The Gates of Ivory*, one of our most acclaimed, most ferociously perceptive writers now widens her creative canvas to bring forth her most powerful, passionate novel yet. Liz Headland, a London psychiatrist blessed with a successful practice, an amicable divorce, and independent children – all the comforts of the modern world – receives a cryptic package in the mail. Inside are drawings of Cambodian temple ruins, fragments of a novel by her old friend Stephen Cox, and two pieces of a human finger bone.

The package is a message, apparently from Stephen, which Liz can decipher only by retracing its sender's journey from the safety of England to the chaos and corruption of Southeast Asia. As Margaret Drabble interweaves the odysseys of Liz and Stephen, she ushers the reader into a world that would be colourful were its horrors not so authentically portrayed – a world of entrepreneurial beauty queens and media superstars, of ideological butchers and permanent refugees.

# Paper 2 Part 2

Choose **one** of the following writing tasks. Write your answer in 220–260 words in an appropriate style.

1  This is part of a letter you receive from an English friend of yours, who works for a hotel company. You are going to reply to the letter.

> We're considering opening a hotel in the place where you live.
> Do you think it would be a good idea to open a large hotel there? Why or why not? If we do go ahead with the idea, what would be the best part of town to open a hotel and why? Do you think we'd be more likely to get business or holiday customers and what sort of facilities should we offer? I'd also, of course, welcome any other suggestions you might have for us.

Write your **letter**.

2  You see this announcement on the notice board of the college where you study English.

> **Can you help others to study well?**
> **Win a prize by sharing your experiences!**
>
> What have you learnt about how to study languages effectively? Write and tell us how it's done!
>
> What advice would you want to give new students about what they should and should not do in order to study well throughout the year and to get good marks in exams? You should explain how your own experiences have informed the advice you give.
>
> The three best entries will each win computer equipment.

Write your **competition entry**.

3  You see this notice in an English language magazine.

> We are planning to publish a regular series reviewing websites. We would like readers to send us reviews of two websites which you know well. The two websites should contrast in some way. Tell us what the websites deal with and how they contrast with each other, what you like or dislike about the sites and who you think would be particularly interested in these sites and why.

Write your **review**.

4  Your teacher has asked you to write a report on the set text you have prepared. Your report should consider whether the text is likely to be of interest to students of both sexes and of all ages and backgrounds.

Write your **report**.

# Paper 3 Part 1

For questions **1–12**, read the text below and decide which word best fits each space. The exercise begins with an example (**0**).

## GRAND CANYON

The motorcycle stuntman Robbie Knievel has fulfilled his father's (**0**) ...A... by soaring across the Grand Canyon on his 500cc machine to (**1**) ............ a new world record.

Millions watched on television as Knievel, 37, son of the (**2**) ............ daredevil Evel Knievel, roared up a ramp at 90 miles per hour and launched himself into the air, sailing 228 feet over a gorge to break his own (**3**) ............ record by 5 feet.

Fireworks erupted and several hundred (**4**) ............ cheered as he slid to safety on the other (**5**) ............ in a cloud of dust, tumbling off his motorcycle into bales of hay. If he had (**6**) ............ , Knievel would have plunged 2,500 feet to the canyon (**7**) ............ on the Hualapai Indian reservation.

He was going to attempt the same jump last month but it was cancelled at the last (**8**) ............ because of wind and cold. "It's a jump my father always wanted to do but never got the (**9**) ............ ," he said. His father, now recovering from a liver (**10**) ............ , said recently: "Robbie is the true (**11**) ............ to the Knievel name. He can not only jump better than me but he does it with no (**12**) ............ on the handlebars."

| | | | | | | | |
|---|---|---|---|---|---|---|---|
| **0** | **A** dream | **B** wish | **C** hope | **D** plan |
| **1** | **A** put | **B** do | **C** set | **D** bring |
| **2** | **A** ancient | **B** antique | **C** veteran | **D** obsolete |
| **3** | **A** earth | **B** world | **C** land | **D** globe |
| **4** | **A** audience | **B** viewers | **C** congregation | **D** spectators |
| **5** | **A** side | **B** edge | **C** bank | **D** rim |
| **6** | **A** mistaken | **B** failed | **C** disappointed | **D** dropped |
| **7** | **A** ground | **B** bottom | **C** earth | **D** floor |
| **8** | **A** point | **B** minute | **C** thing | **D** time |
| **9** | **A** possibility | **B** moment | **C** chance | **D** luck |
| **10** | **A** transplant | **B** transfer | **C** transmission | **D** transport |
| **11** | **A** son | **B** heir | **C** honour | **D** credit |
| **12** | **A** fingers | **B** arms | **C** hands | **D** touch |

# Paper 3 Part 2

For questions **1–15**, complete the following text by writing each missing word in the space provided. **Use only one word for each space**. The exercise begins with an example (**0**).

## THE COST OF TEAM-BUILDING

When it comes to work, we have always followed (**0**) ...*in*... America's footsteps; we work longer hours than other European countries, and more and (**1**) ............ companies book team-building weekends for their employees. The intention is clear – (**2**) ............ raise morale and help people work more effectively together – but the reasoning less (**3**) ............ . It doesn't seem to matter that if you spend most of the week with your colleagues, you may (**4**) ............ want to spend the weekends with them. Especially when it invariably involves doing something absurd (**5**) ............ driving go-karts. This is one of the activities that often tops managers' lists of ideas.

For just under £50 you'll (**6**) ............ issued with a helmet and a small petrol-driven kart. Usually you will have to compete in a championship in the hope of (**7**) ............ a tiny plastic trophy. Of course, there will be one person who will take it all desperately seriously; it is quite possible he will have practised (**8**) ............ the team-building weekend. He is usually the most unpopular person in the office, too.

An even more adrenalin-charged alternative is to arrange a tandem parachute at £235 (**9**) ............ person. Remind the manager that employees should not be forced to jump. Survival weekends, when the department is deposited in the (**10**) ............ of nowhere (usually Wales) and told to find their own food and shelter, are popular.

The theory is (**11**) ............ adversity bonds people together. The reality is quite obviously the opposite. Another dreaded option is paintballing. This is where the office politics start. If you paintball your account manager, will he take it out on you in the office, assigning (**12**) ............ paperclip-counting tasks? And if you don't shoot him, will he forever think you are a gutless wimp and pass you (**13**) ............ for promotion? It's a minefield.

In common with the male-orientated themes of team-building (**14**) ............ not send everyone to a spa for a morale-boosting weekend? Premiership football season tickets are widely used incentives. A one-day hospitality package at a Premiership club will cost from £165. Perhaps, (**15**) ............ all, the most cost-effective option is to take everyone to the pub for an after-work drink.

# Paper 4 Part 4

You will hear five short extracts in which people are talking about holidays.

## TASK ONE

For questions **1–5**, choose from the list **A–H** what was special about the holiday.

## TASK TWO

For questions **6–10**, choose from the list **A–H** the emotion that the speaker remembers most vividly from the holiday.

**While you listen you must complete both tasks**

| | | |
|---|---|---|
| A | It was the speaker's first independent holiday. | |
| B | The speaker was with a lot of people of his/her own age. | Speaker 1 — 1 |
| C | The speaker had a number of lucky escapes. | Speaker 2 — 2 |
| D | It was not possible for the speaker to spend much time or money on a holiday. | Speaker 3 — 3 |
| E | The speaker had not been to a foreign country before. | Speaker 4 — 4 |
| F | It was the speaker's first holiday with his/her partner. | Speaker 5 — 5 |
| G | It was a much more expensive holiday than the speaker was used to. | |
| H | The speaker was earning money while on holiday. | |

| | | |
|---|---|---|
| A | being attracted to some new people | |
| B | feeling exhilarated by the change of scene | Speaker 1 — 6 |
| C | being disappointed by the accommodation | Speaker 2 — 7 |
| D | having nothing much to do | Speaker 3 — 8 |
| E | feeling slightly irritated by his/her companion | Speaker 4 — 9 |
| F | being amazed by the geography of the place | Speaker 5 — 10 |
| G | enjoying learning about a new culture | |
| H | feeling rather afraid | |

# TEST 4 Key

## Paper 1 Part 4

1 E  2 B  3 D  4 G  5 A  6 D  7 E  8 F  9 C
10 B  11 G  12 A  13 F  14 A  15 A  16 D

## Paper 3 Part 1

1 C  2 C  3 B  4 D  5 A  6 B  7 D  8 B  9 C
10 A  11 B  12 C

## Paper 3 Part 2

1 more  2 to  3 so/clear  4 not  5 like  6 be
7 winning/getting  8 before/for  9 per  10 middle
11 that  12 you  13 over  14 why  15 after

## Paper 4 Part 4

1 E  2 G  3 C  4 D  5 A  6 F  7 D  8 H  9 B  10 A

## Tapescript

**Speaker 1:** I spent my first holiday abroad ever in Iceland. I was only eight at the time but it made a very strong impression on me. There were loads of interesting things there. For example, it was the first time I'd ever seen bananas growing. Yeah, not in the Caribbean but in Iceland! Growing in a greenhouse heated by water from natural hot springs. And I remember the strong rotten egg smells from the boiling mud pools. And the fields of lava. And the barren field that had once hosted the oldest parliament in the world. I couldn't get over the fact that there were no trees taller than eight-year-old me there. Or that it was light enough to read a newspaper outside at midnight. I think it's much more interesting for a kid to go somewhere like that than just to a beach which could be anywhere.

**Speaker 2:** When I was at university I was friendly with a girl who came from a very wealthy family. We were both in the same French tutorial group and we used to study together sometimes. Anyway, this poor girl fell in love with someone, went out with him for a year or so and then he dumped her for someone else. She was so upset that she made herself quite ill and her parents decided to take her on a cruise to cheer her up. And they invited me to go along too. It was a real luxury boat going from Southampton through to the eastern Mediterranean. I'd certainly never had an opportunity like that before – and I don't suppose I ever shall again. Yet, oddly enough, my main memory of that holiday is boredom. My friend was getting better but was still too low to want to talk much or to do anything except sleep. We had amazing trips ashore every second day or so but otherwise we were at sea with nothing much to do except sit on deck and eat enormous meals. The average age of the other passengers was at least sixty and I hadn't even taken much to read.

**Speaker 3:** It was the holiday of a lifetime but I still breathed a sigh of relief when we got home. The first thing that happened was that there was an earthquake just as we'd landed in Peru. We couldn't get off the plane for an hour or so and it was very frightening. Mind you, it could have been a lot worse. If we'd touched down five minutes later, we'd have hit the ground just as it started moving and goodness knows what would have happened then. Or we could have arrived a couple of hours earlier which would have meant we were already sightseeing – and one of the main sights of the city was the central square where a tower fell in the quake injuring quite a few people. Then a few days later a storm blew up while we were on a boat trip on Lake Titicaca. We couldn't get back to shore until well after dark and the boat didn't have any lights. I'm sure we weren't in any real danger but some of the people on the tour were getting into a terrible state.

**Speaker 4:** One of my most memorable holidays ever was in England only two hundred miles from home. We were in the Lake District determined to spend every day hill-walking. We'd both had a long hard year at work and were desperate for fresh air and freedom even though we couldn't afford to go far or to be away for long. The weather was lousy and we stayed in a rather grim youth hostel. The warden was horribly bad-tempered, I remember. We were tired and a bit cross as we set off in the drizzle for our first day's walk. Our aim was to get up Scafell which I'd never climbed before. Once we got into our stride things gradually improved. The drizzle petered out and our moods also lightened as we climbed higher and higher. We then actually got as high as the clouds – visibility was poor but the path was clear and Jim had been up Scafell loads of times so we went on. Then, a hundred metres or so from the top we emerged through the clouds into bright sunshine! We were in a different world on a hilltop island with a sea of cloud below us – there were a few more hilltop islands round us also appearing out of the clouds but otherwise nothing else. Magic! I'll always hold that memory with me!

**Speaker 5:** My first ever holiday away from my parents was when a friend and I went on a dig in King's Lynn in Norfolk. We were helping to excavate a sixteenth century warehouse which would have been on the seafront but was now ten miles or so inland. We were working in very smelly mud and it was a very hot summer – I remember how people used to get as far away as possible from us as we walked back to our landlady's in the evenings. Our most exciting find was a perfectly preserved leather boot. The other main thing I remember about that holiday was the fact that there were a couple of very beautiful girls staying at the same landlady's. They were in a play that was on in town while we were there and we didn't see anything like as much of them as we'd have liked to. But we talked about them constantly though I don't suppose they had even noticed our existence.

# 21 Travel broadens the mind

| Genre | Travel writing |
|---|---|
| Topic | Trips and travel |

| Speaking | Holidays and travel |
|---|---|
| Listening | Travel experiences |
| Reading | Extracts from travel writing |
| Vocabulary | Word endings |
| Grammar | Range of grammatical structures |

**Workbook contents**

| Grammar | Range of grammatical structures |
|---|---|
| Vocabulary | Formal and informal vocabulary, completing sentences with words from a box |
| Reading | Matching statements to texts |

## SB pages 130–133

**Lesson planning**

SV   Vocabulary 2 could be set for homework
LV   See extension activities in the Listening, Reading and Grammar sections

## Speaking

Introduce the topic of the unit by referring to the photos. Elicit the types of holiday shown: a package holiday, touring in a mobile home and backpacking.

1   Students should discuss questions a–f, which allow opportunities for personalisation of the topic.

## Listening

1   This pre-listening task provides context for the listening. Words which could be associated with the pictures include:
Picture a: ice cream, hot, sightseeing, monuments
Picture b: current, river, banks, deep, wet
Picture c: lost, phrase book, language, locals, pronunciation

2   This task will help students to understand the gist of the three stories. After checking the task, you may like to ask students to summarise what happened in each story.

**Answers**
a 1a  2e  3g  4b  5c  6d  7f
b 1a  2g  3c  4f  5e  6d  7b
c 1a  2d  3g  4f  5c  6b  7e

3   Refer students to the tapescript which is an extract from Simone's story. Ask them to listen to the recording and complete the gaps.

**Answers**
1 you know  2 not a good idea  3 But  4 So anyway
5 er  6 Why?  7 why did we have to run?

### Tapescript

**Interviewer:** So you were travelling by train into Italy were you?

**Alan:** Yes, yes, it was me and the rest of the family, and we were supposed to be getting eventually to Calabria, way down in the south. And it was a very nice train journey really, through France and then across the Alps. I think it was early morning we arrived in Turin. And it was just supposed to be a short stop and then the train would continue on further south. I mean, I was in one of these wagon-lit sleeping cars. So the train stopped and there was lots of activity, and people got off, and I went back to sleep again, and I thought, well, I'll wake up again a bit later and have my breakfast. And then I woke up again and realised nothing had happened. We were still, sort of stuck at this platform in Turin main station. And I was actually, I was in one compartment, a male, a male only compartment, and my wife and children were in the other compartment. And I realised there was nobody else in my compartment, everybody had gone, I was all on my own. So I walked down the corridor and then found the rest of my family, also totally bewildered. But luckily, this was a wagon-lit thing so there was an attendant at the end, who spoke good English. So the last people left in the carriage, more or less now, we were, there was a few other, other bewildered international travellers, so we asked the wagon-lit attendant and he said, 'Oh, there's a strike. Er, there's a strike of station masters. Nobody else, just station masters have gone on strike.' So all the trains, with one or two odd exceptions, were stuck in the place they'd stopped, that's where we were going to stay until the station masters …

**Interviewer:** So had everyone else got off?

**Alan:** So all the Italians had got off, the local people had got off because there's no point in going any further, and us long-distance travellers then had to decide what to do. There were rumoured to be one or two local stopping trains running and so a lot of people just jumped on those going goodness knows where, somewhere south. And we thought, well, we've a wagon-lit carriage to ourselves, it's bound to start running again some time, and you know, we've got the services of our personal attendant, and it's Turin. So we thought we'll just stay here and see what happens. I mean, in fact, for those few of us who stayed on the train, it was quite nice because they gave us free vouchers to go out to lunch. And eventually they said, 'Oh this train will run again in the evening.' So we had a day in Turin. So we walked around, had an ice cream. It was a Sunday and we went down around the river and had a lovely free lunch. Came back in the evening to discover the strike had now finished and this huge long train finally rolled out of Turin station with about twenty passengers altogether.

**Simone:** So, well, er, basically, we went to Australia for our honeymoon, and we spent three months travelling around Australia, and went all the way round on the bus. On one particular day we were up in the north of Queensland, in this particular place where the rainforest meets the ocean, stuff like that. Anyway, we had about two hours until our coach left to go back south again. And my husband said, 'Oh er, let's go for a walk.' So OK, fine. So we decided to follow the road and then down this path. Anyway, it was lovely, and we lay on this beach, and the beach was fantastic. There was nobody there. The ocean was, you know, fantastic, blue colour and we were lying there thinking, oh, you know, this is the life. And then we looked at our watches and realised actually we were going to miss our bus. So we thought, OK, this is what we're going to do. We're going to take a short cut. Instead of going back to the road and back round to the other side of this hill, we'd just walk over the hill. Simple. So we walked over this hill and then we were sort of confronted with this problem that we had er, this what was, in effect, a river that cut off our side of the beach from the other, which is where our hotel was. So we thought, well, we don't want to walk through the ocean 'cos at that time of the year you've got these er, box jellyfish which are really dangerous so you can't walk in the water. Well, we thought, if we walk in the river, then we'll be safe, you see. So we start walking through this river and you know, I'm thinking, it's only going to go up to my knees so it'll be OK. We get to the middle and it's up to our waist. And you know, I'm thinking this was not a good idea, you know. But we'll walk nice and slowly, we'll get to the other side and we'll just have to sit in wet, wet clothes for about twelve hours while we're travelling south on the bus. So anyway, what happened was, er, we got about half way through and suddenly my husband goes, 'Quick! Run!' And I said, 'Why?' And he said, 'Just run, just run.' So we start running and the water is literally in waves over our head and you know, we get to the other side, and I'm standing there with water dripping off my hair and everything is drenched at this point, and I'm going, er, 'And why did we have to run?' And he goes, 'Well, I just had a really bad feeling.' And I start, you know, you idiot, er, anyway, we just start walking, and I'm going, 'I'm never going to listen to you again, and look at me, and I'm going to have to sit on a bus now for twelve hours and I'm going to be really uncomfortable, and blah, blah'. And we get down there, probably about a hundred yards, and there's this big sign, which you can only see the back of from where we've come. And as we walk round this sign, there's this big billboard, and on the billboard it's got written, 'Crocodile Infested River. Do NOT cross!' So Bill just kind of looked at me, and I just looked at him, and I went, 'OK'. And we didn't say anything else, we just walked to the bus.

**Mick:** Well, this is about something very embarrassing that happened to me about ten years ago. And ten years ago I'd been living in Greece for three years and instead of coming directly back to England from Greece, I thought, well, I'll, I'll come back and take a year and go slowly through all the countries of Europe and er, do it that way. So the first place I was going to visit after Greece was going to be Yugoslavia, and I didn't speak a word of Serbo-Croat, so I thought well, I need a phrase book of some sort. And the only one I could find was in a little shop in the village where I was living in Greece and that was, there was this Greek into Serbo-Croat and well, it was really cheap, and I never thought at the time that that would be a problem. And er, all the way through Greece I kept practising and practising all these phrases. When I finally got into what was then Yugoslavia, er, every time I said something, people would start laughing at me or looking at me really strange and I thought, well, it's the pronunciation, obviously. So after a few weeks of sort of trying different phrases in different ways and different pronunciation, finally I met someone who spoke English there, and they pointed out that I was saying absolutely ridiculous things. And when we looked at the phrase book, the, one page was in Greek and the next, the facing page was, in Serbo-Croat. But when the book had been put together, they got the wrong pages. So I was going round saying, 'Good morning', but what I was actually saying was, 'Can I see the menu, please?' And things like that. So it was no surprise that people were looking at me as if I was completely mad.

4   Ask students to identify the missing words they filled in. Give them an example of a linking device, e.g. *and then*, a filler, e.g. *well* and a word showing feeling, e.g. *unbelievably*.

> **Answers**
> 1 filler   2 feeling   3 linking device   4 linking device
> 5 filler   6 direct speech   7 direct speech

5 People use fillers to gain time to think and to modify what they are going to say. Encourage students to compare the fillers they use when they speak in English to the fillers they use in their own language. The table in the Extension activity provides more examples of fillers from the listening.

> **Extension activity**
>
> Make a table like the one below and complete it with some examples of linking devices, fillers, words which show feeling and direct speech. Then play the recording and ask students to complete the table.
>
> | | Alan | Simone | Mick |
> |---|---|---|---|
> | Linking devices | and, so, also, and then, but, because | so, and, and then, instead of, anyway, because (cos) | and, instead of, so, when ... But |
> | Fillers | er, yes, I mean, well, sort of, more or less now, you know | so, well, er, basically, OK, you know, sort of, what was in effect, you see | well, er |
> | Words that show feeling or attitude | luckily, eventually, bewildered | fine, simple | embarrassing obviously, finally, as if I was completely mad |
> | Direct speech | Oh, there's a strike. Oh, this train will run again in the evening. | Let's go for a walk. Quick! run! Why? Just run. And why did we have to run? I just had a really bad feeling. You idiot. I'm never going to ... blah, blah. OK. | Can I see the menu, please? |

6 Encourage students to use a variety of nouns and adjectives here.

7 Ask students to think back to the story they liked the best and to try to think about what made it a good story. How can students make their own stories more interesting or dramatic?

> **Suggested answers**
> Use of voice: pauses, change of voice/accent, pace
> Exaggeration: facts, size, reactions
> Choice of vocabulary: to make the story funny, exciting, horrific, vivid and so on
> Grammatical forms: direct speech, rhetorical questions

8 Students tell their own stories. Encourage them to try to use some of the features worked on in this section.

## Reading

1 Introduce the topic of the extracts by referring students to the map and showing the route of the journey. Ask students to read the two extracts and to answer the questions.

> **Answers**
> 1 C  2 B  3 A

> **Extension activity**
>
> Students think back to the listening extracts and the two reading extracts.
> Elicit the difference between descriptive/narrative writing and descriptive/narrative speaking. You could write the two headings as below on the board and write up the suggestions the students make.
>
> | Descriptive/narrative writing | Descriptive/narrative speaking |
> |---|---|
> | Vocabulary: a wider range; less repetition<br>More attention paid to style/stylistic devices, e.g. imagery, similes, inversion<br>Grammar: more controlled; a greater range of structures<br>More complex use of subordinate clauses | More informal or dramatic vocabulary<br>Grammar less controlled; some restarting of sentences/ redirection of sentences<br>Use of incomplete sentences |

## Vocabulary

1 Ask students to match the words in italics to their definitions. They should do the exercise without a dictionary, if possible.

> **Answers**
> 1 c  2 f  3 a  4 e  5 d  6 g  7 b

2 Ask students to read the text for gist, deciding as they go along which type of word fills each gap.

> **Answers**
> 1 adjective  2 noun  3 adjective  4 verb  5 adverb
> 6 noun  7 adjective  8 noun

3 Refer students to the Vocabulary spot, then ask them to decide which of the words in the box are adjectives, adverbs, nouns and verbs.

> **Answers**
> aesthetic: adjective   fairy tale: noun   freedom: noun
> gorgeous: adjective   gravitate: verb   ocean: noun
> riot: noun/verb   rowing: adjective/present participle
> visually: adverb.

4   Ask students to fill the gaps with the correct word.

> **Answers**
> 1 gorgeous  2 freedom  3 rowing  4 gravitate
> 5 visually  6 riot  7 aesthetic  8 fairy tale

## Range of grammatical structures

1   The grammar here is covered on page 203 of the Grammar folder. Go through the Exam spot, then refer students back to the text in Vocabulary 2. Ask them to work with a partner and underline the different tenses and grammatical structures.

> **Answers**
> was brought up, didn't really have, was like, we had, used to go, used to sit, I find, gravitate, I've realised, unless I can see …, I don't feel, I've been to, I think, we went, hanging, had, I'd never been, we splurged out, it was, I love staying, when I travel.

2   Ask students to read the whole text first. They should then follow the procedure they used for the text in Vocabulary 2, i.e. decide first which type of word goes in each gap, then fill in the correct word in an appropriate form from the words in brackets.

> **Answers**
> 1 told / had told  2 was going to happen / would happen
> 3 was cycling / had been cycling
> 4 arranged / had arranged  5 lay  6 needed  7 set
> 8 saw  9 was sitting  10 looking  11 turned
> 12 smiled  13 rendered  14 thinking  15 came

3   Ask students to write a paragraph either on their own or in pairs, incorporating a range of structures and a range of descriptive vocabulary. The sentences given are intended as a starting point.

4   Students exchange their paragraphs and highlight any interesting vocabulary and structures.

5   Encourage students to improve on the paragraphs either by adding more descriptive vocabulary or making the structures more varied.

> **Extension activity**
>
> Students could write a story based on their paragraphs for homework.

# Exam folder 9

## SB pages 134–135

## Paper 2 Parts 1 and 2

1   Question 1 checks that students know the content and form of the CAE Writing test (Paper 2).

> **Answers**
> a two
> b one
> c two
> d 1 hour 30 minutes
> e 400–480
> f yes
> g newspaper/magazine articles, contributions to longer pieces, formal and informal letters, reports, reviews, proposals, competition entries, information sheets, essays
> h Part 1 assessment focus: content, effective organisation of input, appropriacy to the intended audience and accuracy
> i Part 2 assessment focus: content, range, style/register with attention to how successfully the candidate has produced the text type required

Go through the Advice box for this paper.

2   Depending on how much support your students need, use this writing task as exam practice.

3   This writing task could be set for homework or done in class as a timed exam-type task.

# 22 Under the weather

| Genre | Interpreting facts and figures |
|---|---|
| Topic | Climate change |

| | |
|---|---|
| Speaking 1 | Discussing the climate |
| Reading | Global climate change |
| Vocabulary | Collocations |
| Grammar | Linking devices |
| Listening | Aspects of climate change |
| Speaking 2 | Life now and in the future |

**Workbook contents**

| | |
|---|---|
| Reading | General comprehension questions, sentence completion |
| Grammar | Linking devices |
| Writing | A paragraph |
| Use of English | Part 4 multiple meanings |

## SB pages 136–139

**Lesson planning**

- **SV** Speaking 2 could be omitted
- **LV** See extension activities in the Speaking 1, Vocabulary and Grammar sections

## Speaking 1

1 As a lead in, elicit from students the meaning of the unit title, *Under the weather* (feeling ill). Then introduce the topic of the weather by asking students which aspects of weather the photos illustrate. Allow students time to discuss questions a–d, then get some feedback from the group as a whole.

> **Extension activity**
>
> Ask students to work in small groups and brainstorm vocabulary for severe weather conditions / natural phenomena. Give an example to get them started, e.g. *earthquake*.
> When they have finished, elicit the vocabulary from the students and write it up on the board.
>
> **Suggested answers**
> aftershock   avalanche   drought   earthquake
> flood   frost   gale   hail(stones)   heatwave
> hurricane   mudslide   ozone layer   storm
> thunder and lightning   tidal wave   tornado/twister

## Reading

1 Elicit students' personal experience of severe weather conditions if this is not distressing.

2 This helps students develop language needed to respond to charts/graphs/diagrams, etc.

> **Answer**
> The vertical Y-axis shows by how many degrees the temperature varied from the norm (what was usual or expected), and the horizontal X-axis represents time (1850–2000).
> This graph shows that global temperatures have been increasing since 1850.

3 The aim of these questions is to raise students' awareness of whether what they read is fact or opinion, or something between the two – an opinion based on fact and an educated guess. Ask students to read the article and answer the questions.

> **Answers**
> a A mixture – there are facts about what scientists have discovered and predictions about the future which are educated guesses.
> b Three: the IPCC, Dr Wainwright and Mark Gibson.
> c **IPCC**
>   debate about how high the rise in temperature will be
>   discovery that Earth is less able to absorb carbon dioxide
>   predictions about what a 4°C increase would mean
>   **Dr Wainwright**
>   feedbacks in global carbon cycle and what that means
>   humans to blame for increase in temperature
>   **Mark Gibson**
>   4°C rise not inevitable
>   ways to mitigate predicted rise in temperature

4 This question deals with recognising how sure people are when they present facts and opinions. Ask students to work on the activity in pairs.

> **Answers**
>
> | IPCC | is more likely | QS |
> |---|---|---|
> | | have discovered | S |
> | | it would wipe out | QS |
> | | would be displaced | QS |
> | | is likely | QS |
> | **Dr Wainwright** | could mean | NSS |
> | | there is little room for doubt | QS |
> | **Mark Gibson** | is not inevitable | S |
> | | If … we could cut | QS |

## Vocabulary

> **Extension activity**
>
> Put these phrases on the board. They are all taken from the magazine article in the Reading section.
> their <u>starkest</u> warning yet
> <u>dire</u> predictions
> it would <u>wipe out</u> hundreds of species
> the 2007 report <u>painted a gloomier picture</u>
> there is <u>little room for doubt</u>
> Ask students to look at the phrases in context in the article and deduce the meaning of the underlined words. Using an English-English dictionary, students could give some examples of the words in phrases or sentences. For example, *stark* can mean 'severe' as in *a stark warning*, or 'desolate' as in *a stark landscape*, or 'absolutely' as in *stark naked*.

1 This exercise practises collocations connected to the topic of weather. Ask students to match a word from the list with another which collocates.

> **Answers**
> a 7  b 8  c 6  d 1  e 2  f 3  g 5  h 9  i 4

2 Students now practise some of the collocations from Vocabulary 1 by putting them into context within the text provided.

> **Answers**
> 1 force nine gale  2 torrential rain  3 ice cap
> 4 high tide(s)  5 sea defences  6 below freezing

## Linking devices

The grammar here is covered on pages 203–204 of the Grammar folder.

> **Extension activity**
>
> Get students to find out about weather in major cities they know and make a similar chart to the one provided (*A snapshot of the world's weather on 16th April*). Alternatively, you could use the Internet to find information about the cities in the chart for the date when you are working on this unit.

Go through the information in the four bullet points which summarises a strategy for interpreting statistics, and then refer students to the Exam spot. Explain that the examples provide phrases which students can adapt and use when talking about statistics.

Here are some further examples of general statements which give examples of different linking devices:

- Britain has a temperate climate. By way of contrast, Hong Kong has a tropical climate.
- In comparison with Mexico, Sweden experiences colder temperatures.
- Many people believe that the whole of the African continent is hot and dry. On the contrary, there is a huge variety of climatic conditions throughout the continent.
- Although some areas of Australia are desert, many others produce lush tropical jungle.
- While Siberia experiences some of the coldest temperatures imaginable, other parts of Russia enjoy a subtropical climate.
- The west of Britain has quite heavy rainfall whereas the east receives comparatively little rain.

1 Students should read the whole text first, then complete the gaps with an appropriate linking device from the box.

> **Answers**
> 1 On the other hand  2 However  3 whereas
> 4 contrary to  5 Indeed  6 because

2 These words will be useful to students when interpreting information in charts, graphs or statistics.

> **Answers**
> increase  rise  fluctuation  decrease
> decline  reduction  fall  drop

3 If students find this exercise very difficult, give them some help by providing the first, fifth, tenth and last word for each sentence.

> **Answers**
> a In conclusion, we can say that the world's temperature has risen significantly over the last couple of decades.
> b On the whole it may be said that / It may be said that, on the whole, we are experiencing more extreme weather conditions.
> c Therefore it can be concluded / It can therefore be concluded / It can be concluded, therefore, that scientists are following all climate changes with increased interest.
> d Given this, it may be deduced that unless countries reduce carbon emissions, the climate is under threat.

**UNDER THE WEATHER**

## Listening

1 Before playing the recording, check that students understand the vocabulary listed in the table.

> **Answers**
> Tim: floods, global warming, greenhouse gas emissions, sea level, storms
> Wendy: El Niño, floods, droughts, global warming, storms

2 Ask students to listen again and make more notes about the speakers' views.

3 Then ask students to work with a partner and compare and contrast the speakers' views, using linking devices as appropriate.

## Tapescript

**Tim:** Some people say, good, it's great if the world's warming up. We'll have better holidays. But if they stopped to think for a second, they'd realise it's serious. I mean, if it gets warmer, it stands to reason that more water will evaporate from the oceans and surely that means more storms somewhere else. There's evidence that there are more storms, hurricanes and so on and that they're more intense. Now that more accurate records are kept we can see that global warming is a fact.

Another aspect of global warming is how this will affect the sea level; it'll definitely rise. I read something recently which suggested that the sea might rise by as much as half a metre over this century, you know, because as the ice melts, the oceans expand. Imagine what effect that'll have on low-lying areas around the world.

Another thing that gets me is that we know all this and yet we're not reducing our greenhouse gas emissions anything like fast enough to stop the effects of climate change. We might be able to slow it down a bit but I think that's all.

**Wendy:** I know it seems as if there are more cases of extreme weather, like floods and droughts, but I wonder if it's only that we hear about them more than before because of the news on TV and the fact that now it's easier to communicate world events to everyone and very quickly. Surely there's always been severe weather. Storms are a natural phenomenon, after all.

OK, I admit there is evidence of global warming, but is there evidence to show that that's what's causing severe weather? Wouldn't we have had these hurricanes and so on anyway? I mean nobody even really knows how storms form and the path they'll take. You see, what it is, is that the consequences are much greater these days. The world is more densely populated so in terms of the effect on population and financial loss the results are more devastating. But perhaps we should study the data more rather than the hype.

Everybody's heard of El Niño and La Niña and I must admit that that must be showing something, but from what I hear, the jury's still out on whether it's global warming that's exacerbating events.

## Speaking 2

1 Ask students to work with a partner. Give Student A a copy of Diary A and Student B a copy of Diary B (in the Photocopiable activities section on page 187 at the back of the book). Students must not look at each other's diaries. Ask students to work together to fill in the missing information in their diaries, using linking devices as appropriate. They should make sure they follow the instructions given in the four bullet points very carefully after they have exchanged the missing information.

2 Ask students to discuss these questions as a class to round up the unit.

# Writing folder 9

## SB page 140–141

## Descriptive writing

1 The aim here is to show that many types of writing requested in the CAE Writing test (Paper 2) include an element of description.

> **Answers**
> A There will be description of schools and their facilities now and in 50 years' time.
> B There will be description of the instruments and performers and the audiences' reactions.
> C There will probably be less description in this task and more advice and recommendations.
> D There will be some description of the offices now and possibly in the future.

2 This task draws students' attention to the importance of planning a piece of writing. Accept any logical order suggested by students.

> **Suggested answers**
> a 7  b 4  c 5  d 10  e 8  f 9  g 3  h 1  i 2  j 6

3 Steps a–f of the writing guide help students to identify the key parts of the question and to organise their ideas.

> **Answers**
> a two music events, review, music website, compare and contrast, the instruments and singers at each event, the ability of the performers, the audiences' reactions, which event you enjoyed more and why
> c people interested in music
> d lively and entertaining
> e instruments: guitar (bass, rhythm, electric, classical), drums, keyboard, synthesiser, violin, cello, double bass, French horn, trumpet, clarinet, flute, fiddle, mouth organ, etc.
> performers: jazz, rave, pop, classical, etc.
> audiences: age (young people, early twenties, middle-aged, older people), size (packed-out hall, half-full club), reactions (a standing ovation, a cool response, slow to warm up, appreciative), etc.
> f Introduction: the occasions when you went to two events
> Second paragraph: the two different bands, their instruments and singers
> Third paragraph: the ability of each band
> Fourth paragraph: the audiences' reactions
> Conclusion: which event you preferred and why

Step g reminds students to use a range of structures in their writing.

> **Suggested answers**
> g past simple ✔              conditional forms ?
> past continuous ✔            passive forms ✔
> past perfect ?               gerunds ✔
> past perfect continuous ✘    infinitives ✔
> present perfect ?            relative clauses ✔
> present perfect continuous ✘
> present simple ✔
> present continuous ?

Students write their first draft, bearing in mind all the points raised in 2.

For step i, explain how you want students to edit each other's first drafts. Go through the correction codes and give an example of each one if necessary. The final version could be set for homework if time is short.

# 23 I'm afraid I really must insist

| Genre | Formal letters |
|---|---|
| Topic | How to complain |

| Speaking 1 | Personality quiz |
| Reading | How to complain |
| Grammar | Phrasal verbs |
| Listening | How to ask for a pay rise |
| Writing | A letter of complaint |
| Speaking 2 | What makes a good communicator |

**Workbook contents**

| Reading | Open gap fill |
| Grammar | Phrasal verbs |
| Vocabulary | Collocations, formal phrases |

## SB pages 142–145

**Lesson planning**

- **SV** Reading 3, Grammar 3 and Writing 2 could be set for homework
- **LV** See extension activity in Speaking 2

## Speaking 1

Introduce the unit by asking what someone might be going to say if they start with the phrase *I'm afraid I really must insist*. Point out that the phrase *I'm afraid* is often used when we are in fact going to complain; it is not always an apology.

1 Explain that the situations in the quiz are ones in which people might feel they want to complain. Ask students to work with a partner and discuss what they would do.

When students have had enough time to talk about the situations, invite them to suggest alternative answers.

Read out the following key and ask students whether or not they agree with the comments.

**Key**
If you have mainly As, people might see you as a doormat; unless you are more assertive when complaining, people might wipe their feet on you.
If you have mainly Bs, it might help if you learn to relax before you complain.
If you have mainly Cs, you have a sensible approach to complaining and should get what you want.

2 Ask students to discuss questions a–c to personalise the topic further.

## Reading

1 This pre-reading question raises students' awareness of the culture of complaining and also how best to use language in difficult circumstances.

2 Ask students not to look at the article while making their list of pieces of advice.

3 Students should now read the article (this could be set for homework if time is short) and match the headings to the paragraphs. Then ask if the advice they came up with in Reading 2 was in fact mentioned in the article.

**Answers**
1 D   2 H   3 F   4 A   5 G   6 C

Check that students have understood the vocabulary in the article, especially idioms such as *spouting hot air* (saying a lot of things in a very angry way) in paragraph 4.

4 Encourage students to give their own views about the advice given in the article. Which three pieces of advice seem the most important?

## Phrasal verbs

The grammar here is covered on page 204 of the Grammar folder.

1 Go through the examples from the article.

2 Ask students to correct the sentences if necessary. You could point out that four of the sentences are correct.

> **Answers**
> a correct
> b I looked through the guarantee but I couldn't find out how long it was valid for.
> c correct
> d correct
> e We don't hold out much hope, but we are still trying to get compensation.
> f Trying to get a satisfactory answer to my queries took up the whole morning.
> g correct
> h I didn't really want to spend so much on a TV, but Frank talked me into buying it.

3 This could be set for homework if time is short. It allows students to use some more phrasal verbs in context.

> **Answers**
> 1 plucked up  2 get on with  3 make out
> 4 stick up for  5 put across  6 sink in
> 7 took to  8 has turned out / turns out

## Listening

1 Ask students to discuss the pre-listening questions a–c with a partner. These should get students thinking about the issue of asking a boss for a pay rise. Allow some time for class feedback.

2 Give students time to read through the questions before playing the recording. Refer them to the Exam spot at this point.

> **Answers**
> 1 C  2 B  3 A  4 A  5 B  6 C

## Tapescript

One of the most important situations in our professional life is when we feel we have to ask for a pay rise. It can be awkward but if you aren't assertive and say what's on your mind, it may lead to you feeling undervalued and having a negative attitude to your work and workplace.

A positive attitude, forward planning and perfect timing are the keys to getting a pay rise. You may be asking for a number of reasons, ranging from a bigger workload or the increased cost of living to the fact that you've found out that a colleague is getting more than you. But these arguments will be secondary to your worth to the company.

Start by taking an objective look at your career. Are you good at your job? Are you punctual and reliable? Do people know who you are, and for the right reasons? Are you worth more than you're getting paid? If so, how much?

Are there any problems that you need to address? If so, make the changes subtly, over a period of time. Bosses are not stupid, and sudden bouts of punctuality just prior to a pay negotiation will seem like the worst type of creeping.

When planning your negotiation, don't base it on your gripes. Even if you think your future in the company doesn't look too rosy, bear in mind the 'what's in it for me?' factor. You may want extra money for all those things that are on your want list, for a holiday or a car, but your boss will be more convinced by an argument based on your quality of work and dedication.

To strengthen your viewpoint, plan for potential objections. If your boss is going to resist, what points is he or she likely to bring up? You could raise some first, along with arguments in your defence. For example, the sort of line you could take is, 'I know most pay rises are linked to set grades in this company, but I believe that my job has changed sufficiently to make this an exceptional case.'

Bartering can be embarrassing, but you will need to feel and sound confident. Remember that negotiations are a normal part of business life. Never pluck a sum out of the air. Know exactly what you will ask for and what you will settle for.

The timing of your communication can be crucial. Keep an eye on the finances and politics of the company to avoid any periods of lay offs or profit dips. If your boss can be moody, get an appointment for his or her most mellow time of the day. Never approach the subject casually. An on the hoof approach will make your boss twitchy.

There's always the chance that you won't get what you ask for. This is often the point at which reasonable demands and negotiations can turn into conflict. Never issue ultimatums, and don't say you'll resign if you don't mean it. Boost your confidence and your argument by having a backup plan (that is, what you'll do if you don't get the pay rise you want). Plan for the future by staying positive, asking when you could next apply and what can be done in the meantime to help your case.

## Writing

1 Refer students back to Unit 5, which also dealt with formal letters. Go through the Exam spot and ask students to bear this in mind when they come to write their letter. Then ask students to read the writing task and discuss questions a and b. Their answers will vary here.

2 If time is short, the letter could be set for homework.

## Speaking 2

1 Go through the bullet points with students and then ask them to tick the features of what they think makes a good communicator. When they have finished, students should compare their suggestions with those of another student. Invite students to suggest more points to add to the list, then refer them to both of the Exam spots.

2 Use this question both as a round up and to personalise the topic for students.

> **Extension activity**
>
> Photocopy the role cards (in the Photocopiable activities section on page 188 at the back of the book). Divide students into pairs. Give one student a Customer role card (e.g. A) and give the other student the corresponding Company role card (i.e. A). Students should use the information on the cards to role play the situation. Monitor students as they work, giving positive feedback and mentioning any points which could be improved.

# Exam folder 10

## SB pages 146–147

## Paper 4 Part 2

1 Questions a–h check that students know what to expect in the CAE Listening test (Paper 4).

> **Answers**
> a four
> b twice
> c sentence completion, multiple choice, multiple matching
> d on the answer sheet
> e one
> f Spelling is expected to be correct.
> g 40 minutes
> h 20%

2 Students should discuss the pre-listening questions with a partner. The answers will be given in the listening text.

3 This is an example of a sentence completion task. In the CAE Listening test there are eight questions in Part 2. Play the recording once.

4 Students go through the Advice box and check their answers with a partner. Stress the importance of checking that the completed sentence makes sense and that the grammar is correct. Remind students also to check their spellings.

5 Students listen again to check their answers.

> **Answers**
> 1 rebellion   2 work pants/trousers
> 3 (an) organic (product)   4 roots/origins
> 5 Asia   6 presidents   7 the knees ripped

## Tapescript

When youth culture emerged in the early 1950s, jeans were a marvellous symbol, along with the explosion of music, films and the whole advent of this thing of youth culture, jeans were adopted as the dress of rebellion. They were frowned upon by your parents if you wore them when you went out. That was considered inappropriate because they were seen as work pants. However, this censorial attitude of parents only resulted in jeans being adopted by youth gradually throughout the world.

And they were saleable across international boundaries because they have fantastic qualities, just as a product in themselves, I mean, they are what I would call an organic product, the more you wear them the better they get; although they're very egalitarian, they just fit you.

And on top of all that you lay upon this, this idea of youthfulness, you put that together with these functional qualities and a symbol of the opening up of America.

Remember, you know, culture in the 50s was all coming from the United States, rock and roll started in America, that's where its roots were, that's where the roots of jeans are.

Some people wonder if jeans have had their day now that that terribly exciting stage is long over. Well, there are those who still wear the classic jeans today but perhaps much more importantly the mass of provincial youth also wear jeans but very different jeans, especially in Europe. They tend to wear imports from Asia, cheaper ones, and they use them not as a symbol of non-conformity but of peer-group conformity. So young men will wear their straight-legged black jeans out to the disco and if you're not wearing that, you're not one of them. So there's diversification of the use of jeans. You've got the clubber, who goes for the brand names but not the classics, and black rather than blue because young men differentiate between everyday wear, that's blue jeans. And then when they go out, they're actually dressing up in these black jeans, smart black jeans, shoes and a shirt.

Some people have suggested that young people are going off jeans because the establishment are wearing them, we've seen presidents wearing them and there is a degree of currency in that but it's how you wear them. You can wear them in a very different way to somebody else. Certain brands have that ability, like the Mini car; it can be driven by pop stars or little old grannies. Certain brands get beyond something that's only worn by one group after a period of time and jeans are certainly in there. So now it's the brand you wear, how you wear them, do you wear them loose or tight, washed out, with a crease down them? The codes become smaller and smaller. And you can still rebel in jeans. If you were to go to a very smart function and you wore jeans with the knees ripped, that would be a symbol of rebellion. And all this means jeans are here to stay, at least for the foreseeable future.

# 24 News and views

| Genre | Investigative journalism |
|---|---|
| Topic | Stories in the news |

| Speaking | Planning a TV schedule |
| Listening | News broadcasts |
| Vocabulary | Homophones |
| Reading | The sweet tooth gene |
| Grammar | Linking devices |

**Workbook contents**

| Use of English | Part 2 open gap fill |
| Grammar | Linking devices |
| Vocabulary | Word webs |
| Use of English | Part 3 word formation |

## SB pages 148–151

**Lesson planning**
- **SV** Vocabulary 2 could be set for homework
- **LV** See the extension activity in the Listening section

## Speaking

1 Ask students to work with a partner to discuss questions a–c.

2 Ask students to get into small groups. They could start their discussion by talking about the Saturday programmes they usually watch.

Remind students to think about the length of programmes and the likely audience.

3 When students have completed their proposed schedule, ask them to form new groups to compare and contrast each choice of schedule. How far do students agree?

## Listening

1 Ask students to listen to the introduction to the news and note down any stories they are particularly interested in. Play only Part One of the recording at this point.

2 Now play Part Two and ask students to complete the table.

**Answers**

| | Where | Who | Topic |
|---|---|---|---|
| Item 1 | Australia | International aid group Oxfam / The Aborigines | The rights of Aborigines |
| Item 2 | Sydney, Australia | A lone athlete / The President | The end of the Paralympics |

**Extension activity**

Ask students to retell the two items in their own words.

3 Elicit what the phrase *labour laws* might refer to and how these might be broken. Answers could include the minimum age at which children can start work, the legal maximum number of hours worked, safety and hygiene regulations and the minimum wage.

4 Ask students to listen and answer questions a–f. Play Part Three of the recording now.

**Answers**
a No
b employing children and not paying workers the minimum wage
c Workers are working illegally and therefore don't want to complain or they are so desperate for the work that they think it's better to have any job rather than no job at all.
d She is sewing clothes in a factory.
e Her boss said he would report her to the authorities and say she had lied about her age.
f No

5 There are two sides to this argument; one is that if malpractice is exposed, it cannot continue, and the other is that malpractice will be driven underground.

## Tapescript

1 *The News Today*. News twenty-four hours a day. It's fifteen hours GMT.
You're listening to *The News Today*. Hello and welcome. Next, a bulletin of world news, followed in five minutes by *News from Around the World*. This week Richard James provides a glimpse of life in North Korea, Mark Holder reviews an album of South American love songs, Michael Martin visits Western Nepal, John Duncan meets the Chileans who live under the ozone hole in

**NEWS AND VIEWS**

South America and Marion Southgate brings us a story of mermaids and diamonds from Angola. That's all in our edition of *News from Around the World* in about five minutes. Later, it'll be politics from Westminster here in London: an analysis of current events in British government. That's all to come in the next hour. But first, here's a bulletin of the latest world news.

2   A report by the International Aid Group Oxfam is investigating Australia's role in protecting the basic rights of its native people, the Aborigines. The report identifies what it calls alarming gaps between the rights and access to services of indigenous people and those available to other Australians. It says there could also be cases of structural discrimination in the country's laws and regulations and calls for an investigation into constitutional change.

   The eleventh Paralympic Games in Sydney, Australia, have ended with a spectacular carnival show and party. A lone athlete made his way to the centre of the arena. His arrival was the cue for a massive pyrotechnic display that raced around the stadium. Then followed displays from circus performers and dancers, huge inflatable animals. The President declared the games the best ever.

3   Working under cover, I have discovered that many companies throughout the world are flouting the child labour laws and minimum-wage laws. And you can't pin this down to one particular part of the world or say that it only happens in big cities as opposed to country areas. I have witnessed with my own eyes child labour in cities in so-called developed nations and workers being paid well below the legal requirements in every type of work you can imagine, from agriculture to clothes factories. Unfortunately it's very difficult to get workers to complain and the reasons are numerous, from they're working illegally and therefore don't want to complain or they're so desperate for the work that they think it's better to have any job rather than no job at all. And unscrupulous employers are cashing in on this.

   This overcrowded, noisy factory is in a city in Europe where outside people are eating pepper steaks in posh restaurants, driving fast cars and earning a fortune. In here it's a different picture; it's like something from another age, rows and rows of women sewing clothes in a factory down a back alley just off a fashionable shopping street. This is what you call sweatshop labour; people working unimaginable hours, for half the minimum wage. I talked to a girl here, let's call her Janine, she's 14 and instead of going to school, she comes here to work to earn money so that she can help out with the finances at home. At first she'd intended to do it for just a couple of weeks during the holiday, but when she suggested that she might leave, her boss told her that if she left, he'd report her and tell the authorities that she'd lied to him about her age. And of course, the more school she missed, the harder it was to go back. A vicious circle.

## Vocabulary

Go through the introduction to this section and ask students if they can think of any more examples.

1   Ask students to read the headlines and to think of a homophone for each of the underlined words.

> **Answers**
> a read   b weigh   c guest   d mail
> e whole   f miner   g jeans

2   Ask students to think of a homophone for each word in the list.

> **Answers**
> a one   b meat   c cell   d sew   e stares   f blew
> g sale   h wear   i waist   j threw

## Reading

1   Students should discuss the pre-reading question a–c as a lead in.

2   Check that students understand the verb in the headline *to binge* (to eat in an uncontrolled way). Then ask them to read the article and decide if the statements are true or false.

> **Answers**
> a true   b false   c false   d true   e false
> f true   g false

3   This question allows students to react to this type of article in a personalised way.

4   Students might mention cloning, designer babies, prolonged lifespans, etc.

## Linking devices

The grammar here is covered on pages 204–205 of the Grammar folder.

1 Remind students to read through the article first before filling the gaps with the linking devices from the box.

**Answers**
1 as  2 because  3 Then  4 So  5 Despite  6 even
7 but  8 And what's more  9 To cap it all  10 By then

2 Ask students this question to round up the activity.

# Writing folder 10

## SB pages 152–153

## Formal writing

1 Go through the two introductory sentences to point out the difference between formal and informal language.

*Give us a ring soon* is informal English, probably spoken and used to someone who the speaker knows well.
*We look forward to hearing from you at your earliest convenience* is formal English, almost certainly written and probably written to someone who the speaker does not know well.

2 It is impossible to be absolutely precise about the ordering of these but they are likely to be in the following order (from the most formal to the least formal).

**Suggested answers**
- proposal to a benefactor on how you would spend the money he might give you
- report for your boss
- contribution to a tourist guidebook
- letter of complaint to a newspaper
- leaflet for a local sports club
- competition entry for an international magazine
- review for an English Club newsletter
- article for a student magazine
- letter to a pen friend

3 Ask students to read through the advice. With a partner, they should then modify the pieces of advice if necessary to make them more appropriate.

**Answers**
- It is not usually appropriate to use verb contractions in formal writing.
- Try to avoid phrasal verbs in formal writing although sometimes there is no alternative or the alternative would sound too stilted to be appropriate.
- Avoid slang or colloquial expressions in formal writing – if they are included, it will be done for some special effect.
- Layout is more fixed in formal contexts.
- Structure is always important, but because you are more likely to be writing formally to someone whom you do not know and with whom you do not have so much shared knowledge, clarity of structure is particularly important.
- Again this is important in all kinds of writing but may perhaps be particularly so in formal writing (as one means of clarifying structure).

4 Tell students that the sentences are all grammatically correct but could be improved stylistically.

**Suggested answers**
a It was somewhat difficult to collect as much data as we had originally hoped.
b The men tended to express views that were slightly more conservative than those of the women.
c A number of our respondents raised some important concerns.
d Interviewees' responses depended on their age, gender, occupation and educational background.
e I would now like to discuss further several important aspects of the survey.

5   Encourage students to use a wide variety of interesting and appropriate adjectives. Note that any word suggested as a replacement for *nice*, *good* or *beautiful* will add something extra and different to the meaning of the sentence.

> **Suggested answers**
> a  lovely, fascinating   b  stimulating, talented
> c  sumptuous, spectacular   d  varied
> e  glamorous, impressive

6   The three texts provide further practice in using linking devices. Remind students to read through each text as a whole before filling in the gaps.

> **Answers**
> a  1 Firstly   2 Secondly   3 Moreover   4 Finally
> b  1 Although   2 So   3 However   4 Consequently
> c  1 then   2 Firstly   3 when   4 Gradually   5 After that
>     6 especially   7 because   8 Finally

7   Students can prepare this writing task in class or it could be set for homework if time is short. Encourage students to bear in mind all the work they have just done on formal writing.

# 25 Powers of observation

| Genre | Academic texts |
|---|---|
| Topic | Research methods |

| Speaking | Study methods |
|---|---|
| Reading | Academic texts |
| Grammar | Complex sentences and adverbial clauses |
| Listening | Devising a good questionnaire |

**Workbook contents**

| Use of English | Part 1 multiple-choice questions |
|---|---|
| Grammar | Complex sentences |
| Vocabulary | Less formal alternatives |

## SB pages 154–157

**Lesson planning**
SV   Listening 3 and 4 could be omitted
LV   See extension activity in the Listening section

## Speaking

1 Ask students to work with a partner and discuss questions a–d. The pictures are provided to generate ideas and stimulate discussion.

## Reading

1 Ask students to discuss what sorts of questions a horse might be asked and by whom. The answers are all revealed in the text. Ask students to read the first part of the text.

2 Encourage students to be inventive about how Hans might have answered the questions, before going on to the rest of the text.

3 Encourage students to draw on their own experience when answering this question.

**4 and 5** If you would like to give students more guidance for this task, you could give them the underlined phrases in the text opposite and ask them to work only on these. Students may suggest other words or phrases which could be made less formal. Accept any reasonable suggestions.

**Suggested answers**
Formal words or phrases are underlined and the informal paraphrase is given in italics afterwards.

We can learn a great deal *a lot* about behaviour by simply *just* observing the actions of others *what other people do*. However, *But* everyday observations are not always made carefully or systematically. Most people do not attempt *try* to control or eliminate *get rid of* factors that might influence the events they are observing. As a consequence, *So* erroneous conclusions are often drawn *we often come to the wrong conclusions*. Consider, *Think about*, for example, the classic case of Clever Hans. Hans was a horse that was said by his owner, a German mathematics teacher, to have amazing talents. Hans could count, do simple addition and subtraction (even involving fractions), read German, answer simple questions ('What is the lady holding in her hands?'), give the date, and tell the time. Hans answered questions by tapping with his forefoot or by pointing with his nose at different alternatives shown to him. His owner considered *thought* Hans to be *was* truly intelligent and denied using *said he didn't use* any tricks to guide his horse's behaviour. And, in fact, Clever Hans was clever even when the questioner was someone other than *wasn't* his owner.

Newspapers carried accounts *published stories* of Hans's performance, and hundreds of people came to view *see* this amazing horse. In 1904, a scientific commission was established *set up* with the goal of discovering *to discover* the basis for Hans's abilities. The scientists found that Hans was no longer clever if either of two circumstances existed. First, Hans did not know the answers to questions if the questioner also did not know the answers. Second, Hans was not very clever if he could not see his questioner. A slight bending forward by the questioner would start Hans tapping, and any movement upward or backward would cause *make* Hans to stop *stop* tapping. The commission demonstrated *showed/proved* that questioners were unintentionally cueing *prompting* Hans in this way.

This famous account *story* of Clever Hans illustrates the fact *shows* that scientific observation (unlike casual observation) is systematic and controlled. Indeed *In fact*, it has been suggested that control is the essential ingredient of *the most important thing in* science, distinguishing it from non-scientific procedures (Boring, 1954; Marx, 1963). In the case of Clever Hans, investigators exercised control by manipulating *changing*, one at a time, conditions such as whether the questioner knew the answer to the question asked and whether Hans could see the questioner. By exercising control, taking care to investigate the effect of various factors one by one, a scientist seeks to gain *tries to get* a clearer picture of the factors that actually produce a phenomenon.

134  POWERS OF OBSERVATION

6   Explain that the aim of this task is to change language from formal to informal register. Students should read both texts first in order to understand the main points and then summarise the content in informal language by filling in the gaps.

> **Suggested answers**
> 1 from somebody in the English Group   2 have to go to
> 3 be a good chance   4 other   5 is/will be   6 sent
> 7 give out

## Complex sentences and adverbial clauses

The grammar here is covered on page 205 of the Grammar folder.

Go through the introduction to complex sentences and adverbial clauses. Discuss the examples of the different types of adverbial clauses with students. The examples provide adverbial clauses of time, place, manner, reason and condition. Refer students to the Exam spot at this point.

1   Ask students to complete the sentences as appropriate.

> **Suggested answers**
> a he could answer any question he was asked.
> b someone other than his owner asked the questions.
> c he could not see the questioner.
> d carefully observing what happened.
> e many people were suspicious of his owner and his act.
> f Hans could see him.

2   Students might say that people today tend to want things scientifically proved before they will believe them.

## Listening

1   The aim of this pre-listening question is to start students thinking about what makes a good questionnaire. Draw their attention to the amateur questionnaire and ask them to think of ways in which it could be improved.

> **Suggested answers**
> a too informal with a question tag, suggests a positive answer
> b does not give the time period (per day/month, etc.)
> c does not indicate how to answer (tick, delete, etc.)
> d too open
> e too open
> f too open
> g not clear what respondents have to do (they could be asked to rank the conditions in order, for example)
> h surely everyone will say yes

2   Play the recording and ask students to compare their notes. They should ensure that the grammar of the sentences makes sense.

> **Answers**
> 1 what information you need to find out
> 2 they are done under time pressure
> 3 inexperienced researchers are often impatient
> 4 decide on the type of questionnaire to be used
> 5 yourself
> 6 items prepared by other researchers
> 7 write a first draft of the questionnaire
> 8 format
> 9 effective wording of questions
> 10 re-examining and rewriting
> 11 people who know about the topic / experts
> 12 eliminate bias
> 13 pretest
> 14 typical of people who will answer the real questionnaire
> 15 ambiguous
> 16 offensive
> 17 interviewers
> 18 edit the questionnaire

### Tapescript

It's important to realise that the results of any survey are useless if the questionnaire was poorly constructed. Although there's no substitute for experience when it comes to preparing a good questionnaire, there are a few basic principles. I'm going to describe six basic steps in preparing a questionnaire.

The first step in questionnaire construction, deciding what information you need to find out, should actually be the first step in planning the survey as a whole. This decision, of course, determines the type of questions to be included in the questionnaire. It's important to project the likely results of the survey if the proposed questionnaire is used and then decide whether these findings will answer the questions the study is intended to address. Surveys are frequently done under considerable time pressure, and inexperienced researchers are especially prone to impatience. Just remember that a poorly conceived questionnaire takes just as much time and effort to administer and analyse as a well-conceived one. The difference is that a well-constructed questionnaire leads to interpretable results. The best we can say for a poorly designed instrument is that it's a good way to learn how important careful deliberation is in the planning stages.

The next step is to decide on the type of questionnaire to be used. For example, will it be self-administered or will trained interviewers be using it? This decision is determined primarily by the survey method you have selected. For instance, for a telephone survey, trained interviewers will be needed. In designing the questionnaire, also consider using items which have been prepared by other researchers. There is no reason to develop your own instrument if a reliable and valid one already exists. Besides, if you use items from a questionnaire which has already been used, you can compare your results directly with those of earlier studies.

If you decide that no available instrument suits your needs, you'll have to take the third step and write a first draft of your questionnaire. You should consider the format and ordering of questions as well as the effective wording of questions.

The fourth step, re-examining and rewriting, is essential. Questions that appear objective and unambiguous to you may strike others as slanted and ambiguous. It's really helpful to have your questionnaire reviewed by experts, both those who have knowledge of survey research methods and those with expertise in the area of your study. For example, if you're doing a survey of students' attitudes towards the campus food service, it would be advisable to have your questionnaire reviewed by the campus food service director. When you're dealing with a controversial topic, ask representatives of both sides of the issue to screen your questions for possible bias.

By far the most crucial step in the development of a sound questionnaire is step five, the pretest. A pretest involves actually administering the questionnaire to a small sample of respondents under conditions as much as possible like those to be used in the final administration of the survey. Pretest respondents must also be typical of those to be included in the final sample; it makes little sense to pretest a survey of nursing home residents by administering the questionnaire to college students. There is one way, however, in which a pretest does differ from the final administration of the survey. Respondents should be interviewed at length regarding their reactions to individual questions and to the questions as a whole. This provides information about potentially ambiguous or offensive items.

The pretest should also serve as a dress rehearsal for interviewers, who should be closely supervised during this stage to ensure that they understand and adhere to the proper procedures for administering the questionnaire. If major changes have to be made as a result of problems arising during the pretest, a second pretest may be needed to determine whether these changes solved the problems. After pretesting is completed, the final step is to edit the questionnaire and specify the procedures to be followed in its final draft.

> **Extension activity**
>
> In order to practise summary skills, ask students to use their notes from the talk they have just heard as an outline and to summarise the talk. This can be either a Speaking or Writing activity.

3   Go through the instructions for the class survey. Put students into small groups and encourage them to bear in mind all the advice about preparing a questionnaire as they write their own questionnaire.

4   Students carry out the survey and then report back to the class.

# UNITS 21-25 Revision

## SB pages 158–159

## Topic review

Follow the standard procedure outlined on page 29 of the Teacher's Book.

## Grammar

1 This activity consolidates the work students have done on linking devices. Answers will vary according to which linking devices students remember from previous units.

2 Ask students to work with a partner. They should read through the text first, then look at the words in italics and decide which category each linking device belongs to.

> **Answers**
> *Whilst* concession  *also* listing
> *As* cause  *then* result

## Reading

1 Encourage students to guess the chracteristics of the roles listed and to speculate about which type of team member they themselves are.

2 Ask students to read the text to find out about the different roles people play.

3 Ask students to match the statements with the different types of team members.

> **Answers**
> 1 diplomat  2 challenger  3 innovator  4 challenger
> 5 innovator, diplomat  6 judge  7 expert  8 expert
> 9 judge, diplomat

4 Encourage students to give a personalised response to questions a–c.

## Vocabulary

1 Ask students to work with a partner and complete all three sentences in each question with the same word.

> **Answers**
> a drive  b path  c team  d test  e gap  f ease

# TEST 5

## Paper 1 Part 4

You are going to read an article that contains information about underground train systems. For questions **1–15**, choose from the cities (**A–D**). The cities may be chosen more than once.

### Of which city's underground system is the following stated?

| | | | |
|---|---|---|---|
| There is only one price for all tickets. | **1** ............ | **2** ............ | **3** ............ |
| Its construction was a historical landmark in the city's development. | **4** ............ | | |
| The underground is a great contrast to the rest of the city. | **5** ............ | | |
| It may require some effort to get to another line. | **6** ............ | | |
| It may be crowded but a train is sure to come along in a short time. | **7** ............ | | |
| You know where to stand to board the train. | **8** ............ | | |
| Passengers use the underground to avoid the pollution in the city. | **9** ............ | | |
| Sometimes extra employees are needed to help people get into crowded trains. | **10** ............ | | |
| Train drivers' wages used to be reduced if their trains were late. | **11** ............ | | |
| Expansion of the system is slow because the lines can pass through several authorities' areas. | **12** ............ | | |
| The city makes using the underground an aesthetic experience. | **13** ............ | **14** ............ | |
| The proportion of users to miles of track is very high. | **15** ............ | | |

**A** Paris

**B** Moscow

**C** Tokyo

**D** Mexico City

### A Paris

**Passengers carried per day:** 4.4 m
**Cost of ticket:** 80p flat fare
**Length:** 131 miles  **Lines:** 14  **Stations:** 297

In Paris there are pleasures for those who use the Metro – many of them aesthetic. The gracefully curvaceous Art Nouveau dragon-fly entrances are just the most prominent on a Metro system which celebrated its centenary by spending 30 million francs (£2.9 million) on making its stations works of art. On my way home I pass Bonne Nouvelle station in the heart of Paris's cinema district. There, during the cinema festival this summer, special lighting effects dapple the platforms and films are projected onto the advertising hoardings.

More than anything the metro is efficient. 'When I worked on line 4,' says a retired driver, 'we had exactly 30 minutes and 15 seconds to complete the journey. If it took any longer, they docked our pay.' But there are drawbacks. Many Metro stations have too many stairs, and changing lines at big interchanges can be tiresome.

### B Moscow

**Passengers carried per day:** 9m
**Cost of ticket:** 12p
**Length:** 164 miles  **Lines:** 11  **Stations:** 162

The first tunnelling for the Moscow Metropolitan started in 1932. Three years later the trains started running. They haven't stopped since – every 90 seconds or two minutes during rush hour, every five minutes the rest of the time, from 6 am till 1 am. There may be a crush but there is seldom a wait.

The trains take you through a parade of marbled, stuccoed, spacious, spotless stations. For tourists it's a major sightseeing draw: from Russian art deco to neo-classical, the Metro stations are not to be missed. In short the Metro was a central, perhaps *the* central, element in Stalin's monumentalism that changed the face of Moscow forever.

### C Tokyo

**Passengers carried per day:** 7 m
**Cost of ticket:** 90p – £1.68
**Length:** 177 miles  **Lines:** 12  **Stations:** 209

Trains do not just arrive on time in Tokyo, they stop right on the platform mark so that passengers can line up knowing exactly where the doors will open. Train driving is a prestigious job for life for which the applicants must pass a rigorous screening of health checks, interviews and written exams before they can don the usually meticulously turned out uniform, cap and white gloves.

However, overcrowding means it is far from a commuter paradise. At peak morning hours, some stations employ part-time platform staff to cram in passengers. Carriages can be filled to 183% of capacity. The main reason for such cramped conditions is that the Tokyo subway system has only 15 miles of track for every 1 million people, compared to 36 on the London Underground. New lines are under construction, but at a cost of £500,000 per metre of rail, progress has been slow.

### D Mexico City

**Passengers carried per day:** 4.2m
**Cost of ticket:** 11p flat fare
**Length:** 99 miles  **Lines:** 11  **Stations:** 175

Fast, relatively safe, and very cheap, Mexico City's underground is an oasis of order and efficiency under the chaos above. The Mexican capital's underground system is the biggest in the continent and one of the most subsidised networks in the world.

Built by the French in the 1960s, it boasts rubber-tyred carriages and long connecting walkways that recall the Paris Metro. An army of vendors wind their way through the cars selling everything from briefcases to potato peelers.

The first trains leave the terminuses at 5 am and the last after midnight as the masses move from the outskirts of the 20 million-strong megacity. Mexico City's Metro also attracts a sizeable contingent of passengers who are unwilling to spend hours in choking traffic jams. Without the Metro the city would grind to a halt, but expansion is desperately needed to relieve the crowding. There is a master plan to build new lines and extend existing ones, but financial constraints complicated by the fact that the system runs through different jurisdictions mean progress is slow.

# Paper 2 Part 1

You **must** answer this question. Write your answer in 180–220 words in an appropriate style.

You are on the committee that organises social events at an international college where you are studying English. Next year the college will be fifty years old and the committee is organising a series of events to mark the occasion. You hope to raise the profile of the college in the local community during this anniversary year. Look at the memo from the college principal together with the outline programme that has been planned, on which you have made some notes.

---

From: College Principal
To: Social Committee

Please could you write an article for the local newspaper in which you outline what we are planning to do next year. As you know, we have had a disappointing lack of local support for our recent concerts – so try to interest people in what we are doing. **NB** We hope that lots of readers will be able to provide photos for the exhibition and may take part in the 'Olympics' and the writing competition as well as attending the other events.

---

### GOLDEN JUBILEE – DRAFT PROGRAMME

| | |
|---|---|
| January: | Photo exhibition – 'Fifty Years of College Life' |
| March: | Reunion party for past students and members of staff *(mention some of the well-known former students and staff who'll be returning)* |
| May: | Open Day – chance for all to see what happens in the different departments of the college |
| July: | Drama production – open air in college gardens *(production not chosen yet – probably comedy or something to interest children too)* |
| September: | College Olympics – variety of sports |
| December: | Competition – best article reminiscing about college prize (deadline 15th Dec.) *(money prize – winner announced 20th Dec.)* |
| Every month: | Different national evenings: Music and Food from around the world *(some evenings already planned – other suggestions welcome)* |

Now write your **article** for the local newspaper. You should use your own words as far as possible.

# Paper 3 Part 3

For questions **1–8**, read the text below. Use the word given in capitals at the end of some of the lines to form a word that fits in the gap in the same line. There is an example at the beginning (**0**).

## CREATIVE JUICES

Can eating certain foods enhance your creativity? Pasta might

stand you in good stead for (**0**) ....*running*.... a marathon, but which       RUN

foods will encourage your creative juices to flow (**1**) ................... ?       FREE

Our lack of (**2**) ................... about the link between food and creativity       KNOW

(**3**) ................... stems from the fact that there are so many myths       DOUBT

surrounding creativity itself. I mean, are we talking one-off *Eureka!*

moments or a steady drizzle of (**4**) ................... throughout a lifetime?       BRILLIANT

In the (**5**) ................... world surely creativity is a case of stimulating       COMMERCE

and sustaining a less (**6**) ................... but ultimately more pragmatic       GLAMOUR

flow of lateral thinking.

What should we be eating to increase our chances of making

inspired (**7**) ................... ? 'You need brain foods,' confirms       CONNECT

Michael Van Straten, author of a recently published book,

*Good Mood Food*. And they are? 'A herb like sage is not called

sage by accident; it was used by the Ancient Greeks and Romans

to enhance creativity. Sage is (**8**) ................... a perfect brain food.       QUESTION

It has very special effects on the memory and also on the logical

thinking processes,' says Van Straten

# Paper 3 Part 4

For questions **1–5**, think of one word which can be used appropriately in all three sentences. Here is an example (**0**).

**Example:**

0   The scholarship includes an ......*allowance*...... of £100 for books.

   As a married man his tax ......*allowance*...... is higher than that of a single person.

   The teacher made ......*allowance*...... for the fact that the student had been ill when she took the exam.

1   In a personal ........................... for money for the victims of the disaster, the President showed great emotion.

   Does the idea of working abroad ........................... to you?

   The accused intends to ........................... against his ten-year prison sentence.

2   ........................... it to me straight. Did you have something to do with the theft?

   The newcomer on the tennis scene can certainly ........................... as good as he gets, as was proved by the results of his last game.

   I'll take an hour to get to the airport, ........................... or take five minutes.

3   That's an interesting idea but not relevant to the ........................... in hand.

   It's one thing to talk about sailing round the world but it's quite another ........................... to actually do it.

   Whether it's better to learn English with a native speaker or a non-native speaker is a ........................... of opinion.

4   There is a clear ........................... of special responsibilities among the teachers.

   She works in the export ........................... of the company.

   The river forms a ........................... between the old and new parts of the city.

5   With only minutes to go, the Brazilian Formula One driver is in the ........................... .

   Do you know who is playing the ........................... in that new Broadway musical about ghosts?

   We always wait for the conductor of the orchestra to give us the ........................... .

# Paper 4 Part 2

You will hear a diver talking about a dive in a small submarine to a coral reef. For questions **1–8**, complete the sentences.

North-east Atlantic coral is similar in shape to [_____] **1**

Another easily recognisable form of plant life is the [_____] **2**

The submarine has a length of 2.5 metres and a width of [_____] **3**

The submarine was put into the water by a [_____] **4**

It was difficult to know exactly where we would touch down because of the [_____] **5**

Water depth can be estimated naturally by the [_____] **6**

Crustaceans which are visible on the reef are shrimps and [_____] **7**

The only sound in the ocean is that of the [_____] **8**

# TEST 5 Key

## Paper 1 Part 4

1 A  2 B  3 D  4 B  5 D
6 A  7 B  8 C  9 D  10 C
11 A  12 D  13 A  14 B  15 C

## Paper 3 Part 3

1 freely  2 knowledge  3 undoubtedly
4 brilliance  5 commercial  6 glamorous
7 connections  8 unquestionably

## Paper 3 Part 4

1 appeal  2 give  3 matter  4 division  5 lead

## Paper 4 Part 2

1 (a) cauliflower  2 sponge  3 one metre/meter
4 crane  5 tidal currents  6 light levels
7 lobsters  8 propellers (of the sub)

## Tapescript

I was really excited as I was standing on the deck of the ship waiting for the moment when I could begin the descent to see one of the ocean's best kept secrets: a giant coral reef complex. These particular corals in the north-east Atlantic create strange cauliflower-shaped patterns.

Back in the past Ice Age, some eight thousand years ago, the continent was locked under ice and as the icebergs broke free and scraped their way across the Norwegian continental shelf, they left their mark on the sea bed, scattering rocks and ploughing boulders to either side. You can still see this today and the grooves have become home to these corals and also a type of yellow-coloured sponge, just like the ones you can get for your bathroom.

We went down to the ocean bed in a tiny sort of submarine, just 2.5 metres long and one metre wide, and altogether we were squeezed into that space for about six hours. As you can imagine, it's hard to move at all once you're inside.

Our sub was launched over the side of the ship. We checked all our equipment and then a crane finally let us down into the water. Then we were towed some distance from the ship and we made our final communication checks before we made the descent.

We began to descend at roughly one metre a second and at that rate it should have taken about a quarter of an hour to reach the bottom. But with the tidal currents it was difficult to predict exactly where you'd touch down. As we descended it was hard to appreciate the force of the currents as we went past swarms of jellyfish and millions of shrimps which were darting around in all directions.

The other thing that changed dramatically was the light level. We knew, even without looking at the instruments, that we were reaching deeper waters as the light level dropped. As we approached the coral reef we put on the sub's lights. We had a sort of plexiglass viewing dome and believe me, the view was extraordinary. The water was, in fact, crystal clear and on this particular reef I soon began to see, amongst the luminous white coral, hundreds of points of light shine back at me – the reflective eyes of shrimps and lobsters. A wonderful sight. Having seen them in their natural habitat, I could never eat a lobster dinner again.

We began to cross the reef and we disturbed rabbitfish and all sorts of exotic creatures, and it was on the top of the reef that we found the largest and healthiest corals. Some of them were several metres in diameter on this top part of the reef. Some corals can reach a height of one metre. As we floated through this scene from some sort of wonderland, the only noise was that of the gentle hum of the propellers of our sub. Finally, we had to turn back. Our journey was over, much too soon.

# 26 Natural wonders

| Genre | Travel articles |
|---|---|
| Topic | Beauty spots |

| Speaking | Beauty spots |
|---|---|
| Listening | Visiting Australia |
| Reading | Travelling through Tibet |
| Vocabulary | Idioms |
| Grammar | *Like, alike, as, so* and *such* |
| Writing | Paraphrasing |

**Workbook contents**

| Reading | Multiple-choice questions |
|---|---|
| Use of English | Part 2 open gap fill |
| Writing | An informal letter |

## SB pages 160–163

**Lesson planning**

- **SV** Reading 3 and 6 and Vocabulary 2 could be set for homework
- **LV** See the extension activity in the Listening section

## Speaking

1 Ask students to work with a partner to discuss questions a and b.

## Listening

1 Ask students to suggest what the seven natural (not man-made) wonders might be. The key below gives one popularly accepted list, compiled in the USA.

**Answers**
the Grand Canyon   the Northern Lights
the Great Barrier Reef   Mount Everest
the Harbour at Rio de Janeiro   Victoria Falls
Paricutin in Mexico

2 Students look at the photos and listen to the recording. They should explain how the photos relate to what they hear on the recording.

The tapescript is on page 182.

3 Students listen again and mark the statements true or false. With a partner, they should make any false statements into true ones.

**Answers**
a false: it is in north-east Australia
b false: it is the gateway to the Barrier Reef but not actually on it
c false: it is the fifth busiest international airport in Australia
d true
e false: it is 6,000 years old
f false: it takes 45 minutes by boat
g false: it is not all under water
h false: *a once-in-a-lifetime experience* means that it is a very special experience, not that you are only allowed to go there once

4 Students should brainstorm all the things that the destination offers, which are underlined in the tapescript on page 182. They then decide which are the three most attractive things for them.

### Extension activity

Because of the importance of the kind of language in this text for CAE, you might also like to read the tapescript with your students and discuss any other aspects of the language that interests them. Point out that, at 270 words, this article is only slightly longer than the text that they are expected to write in Paper 2. Having studied the text, ask them to write a similar article about a tourist area in their own country.

## Reading

1 The text is about Tibet but do not tell students this at this point if they do not guess from the picture.

2 Students read the text first and then complete the notes.

**Answers**
Travelled by: car (Landcruiser)
Driver's aim: to keep the car off the ground as much as possible
How Tashi felt about the journey: he seemed to enjoy it
Difficult aspects of the journey: very bumpy
Good aspects of the journey: good visibility and not much other traffic
Scenery: mountains and river
What could be seen on the river: coracles (small boats)
Boats made of: yak skins, a wooden frame, yak hair and yak butter

3 Students read the second part of the text and underline the relevant words and phrases as they do so.

> **Suggested answers**
> village lined with waving Tibetan children
> single and double storey buildings with walled-in courtyards
> foothills behind the buildings
> solid buildings with walls made of stone up to waist height and mud bricks above
> window ledges with marigolds on them
> black and white buildings
> flags (blue, white, red, green and yellow) on flat roofs standing out against the rich blue sky with pictures of jewelled dragon-horse on them
> copse of trees (willows or poplars) but landscape otherwise treeless
> each courtyard wall piled high with firewood

4 Ask students to look at the photo and see how many of the things they underlined are shown.

5 Ask students to read the questions first and try to predict the answers. They should then read the text and answer the questions.

> **Answers**
> 1 C   2 D   3 D   4 A

## Vocabulary

1 With a partner, students match the idioms with their explanations. They may use an English–English dictionary if necessary.

> **Answers**
> a 6   b 2   c 4   d 5   e 1   f 9   g 7   h 8   i 10   j 3

2 Ask students to complete the sentences, putting some of the idioms into context.

> **Answers**
> a off the beaten track   b hit the road
> c picture-postcard   d black spot
> e no room to swing a cat

3 Students should discuss not only which expressions they would be likely or unlikely to find in a tourist brochure, but also why this would be the case.

> **Answers**
> a picture-postcard, stone's throw from (the beach usually), home from home. These emphasise the attractive aspects of places.
> b black spot, tourist trap, no room to swing a cat. These emphasise the unattractive aspects of places.

## Like, alike, as, so and such

The grammar here is covered on pages 205–206 of the Grammar folder.

1–4 Students should discuss these questions with a partner. They should then check their answers by reading the sections in the Grammar folder.

5 Ask students to discuss sentences a–e with a partner before you check the answers with the class as a whole.

> **Answers**
> a Oxford and Cambridge are alike in some ways.
> b We saw such amazing scenery in the Himalayas.
> c It was so far to the campsite.
> d Our holiday cottage looked just like the one allocated to our friends.
> e She looks as if she has just returned from a tropical holiday.

## Writing

1 Students should identify which sentence belongs to which text. Refer them to the Exam spot at this point.

> **Answers**
> From the informal chatty letter
> It's a great hotel with loads of character. The bedrooms get a bit chilly at night and the uncarpeted corridors can be noisy but it's worth putting up with a few minor inconveniences as it has so much atmosphere in other ways. The food is fantastic and you can stuff yourself at breakfast so you don't need to eat again till the evening.
> From the brochure
> The hotel has a magnificent location overlooking the broad spread of the gulf and most of the bedrooms enjoy sea views. Each room has its own luxuriously-appointed en suite bathroom and is individually decorated with many original finishing touches. The superb restaurant offers a wide range of delicious dishes to suit all tastes.

2 Personalise this reading activity by asking students which of the two hotels they would prefer to stay in and why.

3 Refer students back to text a. Ask them to write a postcard to a friend, describing the hotel and holiday.

4 Ask students to read the guide book entry, and then write an entry in a similar style about Cashel House.

5 This writing task provides an opportunity for students to write a letter in a formal style. Refer students back to the language for complaining in Unit 23.

# Exam folder 11

## SB pages 164–165

## Paper 4 Parts 3 and 4

1 Ask students to discuss a–c with a partner.

2 Students should read through the questions and try to predict any likely answers.

3 Students then listen to the recording and choose their answers.

4 Students check their answers with a partner, then listen again.

> **Answers**
> 1 D   2 B   3 A   4 D   5 C   6 A

## Tapescript

**Interviewer:** With me in the studio today is Julia Crawley, who runs a management consultancy which deals with women in business. Now Julia, if the majority of companies were run by women, what difference do you think it would make? I mean, what did you bring to the company you started?

**Julia:** Many people had warned me of the difficulties of being a female manager – to begin with, getting people to take you seriously. Male friends of mine, in similar management roles always seemed to be worried about how long a woman would stay with a company and whether family commitments would mean she was less loyal than a male manager. I remember when I started as a manager it was natural for me, and I think it is for most women, to want to work with others, to see what they could contribute, and I told them what I was bringing to the table.

**Interviewer:** Mm. It is important that everyone realises they are important in a company, that every individual is as important as any other, isn't it?

**Julia:** One of the first female management gurus, Jennifer Alderton, put forward as her 'articles of faith' respect for all staff. She introduced me to the concept of power with rather than power over. Usually when power is discussed, it's taken to mean having power over someone else, getting that person to do what you want him to do, either through actual physical means or through persuasion.

**Interviewer:** And what do you see as being some of the drawbacks of the traditional male-run business?

**Julia:** Well, we've had hundreds of years of command control, maybe more, and it kind of works, although days can be lost as disputes are debated and in the meantime, machines are standing idle. And it's a very uncomfortable sort of organisation to work in, isn't it? I think now that people want more from their job; they don't want to be treated as an easily replaceable machine.

**Interviewer:** Mm. What other concepts that you value might we find in a female-run business?

**Julia:** Well, it would seek out differences. Say you'd been doing a particular procedure the same way for years and then someone challenged that. By positively encouraging criticism, you'd open up far more creativity and as a result the company would go forward at a faster pace. It's usually the people who have hands-on experience of systems that can see shortcuts.

**Interviewer:** And at the same time recognising that it's crucial for people to have a balance between their work and home life.

**Julia:** Yes, this is an issue which has been widely discussed in many countries and there have been some high-profile men and women who have given up highly-paid, highly-responsible jobs because of the demand it was making on their time to spend more quality time with friends and family. The fact that these people were in the public eye has moved the debate on no end. I think where we need to go with this now is helping other countries where it is less acceptable for people to say, 'It's 6 o'clock so I'm off now' to realise that good workers are alert workers who've enjoyed their free time and have slept well.

**Interviewer:** Is this where you're going to channel your efforts from now on?

**Julia:** It's tempting, because I can see that with better communication skills the work place can become a far more attractive place to spend time. However, I'm getting involved in a scheme which backs small businesses which are struggling to get off the ground due to lack of cash. There are some great ideas out there with a demand for the product; but for a small company they've already invested all they had in setting up and getting a working prototype. So that's what appeals to me at the moment.

**Interviewer:** Well, good luck with that, Julia, and thank you for talking to us today.

5   Go through the information about Part 4 of the CAE Listening test (Paper 4). Ask students to listen to the recording and match the speakers (1–5) with their relationship to Sarah (A–H).

**Answers**
1 D   2 B   3 C   4 G   5 H

6   Students should listen again and match the speakers with their opinions of Sarah. Remind them that in the exam, they will have to complete both tasks as they listen.

Play the recording again for students to check their answers.

**Answers**
1 B   2 C   3 F   4 G   5 A

## Tapescript

**Speaker 1:** It's funny how we became friends, I mean that doesn't usually happen with clients, but Sarah's so outgoing. We got on like a house on fire. We chatted away while I was trimming, colouring or whatever it was and then she started bringing her daughter in too and we'd put the world to rights as I cut. And then one day she said she was having a barbecue and would I like to come along. Not many who come to the salon would do that. And since then we've become good buddies.

**Speaker 2:** At first I thought she was a bit bossy, but after a while I realised that it's just her way of getting things done with the minimum amount of fuss and I must say she's great to share an office with. We work like demons while we're working and then usually take our breaks together. Last year we started going to the gym together after work on Wednesdays. She approaches exercise in the same way as work.

**Speaker 3:** She's been such a help. I mean more and more we rely on parents getting involved and helping out with social events. Sarah's a great organiser. I know if I hand over something to her, it'll be done in a jiffy, before you've had time to blink. Her daughter's the same. We wanted to have a sports day to help raise money for some new equipment that we need for the music department. I just mentioned it to Sarah and the next thing I knew there was a list of activities and who would supervise them on my desk. I wish she worked with me full time!

**Speaker 4:** Gosh, it seems like forever. She's really changed, though. You'd never believe it but she used to be quite shy. She'd never answer questions unless directly asked. But she was a bit of a swot, always did her homework on time. In year eight she won some prize or other for literature, I think. I knew then that she had been quietly developing into a very clever girl. Even though I moved away when I got married, we've kept in touch.

**Speaker 5:** We met while we were both doing push-ups. I'd been going to the gym for ages but could only really do about ten push-ups. She immediately wanted to better my pathetic effort and I must admit it made me work harder too. I'd say she rises to the challenge. I've seen it as she goes round. If she sees another woman can do such and such a thing, she wants to do more. Mind you, I suppose that's how she got where she is.

# 27 The open window

| Genre | Fiction |
| --- | --- |
| Topic | Personality traits |
| Speaking | Personal appearance and character |
| Reading and Listening | A short story |
| Vocabulary | Chunks |
| Grammar | Emphasising |
| Writing | Holding the reader's attention |

**Workbook contents**

| Reading | Pronoun references, comprehension questions |
| --- | --- |
| Vocabulary | Usings phrases in a sentence of your own |
| Grammar | Emphasising |
| Writing | Describing people |

## SB pages 166–169

**Lesson planning**

SV  Writing 4 could be omitted
LV  See extension activities in the Listening and Grammar sections

## Speaking

1 Encourage students to use their imagination to build up possible biographies of at least two of the people in the pictures.

2 This open question allows students to discuss how far they think character can be judged from appearance.

3 Ask students if they know of any character traits sometimes associated with the physical characteristics in the box.

## Reading and Listening

1 Refer students to the Exam spot, then ask them to read the text. They should then decide which of the pictures best matches the story.

**Answer**
picture c

2 Ask students to discuss these questions with a partner.

**Answers**
a We learn that the girl is about 15 and that she is very self-possessed/confident.
b Because he has some kind of nervous problem and needs a rest.
c Because his sister met these people about four years ago and has given him a letter of introduction to them – she thinks he needs to meet people in the country.
d No, he isn't. He seems to have little desire to meet new people.
e We learn that it has French windows (windows that are also doors) and that these are open to a lawn. It also seems to have a slightly masculine rather than feminine atmosphere to it.

3 Students discuss how they think the story might continue.

4 Students read the questions before listening to the next part of the story. As they listen, they mark the statements true or false.

**Answers**
a false – there were three men
b true
c false – the bodies were never found but it was presumed they had drowned in a bog
d true
e false – it was a white raincoat
f true

THE OPEN WINDOW  149

## Tapescript

"Out through that window, three years ago to a day, her husband and her two young brothers went off for their day's shooting. They never came back. In crossing the moor to their favourite snipe-shooting ground they were all three engulfed in a treacherous piece of bog. It had been that dreadful wet summer, you know, and places that were safe in other years gave way suddenly without warning. Their bodies were never recovered. That was the dreadful part of it." Here the child's voice lost its self-possessed note and became falteringly human. "Poor aunt always thinks that they will come back someday, they and the little brown spaniel that was lost with them, and walk in at that window just as they used to do. That is why the window is kept open every evening till it is quite dusk. Poor dear aunt, she has often told me how they went out, her husband with his white waterproof coat over his arm, and Ronnie, her youngest brother, singing 'Bertie, why do you bound?' as he always did to tease her, because she said it got on her nerves. Do you know, sometimes on still, quiet evenings like this, I almost get a creepy feeling that they will all walk in through that window –"

5   Students read the next part of the story and predict how it might end. Encourage them to use their imagination.

6   After listening to the end of the story, students discuss the extent to which their predictions were correct.

## Tapescript

"Here they are at last!" she cried. "Just in time for tea, and don't they look as if they were muddy up to the eyes!"

Framton shivered slightly and turned towards the niece with a look intended to convey sympathetic comprehension. The child was staring out through the open window with a dazed horror in her eyes. In a chill shock of nameless fear Framton swung round in his seat and looked in the same direction.

In the deepening twilight three figures were walking across the lawn towards the window, they all carried guns under their arms, and one of them was additionally burdened with a white coat hung over his shoulders. A tired brown spaniel kept close at their heels. Noiselessly they neared the house, and then a hoarse young voice chanted out of the dusk: "I said, Bertie, why do you bound?"

Framton grabbed wildly at his stick and hat; the hall door, the gravel drive, and the front gate were dimly noted stages in his headlong retreat. A cyclist coming along the road had to run into the hedge to avoid imminent collision.

"Here we are, my dear," said the bearer of the white mackintosh, coming in through the window, "fairly muddy, but most of it's dry. Who was that who bolted out as we came up?"

"A most extraordinary man, a Mr. Nuttel," said Mrs. Sappleton; "could only talk about his illnesses, and dashed off without a word of goodbye or apology when you arrived. One would think he had seen a ghost."

"I expect it was the spaniel," said the niece calmly; "he told me he had a horror of dogs. He was once hunted into a cemetery somewhere on the banks of the Ganges by a pack of pariah dogs, and had to spend the night in a newly dug grave with the creatures snarling and grinning and foaming just above him. Enough to make anyone lose their nerve."

Romance at short notice was her speciality.

> **Extension activity**
>
> Students who enjoy this story might like to read other short stories by Saki, the writer of this one. If you have easy access to any other stories by him – for example, on the Internet – ask students to read one and then to write a review of it for the classroom wall. Although their review should outline the plot, it should be mainly concerned with giving the reviewer's opinion of the story and should either recommend or not recommend it to other students in the class.

## Vocabulary

1   Students discuss the missing words, trying to remember what words are needed to fill the gaps before checking their answers in the text.

| Answers | |
|---|---|
| a undergoing | g paid |
| b soul | h laboured |
| c far | i heels |
| d place | j word |
| e appearance | k ghost |
| f make | l notice |

2   Students could do the exercise either individually at home or together in class.

| Answers |
|---|
| a laugh, sigh, smile |
| b chatted, droned, harped |
| c avert, escape, prevent |
| d a long time, his salary, most of his income |
| e confidence, head, mind |

# Emphasising

The grammar here is covered on page 206 of the Grammar folder.

1 Ask students to look through the examples and discuss what has happened to them to make them more emphatic.

> **Answers**
> *Romance at impressively short notice was her speciality.* (Use of intensifying adverb.)
> *No one was better at romance at short notice than she was.* (Negative or restricting adverbial put at beginning of sentence followed by inversion.)
> *Romance at short notice was her most particular speciality.* (Fronting.)
> *What she did best was romance at short notice.* (Cleft sentence.)
> *What a talent she had for romance at short notice!* (Exclamation.)
> *Romance at short notice was such a speciality of hers!* (Use of *such/so*.)
> *Never could she be bettered as far as romance at short notice was concerned.* (Inversion after negative adverbial.)

2 Ask students to write each of the sentences a–c in three more emphatic ways of their choice.

> **Suggested answers**
> a How unreliable are the conclusions that we draw about people from their appearance!
>   Very unreliable are the conclusions that we draw about people from their appearance.
>   Few are the conclusions that we can reliably draw about people from their appearance.
> b What surprising behaviour from the girl!
>   Surprising indeed was the girl's behaviour!
>   Never in my life have I been so surprised as by the girl's behaviour.
> c How shocked I was by what she said next!
>   Very shocking were her next words!
>   Rarely have I heard such shocking words.

> **Extension activity**
>
> Ask students to think of a particularly memorable occasion. They should write a paragraph about it in which they use as many emphatic sentences as they can. They should use each of the ways of emphasising worked on in this unit at least once.

# Writing

1 Students should be able to find examples of all of these techniques in the story. Ask them to work individually and then compare answers in small groups.

2 Students work with a partner and follow the instructions. After they have done the activity, they could discuss with the class how effectively they felt they were able to use the techniques worked on in this section.

3 Students could do this task for homework. When marking it, pay particular attention to the extent to which the students have used the techniques highlighted in this unit.

# Writing folder 11

## SB pages 170–171

## Informal writing

Read the introduction to the folder with students and check their comprehension with the following questions:

*When in the CAE Writing test might it be appropriate to write informally?* (When writing a letter or note to a friend, possibly also in an article for an informal type of publication like a student newspaper.)

*If you are not sure whether an informal style would be appropriate or not, what should you do?* (Use a neutral style, as that will very rarely be inappropriate.)

Refer students to the Exam spot at this point.

1 Students should underline all the parts of the reference that are too informal.

> **Answers**
> I've known Ted for donkey's years – in fact, ever since we were kids at school together – and he's a really nice guy, one of the best. I'd give him the job like a shot if I were in your boat (excuse the pun!). Don't be put off by the fact that he can sometimes seem a bit bossy – that's just because he's such a well-organised bloke himself, he can't stand it when other people are slow to get their act together. He's got loads of experience of working with other people and he can be relied on to get things going. Go for it and give him the job – you won't regret it.

2 Students should now rewrite the paragraph, replacing everything they have underlined with a more appropriate equivalent.

> **Suggested answer**
> I have known Ted for a long time – in fact, ever since we were children at school together – and he is a very warm-hearted, responsible person. I would give him the job immediately if I were in your position. You should disregard the fact that he can sometimes seem rather assertive – that is just because he is such a well-organised person himself, he can find it difficult when other people are slow to organise themselves. He has a great deal of experience of working with other people and he can be relied on to be motivated. I would recommend that you take the decision to give him the job – you wil not regret it.

3 Go through any problematic vocabulary before students begin this exercise. Ask them to mark the words which are inappropriately formal or inappropriately informal. They should then write two sets of sentences: one set should be consistently formal and the other consistently informal.

> **Answers**
> The informal words are marked I and the formal ones are marked F.
> a It's daft (I) to alight (F) from a bus while it is moving.
> b Jack lives in a flat adjacent (F) to the local chippie (I).
> c Julia always wears very snazzy (I) apparel (F).
> d John's life was torn asunder (F) by the death of his missus (I).
> e When talking to the fuzz (I), it behoves you (F) to be polite.
> f Jenny's birthday bash (I) ceased (F) at midnight.
> g The deceased (F) man left all his clobber (I) to his nephew.
> h You must give the office a bell (I) if you intend to make any change of domicile (F).
> i Lawrence dwelt (F) in a remote village in Tibet for yonks (I).
> j Richard is an erstwhile (F) mate (I) of my husband's.
>
> **Formal versions**
> a It is imprudent to alight from a bus while it is moving.
> b Jack lives in a flat adjacent to the local takeaway restaurant.
> c Julia always wears very stylish apparel.
> d John's life was torn asunder by the death of his wife.
> e When talking to the constabulary, it behoves you to be polite.
> f Jenny's birthday celebrations ceased at midnight.
> g The deceased man left all his worldly goods to his nephew.
> h You must telephone the office if you intend to change your domicile.
> i Lawrence dwelt in a remote village in Tibet for many years.
> j Richard is an erstwhile friend of my husband's.
>
> **Informal versions**
> a It's daft to get off a bus while it is moving.
> b Jack lives in a flat right next to the local chippie.
> c Julia always wears very snazzy gear.
> d John's life was ripped apart by the death of his missus.
> e When talking to the fuzz, it's a good idea to be polite.
> f Jenny's birthday bash stopped at midnight.
> g The dead man left all his clobber to his nephew.
> h You must give the office a bell if you intend to change your address.
> i Lawrence hung out in a remote village in Tibet for yonks.
> j Richard is an ex-mate of my husband's.

**4** Students work on this exercise with a partner, using an English–English dictionary if necessary.

**Answers**
a 7  b 5  c 15  d 18  e 11  f 17  g 3  h 1  i 2  j 10
k 12  l 4  m 16  n 9  o 6  p 14  q 13  r 8  s 19

**5** Students do this exercise to put some of the slang expressions or colloquial words into context.

**Answers**
a oodles  b bubbly  c chuck  d chomp  e mega
f higgledy-piggledy  g beasties  h broke  i slog

**6** Ask students to underline all the informal words and expressions. They should then write an answer to the email using a similar style.

**Answers**
You'll never guess  drop by  hit the town  reckon
into  have a bite  fancy  mo  prezzie  crash  chocs
bottle  wild about  brave it

WRITING FOLDER 11  153

# 28 Weighing up the pros and cons

| Genre | Discursive articles |
|---|---|
| Topic | Air transport |

| Speaking 1 | Flying |
| Reading | Problems with air transport |
| Vocabulary | Word formation |
| Grammar | Adverbials expressing opinion |
| Listening | Different means of transport |
| Speaking 2 | Discourse markers |

**Workbook contents**

| Grammar | Adverbials expressing opinion |
| Vocabulary | Word formation |
| Use of English | Part 1 multiple-choice gap fill |
| Writing | A discursive article |

## SB pages 172–175

**Lesson planning**

SV  Reading 1 could be done at home
LV  See extension activities in the Reading and Grammar sections

## Speaking 1

1 Elicit definitions of each of the words in the box and ask students to match the words to the pictures.

> **Answers**
> a carry-on luggage  b the carousel  c to board
> d the hold  e the check-in  f overhead bin

2 Divide students into three groups – A, B and C. Give each group their corresponding role and explain that that is the part they are going to play.

Allow them a few minutes in those groups to discuss how they might feel and behave in such a situation.

3 Now put students into new groups with one student from group A, one from group B and one from group C. If possible, A should be behind a desk and should be approached by B and then C. Ask students to role play the scene.

4 Allow time after the role play for students to discuss how their characters felt and any other issues that arise.

5 As a class, discuss whether anyone has had a similar experience that they would like to share.

## Reading

1 Questions a–c are intended to focus students on the meaning of the text. Allow students time to read the text silently as they think about the questions.

> **Answers**
> a noisy children on planes
>   excessive carry-on luggage
>   luggage going missing on planes
>   poor compensation for lost luggage
> b The article suggests that noisy children could be seated with their parents behind a screen at the back of the plane. It also suggests – though not seriously, of course – that children could be put in the hold!
>   To solve the problem of excessive carry-on luggage, it suggests that airlines should be stricter about sticking to regulations concerning the permitted size and weight of hand luggage.
>   Nothing is suggested directly for dealing with the problem of luggage going astray.
>   To solve the problem of inadequate compensation, it suggests that at least triple frequent-flier air miles should be awarded for distances travelled by one's luggage.

2 The aim of the questions here is to focus on the article in detail. Ask students to work through questions a–i with a partner.

> **Teaching extra**
>
> The article makes effective use of a number of puns. The title of the article is a pun. The pun is based on the expression *carry on*. This can mean to carry luggage on (to a plane). It can also mean a show of annoyance, excitement or anxiety as in the slightly outdated expression *What a carry on!* There is also a pun in the first sentence – *to go on a diet* and *to go on a plane*.
> There is also a play on words at the end of the first paragraph where there is a comment about children *being screened and not heard*. This sentence makes people think of the Victorian maxim *Children should be seen and not heard*.

154 WEIGHING UP THE PROS AND CONS

**Answers**
a A quotation may say something in a memorable way, perhaps because it is succinct, well-expressed or amusing. Using a quotation allows the writer to make a strong first impression at the beginning of a piece of writing.
b *Negative externality* is not a phrase in common usage but it is explained in the text. It means doing something that is nice for one person but causes problems for others.
c *Outrage*, i.e. extreme anger or fury.
d *Lug* gives the idea of carrying something that is heavy and awkward to move. *Take* does not have these connotations and so is a much less appropriate word to use.
e *Luggage* is personified (spoken about as if it were human) in the sentence *You took a flight from London to Tokyo; your luggage and your smart clothes decided to hop on to one to Los Angeles.*
f *Paltry* means ridiculously small.
g Wal-Mart sells cheap clothes whereas clothes at Armani are very expensive. Although it is not possible to work out which is the expensive company and which is the cheaper one, it should be clear from the context that the prices at the two kinds of shops are very different.
h It is inserted to make it clear that the writer is deliberately referring to the traveller with a lot of hand luggage as *a man* and is not merely using *his* as a generic pronoun to stand for either *his* or *her*. The writer is pointing out that it is usually men who have heavy hand luggage.
i These two sentences make the point that if you *fight the flab*, i.e. go on a diet and lose weight, you will be able to take more luggage on board as hand luggage. The last sentence reminds the reader of the opening quotation of the article where Jean Kerr linked diets and planes.

# Extension activity

Suggest that students identify all the connecting words and phrases used in the article. Use this activity as a way of encouraging students to use this kind of language in their own writing. Point out that linking devices should be used accurately and appropriately.

The connecting words and phrases used in the article include the following:

but   especially   just like   i.e.   which   rather than
because   instead   as if   once   and   regardless of
therefore   also   as well as   in addition   better still
then   before

As can be seen, the writer uses a good variety of connecting words and phrases. These are used appropriately to show the links between the different stages in the writer's argument. This varied and appropriate use of connecting words and phrases could be usefully applied in the CAE Writing test (Paper 2).

# Vocabulary

1 Students should complete the table, then compare their own answers with those of other students. They should add any other good phrases thought of by other students.

| Suggested answers | | |
|---|---|---|
| Words from the text | Meaning | Other words from same root (in typical phrase) |
| agree | have the same opinion | to disagree with someone; an amicable agreement; a(n) (dis)agreeable person; the agreed outcome |
| undeterred | not discouraged | a nuclear deterrent, an effective deterrent; to deter an attack |
| excessive | too much | excess baggage; to exceed the speed limit; excessively violent; excesses of behaviour |
| concede | admit reluctantly | to make no concessions; concessionary tickets; concessive clause |
| forcibly | using strength or power | force of will; forced laughter; a forceful character; a force to be reckoned with; forces in physics |
| frequent | happening often | frequently absent; word frequency; to frequent a place (note stress on verb is on the second syllable, not the first as in the adjective) |
| compensation | payment for loss or damage | to compensate for bad weather; compensatory benefits |
| correlation | connection | to correlate statistically; smoking and heart disease are correlated |

2 Students work on this exercise to contextualise the words in Vocabulary 1.

**Answers**
a stressful   b disagreeable   c deterrent
d exceeding   e concession   f enforce
g frequency   h correlation   i compensation

# Adverbials expressing opinion

The grammar here is covered on page 206 of the Grammar folder.

1 Look at the sentences and ask students what the words in bold tell us about the opinion of the writer.

> **Answers**
> a The writer seems to be in favour of putting children behind screens at the back of the plane and thinks it is a pity that this idea has not been taken up by airlines.
> b The writer thinks it is correct of the airlines to be strict about the weight and size of what is permitted as hand luggage.
> c The writer understands why people want to carry their luggage on board as it is often necessary to wait for a long time to retrieve luggage from the hold and sometimes you wait in vain for your cases.

2 Ensure that students understand all these adverbials before asking them to match them to the sentences.

> **Answers**
> a fortunately  b apparently, evidently
> c indisputably, undoubtedly  d inevitably, predictably
> e surprisingly, unbelievably  f ironically

3 Students complete this exercise to put the adverbials into context.

> **Answers**
> a Fortunately  b inevitably
> c Predictably  d apparently

> **Extension activity**
>
> Write this sentence on the board:
> *Travelling by car is undoubtedly safer than it used to be.*
> Ask how this could be changed by adding a different adverbial – encourage students to think also of adverbials that are not in the book. They may come up with:
> *Travelling by car is arguably safer than it used to be.*
> *Travelling by car is questionably safer than it used to be.*
> *Travelling by car is possibly safer than it used to be.*
> *Surprisingly, travelling by car is safer than it used to be.*
> *Fortunately, travelling by car is undoubtedly safer than it used to be.*
> Having made a list of possible sentences like this, ask students which one they feel they themselves would be most likely to use and why.

# Listening

1 With the class, discuss the advantages and disadvantages of travelling by plane, train and bicycle. This prediction activity should make it much easier for students to understand the discussion when they listen to it.

2 Play the recording and ask students to list the advantages and disadvantages of each method of transport.

> **Answers**
> **Flying**
> Advantages: Fast; comfortable; you get well treated; minimal carrying of luggage.
> Disadvantages: Cost; long waits at airports; luggage can get lost.
> **Rail travel**
> Advantages: See the countryside as you travel through it; more flexibility to travel when you want; more relaxing; suitable for shorter journeys.
> Disadvantages: Not always reliable.
> **Cycling**
> Advantages: Freedom to go where you want, stop where you want; healthy; exhilarating.
> Disadvantages: Not so good if it's cold and windy or very wet; you have to be fit.

## Tapescript

**Interviewer:** This article says that your personality is revealed by the kind of transport that you like best. What's your favourite means of transport, Jack?

**Jack:** <u>Oh, well</u> there's no doubt about that, flying. Flying is my number one choice. It's <u>undoubtedly</u> the fastest of any option available. It's <u>generally speaking</u> the most comfortable if you're prepared to pay a little money and you get treated very well. Your luggage gets taken care of. You just hand it all in. It's all sorted for you. I think it's a wonderful –

**Stephen:** <u>Sorry</u>, you say your luggage gets taken care of for you? I think one of the biggest disadvantages in air travel is the way your luggage can disappear and get sent off all over the world, don't you? Have you not found that?

**Interviewer:** I agree with that, <u>yes</u>.

**Jack:** <u>Um, well</u> not in my experience but <u>you know</u>, if that occasionally happens, <u>well</u>, it's going to happen anywhere isn't it?

**Stephen:** Occasionally! It's almost a predictable thing now, I think, with air travel.

**Katie:** I think you're very fortunate if you don't get your bag missing. <u>I mean</u> the other thing that I find amazing that you didn't mention was the predictably long waits. <u>I mean</u> you can be stood there, looking at the board, waiting for your flight and you could have been on holiday already –

WEIGHING UP THE PROS AND CONS

**Stephen:** If you've got a family with you it's an unbelievably long time. It's horrendous. Do you not find that?
**Jack:** No, I'm a fan, <u>I'm afraid</u>. I couldn't live without it.
**Katie:** <u>Alright then</u>.
**Interviewer:** What about you, Katie?
**Katie:** <u>Well</u>, I'm a great one for rail travel. I've got a railcard and it gets me everywhere I want to go. <u>You know</u>, I get the opportunity to see the countryside which is something I love because I was brought up in the country and you get to see such a different sort of terrain and I feel very fortunate. I think it's really flexible. I can ring up, I can change my ticket at the last minute, I can get to all sorts of places and I can just sit back and relax. I love it.
**Stephen:** Do you trust it? <u>I mean</u> is it a reliable form of transport?
**Katie:** <u>OK, well</u> –
**Stephen:** It's not, is it?
**Katie:** <u>In short</u>, not always, no.
**Jack:** And it's slow, isn't it? <u>I mean</u> it's – you can't say it's quicker than flying, can you?
**Katie:** No, but you'd hardly want to fly from Birmingham to Barnsley, would you? <u>I mean</u> it's <u>like</u> – <u>you know</u>, it's just something that, that you do really. It's enjoyable.
**Stephen:** <u>Well, I don't know</u>, it's not for me.
**Interviewer:** <u>And</u> what's your view on this, Stephen?
**Stephen:** <u>Oh</u>, I'm a passionate believer in exercise. I'm very keen on fitness, outdoor life. I cycle everywhere, long distance cycling. That's my way of getting round and I like it very much. I can set off when I want, I can do what I want. It's healthy, it's exhilarating, choose exactly where I want to go, see the things I want to see, stop when I want to stop and start when I want to start.
**Katie:** You must be unbelievably fit to do that.
**Stephen:** <u>Well</u> thank you very much, I am. I am pretty fit. But –
**Jack:** When do you eat? <u>I mean</u> –
**Stephen:** When you stop, <u>you know</u> I stop at <u>like</u> a little pub or –
**Jack:** <u>But then</u> you have to stop, don't you? <u>I mean</u> you don't really get anywhere.
**Stephen:** Sorry?
**Katie:** I was just going to say how cold you'd get. You'd have to stop and eat quite often to keep warm.
**Stephen:** <u>What</u>, just to keep warm?
**Jack:** And wet. <u>Certainly</u> if you're cycling here. <u>I mean</u> –
**Katie:** <u>Yeah, and</u> hills as well. I think just sit back and relax.
**Stephen:** Really? I'd love to see you two on a bicycle.
**Katie:** A tandem?
**Jack:** <u>Oh alright then</u>.

3   This is an opportunity for students to listen again and think specifically about discourse markers. Point out to students that discourse markers are a very important element of language use. They signal changes of direction or different stages in a conversation. They also give important indications as to how speakers feel about the people they are speaking to or about what they are saying. Refer students to the Vocabulary spot at this point.

The discourse markers are underlined in the tapescript. Their functions include: to introduce a new topic; to allow the speaker time to think; to organise an argument; to help convey an opinion; to reformulate what has already been said; and to suggest agreement or disagreement.

## Speaking 2

1   Students should complete the dialogue with the expressions from the box.

> **Answers**
> 1 as I was saying   2 I know   3 so   4 then   5 stupidly
> 6 you mean   7 just my luck   8 I suppose   9 certainly

2   Encourage students to use the discourse markers they have worked on in this unit as they prepare their dialogues.

3   Students should perform their dialogues in turn. The other students should note down the discourse markers they hear.

# Exam folder 12

## SB pages 176–177

## Paper 5 Speaking

This Exam folder provides practice in all four parts of the CAE Speaking test (Paper 5). Refer students to the introduction, then go through the Advice box with them.

1 This question helps to prepare students for Part One of the test. Encourage students to expand their answers and to answer the question precisely.

2 This question helps to prepare students for Part Two of the test, when they are asked to comment on and/or react to a set of pictures or photographs.

3 Students should work in pairs for this question, which helps to prepare them for Part Three of the test. Students need not agree with each other, but should reach a conclusion.

4 This question helps to prepare students for Part Four of the test, in which students participate in a wider discussion of the issues raised in Part Three.

As far as possible, give each student a mark out of five for each of these criteria used by the oral examiners in the CAE Speaking test:
- grammar and vocabulary
- discourse management
- pronunciation
- interactive communication.

# 29 A testing question

| Genre | Debates |
|---|---|
| Topic | Education |

| Speaking 1 | Schooldays |
| Listening | Educational issues |
| Reading | The value of exams |
| Vocabulary | Collocations |
| Grammar | Gerunds and infinitives |
| Speaking 2 | How to pass exams |

**Workbook contents**

| Reading | Putting paragraphs into gaps |
| Grammar | Gerunds and infinitives |
| Use of English | Part 3 word formation |

## SB pages 178–181

**Lesson planning**

SV  Reading 3 and Vocabulary 3 could be set for homework

LV  See the extension activity in the Speaking 2 section

## Speaking 1

1 Students should discuss questions a–d in small groups. If possible, group students with different school experiences together.

## Listening

1 Ask these prediction questions to prepare students for dealing with the topics on the recording.

2 Play the recording and ask students to listen and take notes. They should note both the main arguments made by each speaker and the points made against these arguments by other speakers.

**Answers**

1
- System based on tests makes children hate school and learning.
- Schools should be freer – pupils should study what and when they want.
- Portfolios of work and references from teachers are better than tests.
- Testing creates too much pressure – children are stressed.

**Arguments against**
- Children need boundaries, discipline.
- Good to ask them to show what they can do under pressure.

2
- Summer holidays are too long – children forget what they've learnt.
- Short terms and short school days make life very difficult for working parents.
- Extra time at school could be used for music, sport, drama.

**Arguments against**
- Children already spend a lot of time at school.
- They need unstructured leisure time.
- Separation of worktime and playtime is a good thing.

3
- Expensive private schools take the best teachers and students.
- Not fair for some children to get a worse education because their parents have less money.
- Free education would mean equal opportunity for all.

**Arguments against**
- People should be free to choose how they spend their money.
- If some schools are funded privately, the state has more money to spend on state schools.

## Tapescript

1

**First man:** My feeling really is that children at school are just disciplined too much these days. I mean, I just think that basing an education, an education system on tests and then punishing children if they don't do very well in them or they don't do what's expected, it's just a sure way to make most pupils hate school and hate learning, and just not want to participate at all. I think it would be so much better if schools were just kind of freer places where pupils could study what they wanted to and when they wanted to. And instead of all these tests all the time, why don't students – it would be so much better if they were just simply able to show future employers or universities or whatever portfolios of their own work and together with personal references from their teachers.

**Second man:** I don't know, sounds like a logistical nightmare to me doesn't it? I mean –

**Woman:** I mean, children, they do need boundaries, they do need some sort of discipline don't they? They need to be told what and, you know, where they can go, what they can do. If they don't, they just go mad. They go wild. And it helps them, I think.

**First man:** But there's so much pressure on them, I just think, from all these tests all the time.

**Second man:** Isn't that good, though? I mean, just putting them under, I agree we don't want too much pressure but isn't it good that actually they have to try and show what they can do under pressure situations?

**First man:** I think it's good if you respond well to the pressure but if you don't then, you know, so many kids are just, are so stressed. I mean, you get four and five year olds who, or seven year olds, this first seven-year-old test, who are apparently, you know, stressed because they've got to do their SATs tests at seven.

**Second man:** But if it's all portfolios of work, it'll end up being, you know, a lot of the parents' work, won't it?

**Woman:** Yeah.

**First man:** Well, yeah, that's true.

2

**Woman:** Well, I actually believe that term time is too short. The summer holidays just seem to go on for an eternity and during that time, the kids, they forget everything they've learnt from school. I just, I do actually think they need a longer time in class. The days are just, they're just far too short and with me having, you know, to work and having to get back for half past three, half past four, whichever child it is, I just can't cope with that time. I think it would do the kids really – I think they'd benefit if they could stay longer at school. It doesn't have to be work but if they just stayed there and, you know, I don't know, did music or sport, drama – I mean Phoebe loves doing drama – it would just be, well, it would help me and I think they'd benefit, don't you think?

**First man:** Well, I mean frankly I don't. I think it depends, again it depends on the child and I think kids actually spend a lot of time at school and it means that they don't get any time at home and they don't get any time to kind of just sit around and –

**Woman:** Well, they've got all weekend.

**First man:** Yeah, but that's not very long. I mean, a lot of these kids, you know, if they're young children, to be at school from kind of nine in the morning until six at night when their parents who work come and pick them up, that's a hell of a long time to be at school.

**Second man:** And I think it's good that the kids learn, you know, when is worktime and when is playtime and once they've separated those, I think that's that's a good thing, isn't it?

**Woman:** No, I think you can combine the two and I think they can learn a lot from the other children. If they're always at home with their parents or their siblings, I just think it's really good they're working, you know, different classes, different ethnic communities all the time. I don't know. I just really feel that they'd benefit a lot more than being at home and being in a routine. Which we do have to have, a routine.

**First man:** But with more classes as well, I mean, I do think schools are asking more and more of kids and actually it can be quite stressful for them.

3

**First man:** One thing that does make me angry about all this, though, is how much education costs. I mean the bottom line is I think education should be free for everybody because the, you know, a lot of poorer people in society just don't have that money. They don't have that money to send their kids to the better schools and what happens then is that the comprehensive schools are not as good because the private schools take all, they take the best teachers, they take the best students. I really believe very strongly that education should be free for everybody and you have a level playing field.

**Second man:** Well, it's great in theory but I always think that in the end if people have the money and they want to spend it on their children's education, then they should be allowed to.

**Woman:** Absolutely, and also if, you know, for those people that can afford private education, that releases more money for the state, for the state schools, doesn't it?

**First man:** Well, does it? Does the money get back there? Do you really think that goes back down to the ground roots? I don't think it does.

3  Students should discuss this question in groups. Round up by taking a vote on each of the three issues.

## Reading

1  Discuss the question briefly with the class. Remind students that reading the title is important, as it can help them to understand the text as a whole.

2  Ask students to read the text and answer the questions.

> **Answers**
> a  head of Dulwich College Preparatory School in London
> b  School should be fun and should not be dominated by exams. Children should be sheltered from exam pressures while they are young.
> c  The writer of the article clearly doesn't agree with him, though children and many parents probably would!

3 Ask students to divide the words and expressions into two groups: positive and negative. They may use an English–English dictionary if necessary. Point out that they should look at the words in the context of the reading text, as in different contexts some of them would have different associations.

**Answers**

Positive words: rousing, nurtured, rounded, cushion, sheltering

Negative words: burnout, hothouse flower children, wilt, scream, sin, showered, blasphemy, boot camp, misguided, cosseting, smothering

What the words suggest:

| | |
|---|---|
| rousing | that the speech made people feel vigorous and inspired |
| nurtured | that something is lovingly cared for |
| rounded | (of an education) well balanced and not too narrowly academic |
| cushion | protect from accidents or problems |
| sheltering | protecting from difficulties |
| burnout | when someone has pushed themselves so hard that they have no energy or enthusiasm left |
| hothouse flower children | pushed to achieve too much at too early an age for their own good |
| wilt | die from lack of water or nourishment |
| scream | call out loudly (it suggests that the headlines are large and eye-catching) |
| sin | evil, against the will of God (this word has strong religious associations) |
| showered | given a lot of something without having to make any effort |
| blasphemy | terrible thing to say (like cursing a religious person) |
| boot camp | a tough place where army cadets train |
| misguided | having the wrong ideas |
| cosseting | treating too softly |
| smothering | over-protecting |

4 Invite students to express their own personal reaction to the article. Refer them to the Exam spot at this point.

# Vocabulary

1 Ask students first to cover up the right hand column and see how many of the collocations they can remember from the article. They may of course come up with other collocations. Accept any good ones that are suggested.

**Answers**
a 9  b 6  c 1  d 5  e 7  f 10  g 8
h 4  i 2  j 3

2 Students could do this exercise individually and then check their answers with the class as a whole.

**Answers**
a to treat someone with kid gloves
b the current climate   c to achieve a qualification
d the real world   e at the end of your tether
f in the long run   g a rousing speech   h pocket money
i to do someone a favour   j to reach a stage

3 This exercise provides further practice of the collocations in context.

**Answers**
a in the long run   b do me a favour
c at the end of her tether   d the current climate
e to treat me with kid gloves   f the real world
g reached a stage   h pocket money

# Gerunds and infinitives

The grammar here is covered on pages 206–207 of the Grammar folder.

1 Ask students first to identify the uses of the gerund and the infinitive and then to explain why they are used in each case.

**Answers**
a to learn   to achieve
(two examples of the infinitive of purpose)
to accept
(infinitive is used after the verb *want*)
b to spray   to protect
(*to protect* is an example of the infinitive of purpose)
c growing   sheltering   smothering
(gerund is needed after prepositions)
d to do   to get
(infinitive is used after verbs such as *want* and *tell*)

2 Elicit the rules for the use of gerunds and infinitives by asking students to complete the gaps.

**Answers**
a gerund   b gerund   c infinitive
d infinitive   e gerund

A TESTING QUESTION

3 Students should separate the verbs into two lists: those followed by a gerund and those followed by an infinitive.

> **Answers**
> Verbs followed by a gerund: mind, feel like, deny, enjoy, risk, suggest, give up
> Verbs followed by an infinitive: promise, refuse, arrange, tend, offer, expect, decide, agree, manage

4 Ask students to divide the verbs into three groups. Give students an example of each to get them started.

> **Answers**
> A forget, regret, go on, remember, try
> B start, intend, begin, continue, can't bear
> C permit, advise, allow, forbid

5 Students now put some of the verbs into context by rewriting each sentence using the word in brackets in an appropriate form.

> **Answers**
> a Jack suggested going to the new Chinese restaurant.
> b Students are not permitted to eat in the classrooms.
> c The police officer forbade anyone to enter the building.
> d Would you mind opening the window?
> e Melinda offered to paint my son's portrait.
> f I hope you didn't forget to buy some apples.
> g I regret wasting so much of my time at school.
> h Despite his injury, he went on playing his violin.
> i Everyone expects him to do well in his exams.
> j Smoking is not allowed on any of that airline's flights.

# Speaking 2

1 Play the recording and ask students if they know anyone like the types of examinees mentioned. They then complete the notes.

> **Answers**
> Aim of exams: to find out which pupils can remember what they've been taught
> Types of examinees:
> 1 The petrified
>   a persuade yourself that there is nothing to worry about
>   b make a plan of campaign
> 2 The disorganised
>   a draw up a timetable
>   b find a study partner

## Tapescript

At the end of the day, no matter how you look at it, you are at school to learn. And to remember. And it is this last bit that causes all the problems. So they have exams. That way, those in charge can find out which of their pupils remembers x = y x 4t and which haven't a clue what x is in the first place.

Not everyone approaches exams in the same way and not everyone revises in the same way. It does help if you can identify what sort of examinee you are and how to get the best out of yourself.

**1 The petrified**
These are the people for whom the word 'exam' induces a massive upsurge in heart rate, clammy palms and a desire to run very far away and never come back. Never mind that all through the terms they can get eight out of ten without really trying, sit them in a silent classroom with a clock ticking away the minutes and a pile of spotless white paper before them, and everything they ever knew vanishes from their minds.
If you are one of these, here is what to do:
a) About three weeks before the exam, sit yourself down firmly and have a chat with yourself. What is an exam? A test. How many tests do you have every term? Dozens. How do you get on? Fine. Right, so why worry because they have called this one an exam? Would you stop eating burgers if they suddenly called them calorie challenged stomach fillers?
b) Draw up a plan of campaign for the first five minutes of the exam. It is known that 80% of all panicking occurs in the first few moments after the invigilator says 'You may now turn over your papers.' Count slowly to ten, then back to one. Take three deep breaths and tell yourself that even if you could not answer a single question, the sun would still rise tomorrow. Life would go on and you would have another chance. There is always another chance; you never blow life in one go.

**2 The disorganised**
This is the soul who works flat out for German literature for days and days and then wakes up to discover that German literature isn't till next week and she has two hours to master three terms of physics. This species is also likely to start rereading *Vanity Fair* (the classic novel) and then find a fascinating piece about hair highlights in *Vanity Fair* (the magazine) and waste a whole evening.
This is what you do:
a) Draw up a timetable. Set yourself one hour for a specific topic and then schedule yourself a fifteen minute break. That break can be used for anything from making Marmite and cheese sandwiches (marvellous for the brainpower) to washing your hair. But when it is over, it is back for the second hour.

b) Find a study partner. If you are not the most orderly person, it can be a real bonus to have a friend who is studying the same subjects to keep you on the straight and narrow. Again, allow yourself little treats during the evening and nag each other into completing the task in hand.

2 Students have to imagine they heard the talk but their best friend didn't. They now have to summarise the key points that the speaker made in the talk. Allow a few minutes for students to think about how they would summarise it. Ask one student to summarise the talk for the other students. Then ask the other students whether the summary they heard was effective. Would they have omitted anything that the speaker said or included anything that the speaker did not say?

3 Make sure that the groups know that someone from their group will be summarising the discussion for the other groups but do not tell them in advance who will do this. At the end of the discussion, assign one person from each group to summarise the discussion of their group. Allow time for the group to help this person to prepare notes.

The assigned students then take it in turns to give feedback from their groups.

> **E**xtension activity
>
> Ask students to prepare wall posters listing the key pieces of advice that their group came up with.

# Writing folder 12

## SB pages 182–183

## Descriptive, narrative and discursive articles

1 Refer students to the Exam spot, then ask them to look at the writing tasks and answer questions a and b.

> **Suggested answers**
> a
> A You have to describe the difficult conditions that students have to live in and you have to discuss ways of making the best of those conditions. You have to narrate examples from your own friends' experience.
> B You have to describe one modern means of communication and you have to discuss how it has changed your life (in both positive and negative ways). There will be a narrative element in the examples that you give from your own experience of this means of communication.
> C You have to describe the week's work experience programme that you took part in (this will include an element of narration) and you have to discuss how the programme could be improved.
> D You have to describe what facilities are already available and you have to discuss why one particular additional facility would be of benefit to your community.
> E You have to describe the types of punishments and rewards used in schools in your country and you have to discuss what you think is good and bad about this system, including suggestions for improvements. There will be some narration in your account of your own experience of punishments and rewards at school.
> b
> No narrative element is appropriate in D as it is a formal proposal.

2 Ask students to read the instructions and make notes on how they would proceed with each of the tasks.

3 Now ask students to focus on the narrative parts of the tasks. Encourage them to use ideas from their own experience.

4 Students should now focus on the discursive parts of each of the tasks.

5 Ask students to discuss which of the approaches listed would work best for each of the five writing tasks.

6 Students should write an answer to two of the five tasks worked on in this Writing folder, bearing in mind all the issues raised here.

# 30 Why should we employ you?

| Genre | Interviews |
|---|---|
| Topic | Job interviews |

| | |
|---|---|
| Speaking 1 | Experience of interviews |
| Reading | How to deal with interview questions |
| Listening | Interviews – different ways of answering questions |
| Grammar | Using a range of structures |
| Vocabulary | Using a range of vocabulary |
| Speaking 2 | Speaking clearly in the CAE Speaking test (Paper 5) |

**Workbook contents**

| | |
|---|---|
| Use of English | Part 2 open gap fill |
| Use of English | Part 4 multiple meanings |
| Use of English | Part 5 key word transformations |
| Vocabulary | Formal and informal language |
| Writing | A competition entry |

## SB pages 184–187

**Lesson planning**

SV  Reading 2 and Grammar 2 could be set for homework
LV  See extension activities in the Listening and Vocabulary sections

## Speaking 1

Refer students to the pictures and ask them to discuss questions a–d.

## Reading

1  Students discuss these questions with a partner and then compare their answers with those of other students in the class.

2  Students match the questions a–h in Reading 1 to the answers 1–8 in the reading text.

**Answers**
a 3  b 8  c 1  d 5  e 4  f 7  g 2  h 6

3  Discuss this question with the class as a whole. If students do not yet have very clear career plans, ask them to answer it from the point of view of someone applying for a teaching job in the school where the class is taking place. That will at least help them to focus on a concrete and familiar context.

## Listening

1  Students should listen to the recording and complete the table. They should bear in mind the answers given in the reading text as they answer.

**Answers**
Better answer from Mr Higgins: 2, 3, 4
Better answer from Miss Smith: 1

2  Play the recording again and ask students to complete the table.

**Answers**

| Phrase | Used by | Context |
|---|---|---|
| badly need | Mr Higgins | I badly need this job |
| take instructions | Miss Smith | I can take instructions |
| I wonder if | Miss Smith | I wonder if you could define calculated risks |
| good and bad points | Mr Higgins | All my jobs had their good and bad points |
| which is why | Mr Higgins | which is why I'm here now |
| it's hard to know | Miss Smith | It's hard to know where to begin |

### Tapescript

**Interviewer:** Why should we employ you, Mr Higgins?
**Mr Higgins:** You won't find anyone better suited to this job than I am. I've usually made a great success of any jobs that I've taken on. And I badly need this job because my wife is expecting and I've been out of work for six months now.
**Interviewer:** Why should we employ you, Miss Smith?
**Miss Smith:** As we've been discussing, I have the experience and qualifications that you ask for in your advertisement for the post. I'm a good team player. I can take the instructions and I have the desire to make a thorough success of this job.
**Interviewer:** Are you willing to take calculated risks, Mr Higgins?

**Mr Higgins:** Oh yes, most certainly. Life is a risk. All business involves risk and you can't win anything if you don't take risks.

**Interviewer:** And are you willing to take calculated risks, Miss Smith?

**Miss Smith:** I wonder if you could define calculated risks for me? Perhaps you could give me an example of the sort of risk that you have in mind and the stakes that are involved?

**Interviewer:** Which of the jobs you have held have you liked least, Mr Higgins?

**Mr Higgins:** All my jobs had their good and bad points, but I've always found that if you want to learn, there's plenty to be picked up along the way. Each experience was valuable. In my first job, I had, of course, to do a lot of very straightforward, routine jobs but I used the spare time and energy I had to learn as much as I could about office procedures, which has I think stood me in very good stead in later jobs.

**Interviewer:** And which of the jobs you have held have you liked least, Miss Smith?

**Miss Smith:** I suppose the job I last held was the worst. The people I was working with were very backbiting and unpleasant and management were pretty inefficient. The job was also not nearly challenging enough for me at this stage in my career, which is why I decided it was time to move on.

**Interviewer:** Now, Mr Higgins, in what areas do you feel that your last boss could have done a better job?

**Mr Higgins:** Oh, I've always had the highest respect for my last boss. He has taught me so much that I don't think he really could have done a better job. He's really brought me to the point where I'm ready for greater challenges, which is why I'm here now.

**Interviewer:** Now, Miss Smith, in what areas do you feel that your last boss could have done a better job?

**Miss Smith:** It's hard to know where to begin. He's lazy. He's inconsistent in his judgments and he is very poor at motivating people and at delegating work. It is hard for me to see how he ever got to a management position being as incompetent as he is.

3 Ask this question to round off the exercise.

> **Extension activity**
>
> Students could now role play a job interview. Group students in threes with two interviewers and one interviewee. Any question from those worked on in the Reading and Listening sections may be used. The candidates should try to answer as well as they can.

# Using a range of structures

The grammar here is covered on page 207 of the Grammar folder.

1 Ask students to discuss these questions with a partner.

| **Suggested answers** | |
|---|---|
| **a** | |
| conditionals | If I were you, I'd stop taking taxis. |
| modals | You should use your mobile phone less. |
| inversion | Were you to use your bike rather than your car, you'd save a lot of money. |
| present simple | People who eat at home rather than in restaurants spend a lot less money. |
| **b** | |
| used to | I used to love art at school. |
| would | I would always go in the art room at lunch time. |
| past simple | We had one very eccentric teacher. |
| present perfect | I've never met anyone else quite like my very first school teacher. |
| **c** | |
| past simple | We called the police. |
| past continuous | It was late at night and we were getting ready for bed. |
| past perfect | I had just cleaned my teeth when I heard a knock at the door. |
| inversion | Never have I been quite so terrified as I was that night. |
| **d** | |
| conditionals | I could have played rugby. |
| wish | I wish we girls had done metalwork rather than sewing. |
| indirect questions | I wonder how it feels to be a boy. |
| inversion | Little can we really imagine what it is like to be in anyone else's skin, let alone someone of the opposite sex. |

2 Point out that it may help students to refer back to the instructions for the previous exercise.

> **Answers**
> a 1 walked/cycled 2 should 3 saves
> b 1 used 2 went 3 would 4 been 5 got/had
> c 1 had 2 was 3 realised 4 would 5 had 6 was
> d 1 how/if/whether 2 had 3 would 4 had 5 Had 6 been 7 have 8 was/were 9 have 10 am

3 Ask students to improve both paragraphs as much as they can. Point out that the paragraphs are grammatically correct.

   A This paragraph is correct but it is predictable and rather dull, with sentences all of much the same length and all (apart from the first one) beginning with a similar kind of discourse marker and using the same structures. It needs to have at least one rather longer sentence and a bit more variety in structure.

B This paragraph is correct but it does not use a good range of vocabulary. The *I liked / loved* is repetitive. To improve the text, it needs some more interesting and contrasting vocabulary.

Students could write improved versions of these paragraphs as homework.

## Vocabulary

1 Refer students to the Vocabulary spot, then discuss this exercise with the class as a whole. Aim to get at least three alternatives for each underlined word.

**Suggested answers**
a astounded / amazed / astonished
b wandering / strolling / ambling
c promised / insisted / claimed
d enjoyable / rewarding / exciting
e businessman / boy / soldier
f buy / purchase / acquire

2 Students do this exercise with a partner, using an English–English dictionary if necessary to help them.

**Answers**
A a 4  b 1  c 2  d 3
B a 3  b 4  c 2  d 1

3 Students should try to suggest new words for each of the two lists.

**Suggested answers**
Ways of walking – crawl, creep, totter, march, stumble, hike
Ways of speaking – argue, boast, whisper, grumble, beg, suggest, warn

4 Encourage students to use a variety of different adjectives for this exercise.

### Extension activity

Working in pairs or individually, students have to try to find an adjective that could be used to describe a person and a place beginning with each of the letters of the alphabet.
For example,
an ambitious person    an awe-inspiring place
a boastful person      a barren place

## Speaking 2

1 Discuss these pieces of advice with the whole class.

**Answers**
a bad advice – it will be hard to hear you.
b bad advice – both should hear you, but you should be talking to your partner rather than the examiner.
c bad advice – you will probably be harder to understand if you talk too quickly. Neither too fast nor too slow is ideal.
d bad advice – just speak clearly.
e bad advice – this is going too far. Of course you must speak clearly and not too fast but it is not natural to say every word distinctly in English. Little words like *of* and *the* are often swallowed. It will sound unnatural if you give too much stress to unimportant words.
f good advice
g bad advice – it is certainly good advice to make eye contact with the examiner but all the time would be inappropriate and would make the examiner feel uncomfortable. In Part 3 for example, you are talking to the other candidate and not to the examiner.
h bad advice – you must talk distinctly. You can't get any marks unless the examiner can hear and understand what you are saying.

2 Students should do this exercise with a partner.

**Suggested answers**
a Keep your head up when you are speaking.
b When you are talking to your partner, it is important that both your partner and the examiner should be able to hear you.
c You will sound more natural if you talk neither too quickly nor too slowly.
d It is not a good idea to shout at the examiner – just speak clearly.
e Speak clearly but do not give too much prominence to unstressed words like *of* and *and*.
g Make regular eye contact with the examiner.
h Speak distinctly or you cannot get any marks.

3 Divide students into groups of four. In each group, two students will be the examiners and two the candidates.

Ask the first pair of candidates to look at the pictures in Task A. They should discuss which two of the jobs they would like to do least and which two most, and why. The pair of examiners should then comment on their performance.

The students should then swap roles. Ask the second pair of candidates to look at the pictures in Task B. They should discuss which procedures they think would be most useful in choosing a new teacher, which would be least useful, and why. The pair of examiners should then comment on their performance.

# UNITS 26–30 Revision

## SB pages 188–189

### Topic review

Follow the standard procedure outlined on page 29 of the Teacher's Book.

### Vocabulary

1 Ask students to fill the gaps with a word based on the word in brackets at the end of each sentence.

> **Answers**
> a scenery  b exposure  c erosion  d Predictably
> e unexpected  f regardless

### Reading

1 Ask students to read the text and choose the correct option, A, B, C or D.

> **Answers**
> 1 B  2 C  3 A  4 D  5 B  6 A  7 C  8 C

### Grammar

1 Ask students to read the text through first, then fill each gap with one missing word.

> **Answers**
> 1 an  2 work/write  3 to  4 had  5 no  6 for
> 7 how  8 were  9 do/perform  10 so

### Speaking

1 and 2 Allow plenty of time to discuss these questions fully with your class. Come prepared with your own suggestions about appropriate ways your students can keep up their English.

# Paper 1 Part 3

You are going to read an extract from a book. For questions **1–7**, choose the answer (**A**, **B**, **C** or **D**) which you think fits best according to the text.

## THE LIFE OF DIPLOMATS' CHILDREN

During the writing of this book about the lives of diplomatic wives, I was reminiscing with my oldest friend, a diplomat's child like myself, whom I have known since we were at boarding school together, aged ten. I was not at all surprised to find that, like me, she has the most vivid memories surrounding the arrival of the post: the staircase, the old chest, the anxious craning over the banisters for that glimpse of a familiar envelope or handwriting. 'There was one time when I did not hear from my parents for nearly three months,' she recalls. 'I thought they must be dead.' Now an English literature academic, she believes that her chosen field of expertise – eighteenth century epistolary novels and letters – is no accident.

Like that of our mothers, the experience of diplomatic children is enormously varied. 'The myth is that diplomatic life, with all the travelling, new places, new faces, is attractive and exciting for children,' wrote Jane Ewart-Biggs, 'but I believe that nothing could be further from the truth.' Although the necessity of changing houses, schools, friends, food and even languages every few years can be problematic for many children, others happily adapt.

My own feelings, while principally positive, are not wholly uncomplicated. I was brought up in Spain (in Madrid and Bilbao) and in Singapore. My memories of both places are startlingly happy. In Bilbao, when I was six, we lived in an apartment overlooking the sea. I learnt not only to speak but to read and write Spanish; I came top in catechism (I was the only Protestant child in a Catholic convent) and bottom in English. I developed a love for Velazquez and the gorier paintings of Goya. 'My father is a Consel. If any person from England, Scotland, Wales or Irland is in trouble in any kind of way my Father has to go and lock after them,' I wrote, to my parents' mingled pride and despair, in one of my first essays. 'My father job is very very important. If ther wer no consels ther wode be pepole diing without help and all kids of thing. If he doset like eny person he must not say o I dont like yo I don't want to help you. He must be nice and help hem.'

In Singapore, when I was eight, my brother and I ran wild in a tropical garden filled with bougainvillaea and frangipane trees. We swam in jellyfish-infested seas and went barefoot for two years. I wrote my first stories and it was always hot. England was a faraway, drizzle-grey dream, from whence letters and comics turned up occasionally, as emotionally distant as the moon. The utter despair, which I experienced two years later, when I was sent to boarding school there, has stayed with me all my life.

Adults are often tempted to believe that, because children are not yet physically or emotionally mature, they do not experience the 'big' emotions of grief or rage in quite the same way that we do. The pain I experienced on being separated from my family was like a bereavement. For many children in boarding school for the first time, it is the nights which are the worst, but for me it was always the mornings. I would wake up in the cold first light to see the stark little chest of drawers at the foot of my bed with its one regulation photograph frame, and beyond it the melancholy autumn beech leaves, dripping and tapping at the window panes. Then I would hide under the bedclothes, sick in my stomach at the thought of another day to get through.

After half a term of this complete misery – after which I was supposed to have 'settled in' like everyone else – in some trepidation, I wrote a letter: 'Mummy, Mummy, Mummy, Oh my Mummy…' it began. I don't remember the exact wording of the rest of the letter, but I was sure that the hidden message which lay behind these words, the plea to be taken away, could not be mistaken. It was the only letter to which, although I doubtless received a letter back, I never received a reply. So I stayed at school and learnt to survive.

1 What is the main theme of the first paragraph?
   A The children's fear of something bad happening to their parents.
   B The importance of letters in the lives of boarding school pupils.
   C The close friendships made by boarding school children at school.
   D The fact that the children of diplomats attended similar schools.

2 What did Jane Ewart-Biggs believe about diplomatic children?
   A They love the excitement of a life full of change.
   B They are often unhappy.
   C They adjust to change more easily than other children.
   D Their happiness depends on their mothers.

3 Which of these points does the writer make about her schooling in Spain?
   A She was very unsuccessful at school.
   B She tried to impress others with stories of her father's importance.
   C She felt uncomfortable at school there.
   D She was good and bad in unexpected areas.

4 Why did her parents experience some despair when they read the essay the author quotes?
   A She made a lot of spelling mistakes.
   B She was not as clever as the rest of her family.
   C She didn't understand what her father's job involved.
   D Her handwriting was very poor.

5 How did the writer feel about England when she was in Singapore?
   A It was cold and grey.
   B Good comics came from there.
   C Children were not as free there.
   D It had no real significance for her.

6 Which phrase best sums up how the writer first felt at boarding school?
   A extremely angry
   B very cold
   C desperately unhappy
   D rather ill

7 What response did her parents make to the letter described in the last paragraph?
   A They ignored her pleas.
   B They refused her request.
   C They told her that she'd learn to survive.
   D They were too busy to reply to her.

# Paper 1 Part 4

You are going to read seven film reviews. For questons 1–11, choose from the film titles (**A–G**). The film titles may be chosen more than once.

| Which film or films | | |
|---|---|---|
| has a political message? | **1** .............. | |
| have long pauses where little is said? | **2** .............. | |
| | **3** .............. | **A** *Chocolat* |
| is accompanied by some unconvincing publicity material? | **4** .............. | **B** *Heartbreakers* |
| have plots which revolve around relationships between women in the same family? | **5** .............. | **C** *Josie and the Pussycats* |
| | **6** .............. | **D** *Crocodile Dundee in Los Angeles* |
| has acting that is praised? | **7** .............. | **E** *Tears of the Black Tiger* |
| has acting that is criticised? | **8** .............. | **F** *Le Secret* |
| have photography which receives special comment? | **9** .............. | **G** *At the Height of Summer* |
| | **10** .............. | |
| has a plot which is criticised for being hypocritical? | **11** .............. | |

**This week's films**
***** Excellent **** Very good *** Good ** Poor * Give it a miss

**A  CHOCOLAT** ****
*Buena Vista, 12, 121 mins, 2000; rental*
Now that the summer is drawing to a close, a chance to relive those blissful days in France, even if the weather that visits the opening scene of Lasse Hallström's delicious film is snow followed by wind. Delicious? Damn, I vowed I wouldn't put that. Based on Joanne Harris's novel, this story of one scarlet woman's effect on a seemingly time-warped northern French village really is a heart-warmingly delightful affair, in which confectionery is the engine for change. Juliette Binoche is the unmarried gal who opens a chocolaterie and gets right up the nostrils of Alfred Molina's mayor. Blissful but never escapist stuff, with Judi Dench, Johnny Depp and Lena Olin putting in fine performances. Afterwards, I devoured an Aero.

**B  HEARTBREAKERS** **
*124 mins, 15*
This is a mother-daughter relationship movie with a difference – the siren-like Max (Sigourney Weaver) and her daughter, Page (Jennifer Love Hewitt), are con artists who prey on men. Max gets them to the wedding altar, Page leads them into temptation, and, once caught, the victim has to deliver a fat divorce settlement. Page has reached that age where she wants to strike out on her own. Her manipulative mom promises her freedom if they pull one more scam. Off they head to Palm Beach to bag a multimillionaire. Max settles on William B Tensy (Gene Hackman), a stinky, chain-smoking tobacco baron. Page, meanwhile, goes for nice guy Jack (Jason Lee), who is set to make millions on a property deal. The director, David Mirkin (a longtime producer/writer for *The Simpsons*), obviously wanted to make a sophisticated Hollywood comedy of the Preston Sturges kind. But his lines aren't witty enough, and Max and Page have no redeeming qualities: Mom is a cruel control freak and her daughter scheming and selfish.

**C   JOSIE AND THE PUSSYCATS   ***
*98 mins, PG*

Based on the Archie comic books of the 1960s, this is a cartoon caper about an all-girl power-pop band who overnight become the next big thing. Josie (Rachael Leigh Cook) and her Pussycats – bassist Valerie (Rosario Dawson) and drummer Melody (Tara Reid) – are stuck in a small town with big dreams of rock'n'roll fame. Along comes a bigwig bad-guy manager, Wyatt Frame (Alan Cumming), and before you can say "a-1-2-3-4!", the girls are signed, sealed and delivered into the evil hands of the CEO of MegaRecords, Fiona (Parker Posey). She, along with the US government, is using pop music to send subliminal messages in order to brainwash American youth into following trends and keeping the wheels of mindless consumerism turning. We see numerous hysterical teenage girls saying things like: "Orange is the new pink ... Heath Ledger is the new Matt Damon." It's a bit rich being lectured about consumerism by a film that has more product placement in it than a Harrods window display. The band may rock, but the film sucks. What should be frothy fun is actually a tired old neo-Marxist critique of mass culture: Archie meets Theodor Adorno.

**D   CROCODILE DUNDEE IN LOS ANGELES   ***
*95 mins, PG*

Even by the standards of these things, the PR bumf that accompanies this belated sequel is laughably disingenuous. Why has Paul Hogan decided to resurrect the genial, croc-hunting Mick Dundee after a 13-year gap? Not, apparently, because he hasn't had a hit in ages, but because the Mick-in-LA idea was so inspired as to be irresistible. And why was the film made independently, without studio backing? Because Hogan likes to be his own boss is why. Well, whatever you say ... and if DreamWorks had offered a blank cheque, I'm sure he'd have told them where to shove it. This Panglossian publicity might have been a bit more convincing if the film was any good, but it most definitely isn't. Despite the new setting, the Aussie-abroad gags are largely recycled from Mick's antics in New York in the previous two films (1986 and 1988) – except that this time, under the direction of Simon Wincer, Hogan and his co-stars read their lines as though for a casual rehearsal, and plod around as if wading through a foot of margarine.

**E   TEARS OF THE BLACK TIGER   ******
*101 mins, 18*

By paying absolutely no heed to the constraints of history, geography or cinematic genre, this Thai film (written and directed by Wisit Sartsanatieng) is able to offer something for everyone. For a start, there is romance, in the story of a young man (Chartchai Ngamsam) and a beautiful woman (Stella Malucchi) whose love for each other is obstructed at every turn by malign fate. This is balanced by plenty of action, provided by the hero's decision to join a band of horse-riding bandits. The fact that these outlaws dress in the style of the Lone Ranger – despite the story being set not only in Thailand but (seemingly) in the 1950s – points to the movie's third key ingredient: a spirit of camp *joie de vivre* that informs not only the fantastical plot, but the film's visual style, whereby each scene is tinted with bright, icing-sugar colours to create a glowing facsimile of old-fashioned Technicolor. The reported fact that all of this amounts to a pastiche of vintage Thai movies may mean nothing to western viewers, but it need not keep anyone from enjoying the film as a delightful novelty.

**F   LE SECRET   ****
*109 mins, 18*

Directed and co-written by Virginie Wagon (who also co-wrote the acclaimed *The Dream Life of Angels*), this French film is about the unpredictability of romantic emotions. As is often the way with such films, it seems to us that unpredictability is an excuse for making its characters opaque and its story inconclusive. Anne Coesens plays (with undoubted charm) a chic middle-class woman who loves her husband and positively adores her little son, but still can't resist a fling with a virile black American whom she meets in the course of her work as an encyclopedia saleswoman. Although various motives are hinted at, the bottom line is that she is driven by feelings that neither she nor the viewer can hope to fathom. Thus, when she finally drifts, in a slightly ambiguous way, back to her husband, you have to accept this as a credible ending, but you can't shake the suspicion that any other outcome might have seemed equally apt if filled with just as many meaningful glances and long pauses.

**G   AT THE HEIGHT OF SUMMER   ****
*112 mins, PG*

If you enjoyed the lyrical Vietnamese drama *The Scent of Green Papaya*, and felt let down when its director, Tran Anh Hung, followed it with the off-putting *Cyclo*, then you might like to know that Tran's third movie marks his return to more delicate film-making. Set in modern-day Hanoi, the soap-opera plot concerns three sisters, each keeping a secret from her siblings: the eldest knows that her husband has a child by another woman; the middle sister is pregnant; and the youngest has just embarked on her first serious romance. These narratives and their offshoots make for a sensitive survey of emotional crises and how to cope with them, but the proceedings never become really gripping, and your attention is soon monopolised by Mark Lee's photography, which lingers on such reliably pretty subjects as fruit, foliage and diaphanous, sun-lit curtains. Such is the beauty of these images that Tran's willingness to indulge Lee at first seems wise. Eventually, though, all those minutes of silent scenery begin to look suspiciously like mere padding.

# Paper 2 Part 2

Write an answer to **one** of the questions **1–4** in this part. Write your answer in 220–260 words in an appropriate style.

1   An international company is offering money to the charity which the company feels is most deserving. The charity may be dedicated to either health, social welfare or the environment and its work should benefit as many people as possible. Members of the public have been asked to send in proposals nominating a charity that they support. Proposals should describe the charity and must explain how its work is of benefit to a large number of people.

   Write your **proposal**.

2   You see this announcement in an international magazine.

> We are preparing an article on the extent to which people's characters are affected by the geography of the places where they live. We would like readers to contribute answers to these questions:
> - What are the significant characteristics of the geography of your country?
> - In what ways might this geography affect the character of people from your country?
> - To what extent do you think your own character is influenced by the geography of your country?
>
> We will use a range of readers' contributions in our article which will be published next month.

   Write your **contribution**.

3   You have been asked to write an information sheet for new students at the international college where you study English. The sheet is to be entitled *Five Good Ways To Spend Sundays* and it should deal with five contrasting ways in which students can spend non-study days in the place where you are studying. It is aimed at students who are new to the area.

   Write your **information sheet**.

4   Your teacher has asked you to write an essay on the set text which you have worked on. Your essay should focus on one of the characters in the text who reminds you of someone you know. You should describe this character and comment on ways in which he or she does and does not resemble the person you know.

   Write your **essay**.

# Paper 3 Part 3

Use the word given in capitals at the end of some of the lines to form a word that fits in the gap in the same line. There is an example at the beginning (**0**).

**EATING OUT IN LONDON**

London is now one of the world's top cities for dining out,
according to the (**0**) ....*founder*.... of a survey that covers 70     **0** FOUND
cities worldwide. Tim Zagat of the Zagat Survey said yesterday
that the sixth (**1**) .................... of his survey showed how much     **1** EDIT
(**2**) .................... London had made. He said: 'In many ways I think     **2** IMPROVE
that London is now more (**3**) .................... than most other European     **3** REMARK
capitals. It is the (**4**) .................... of types of cuisine that makes     **4** VARY
London special.' He added that British people are becoming
much more (**5**) .................... with regard to food. Top restaurant was     **5** DISCRIMINATE
Gordon Ramsay's where the food was called '(**6**) ....................     **6** DESCRIBE
wonderful if rather (**7**) .................... '.     **7** PRICE

In addition to Ramsay's justifiably famous place in Chelsea,
the survey draws attention to the (**8**) .................... of a number of     **8** EXIST
other restaurants which were felt to be of an (**9**) .................... high     **9** EXCEPTION
standard. Although there are still many London restaurants which
remain (**10**) .................... , overall the standard is getting much better.     **10** SUCCESS

# Paper 3 Part 4

For questions **1–5** think of one word only that can be used appropriately in all three sentences. There is one example (0)

## Example

**0**  When I woke up this morning I was surprised to find there had been a ............... frost overnight.

Both my grandparents have become a little ............... of hearing in their old age.

This term you will all have to work very ............... on your projects if you are to finish them on time.

**Answer: 0**  *hard*

**1**  Soldiers must take up their positions as soon as the officer in charge gives the ............... .

Janie's brother insists on having all his CDs arranged in alphabetical ............... .

Most of the students here are taking the course in ............... to improve their chances of getting a good job.

**2**  Both boys were a real ............... to their parents when they were teenagers.

Kim is on ............... at the office for a month and then, if they are satisfied, they'll give her a proper contract.

It is a very complicated ............... and the jury may have to be there for months.

**3**  She had never had to ............... such a large office before but she managed very successfully.

Has it been announced yet whether Brown is or is not going to ............... for President?

You're going to have to ............... if you want to catch that bus.

**4**  We have a wide range of ............... drinks on sale in the buffet car,

Sharon thinks her husband is too ............... on the children when they behave badly.

These shoes are made of lovely ............... leather – were they very expensive?

**5**  When does school ............... up for the holidays?

They always tried to be very careful not to ............... the law.

Boys' voices usually begin to ............... in their early teens.

# Paper 3 Part 5

For questions **1–8**, complete the second sentence so that it has a similar meaning to the first, using the word given. **Do not change the word given**. You must use between **three** and **six** words including the word given. Here is an example (**0**).

**Example**

0   You should try to think only about your own work and not bother about mine.

   **on**

   You should try to ............................................. you need to do and not bother about my work.

**Answer:  0**   *concentrate on what*

1   If you should see Paul at the weekend, you could ask him for help.

   **into**

   Were ............................................. at the weekend, you could ask him for help.

2   Someone is going to install cable TV in my new flat this afternoon.

   **put**

   I'm going ............................................. in my new flat this afternoon.

3   I really hate that kind of film.

   **aversion**

   I ............................................. that kind of film.

4   Don't forget to discuss these factors in your essay.

   **consideration**

   Remember ............................................. in your essay.

5   All parents want only the best for their children.

   **nothing**

   Every ............................................. for their children.

6   Sally often reminds me of my younger sister.

   **think**

   Sally often ............................................. younger sister.

7   Tim didn't object to me taking responsibility for the project.

   **raised**

   Tim ............................................. in charge of the project.

8   The odds are against Maria getting such an important job.

   **likely**

   Maria ............................................. such an important job.

# Paper 4 Part 4

You will hear five people talking about how they met their husband or wife.

## TASK ONE

For questions **1–5**, choose from the list **A–H** the occupation of each speaker.

## TASK TWO

For questions **6–10**, choose from the list **A–H** the place where the meeting occurred.

**While you listen you must complete both tasks**

| | |
|---|---|
| **A** | journalist |
| **B** | economist |
| **C** | cook |
| **D** | translator |
| **E** | doctor |
| **F** | historian |
| **G** | actor |
| **H** | designer |

Speaker 1 — 1
Speaker 2 — 2
Speaker 3 — 3
Speaker 4 — 4
Speaker 5 — 5

| | |
|---|---|
| **A** | restaurant |
| **B** | university lecture room |
| **C** | theatre |
| **D** | school |
| **E** | newspaper office |
| **F** | railway station |
| **G** | park |
| **H** | train |

Speaker 1 — 6
Speaker 2 — 7
Speaker 3 — 8
Speaker 4 — 9
Speaker 5 — 10

# TEST 6 Key

## Paper 1 Part 3

1 B  2 B  3 D  4 A  5 D  6 C  7 A

## Paper 1 Part 4

1 C  2 F  3 G  4 D  5 B  6 G  7 A  8 D  9 E  10 G
11 C

## Paper 3 Part 3

1 edition  2 improvement  3 remarkable  4 variety
5 discriminating  6 indescribably  7 pricey  8 existence
9 exceptionally  10 unsuccessful

## Paper 3 Part 4

1 order  2 trial  3 run  4 soft  5 break

## Paper 3 Part 5

1 you to bump/run into Paul
2 to have cable TV put in
3 have an aversion to
4 to take these factors into consideration
5 parent wants nothing but the best
6 makes me think of my
7 raised no objection to me/my being
8 is not (very) likely to get

## Paper 4 Part 4

1 E  2 H  3 A  4 D  5 F  6 G  7 D  8 C  9 F  10 H

## Tapescript

**Speaker 1:** Jane and I met when we were both at university. She was doing economics and I was in my last year as a medical student. We'd both been there for three years and yet our paths had never crossed – even though in Jane's first year we'd actually been living on the same street. It was quite romantic really how we eventually met. We'd both been working really hard for our final exams and had decided to go for a walk in the local park, you know, to blow some cobwebs away. It started to rain very heavily and we both took shelter under a huge beech tree. We got married six months later and now have three grown-up children. Our eldest daughter wants to be a doctor too and she may be starting at our old university next year.

**Speaker 2:** Some people say that they know at once when they meet the person they're going to marry but it wasn't like that at all for me and Paul. In fact, we hated each other at first. He was my best friend's first boyfriend – we were all in the same class at school – and I think I was a bit jealous of him taking her away from me. Also, he always got better marks than me even though he didn't seem to work as hard as I did – that really infuriated me. His relationship with my girlfriend didn't last long but I didn't start to like him until we ended up working in the same restaurant. He'd become a chef by then and I'd been called in to redesign the place to give it more atmosphere. They were so pleased with my work that I had free meals there whenever I wanted them. Needless to say, I became a regular though I'd have happily paid for the meals anyway. Paul's cooking is amazing and I'd realised that I'd changed my mind about him too.

**Speaker 3:** Where did I meet my wife? Well, would you believe it, we have different views on that. She says we first met in the interval during a rather dull performance of *Hamlet* where I helped her find her contact lens which she'd somehow managed to drop on the floor. I remember the performance because I had to review it and had to be tactful as my editor's wife was playing Ophelia. I do vaguely remember helping someone find their contact lens but I thought it was someone who didn't look at all like Sophie. My version is that we met backstage many years later when Sophie was herself becoming quite a successful actress and I had to interview her for the local paper. But I guess Sophie is probably right – women do seem to remember faces better.

**Speaker 4:** I'll never forget our first meeting even though it's a long time ago now. I was studying Russian and was on my first ever trip there. I was with a group of students – all of us from Scotland – but I was the only one who spoke any Russian. I think it's probably what made me decide to go into translating when I graduated. It was in Soviet times and ours was one of the first such visits during the thaw in the sixties. We stepped off the train after the two-and-a-half-day journey from London and there he was waiting to meet us with a bunch of beautiful flowers, the traditional Russian way of greeting travellers. He was a law student and had been told he had to show this group of foreigners what a great place Leningrad was. I was instantly captivated both by the place and by him.

**Speaker 5:** I guess ours is a fairly typical story. I'd just got my first university job and Maria was one of the mature students – she was taking my course on Europe in the Middle Ages. Mind you, that isn't really where we first met. Maria knew me because she'd been to my lectures but I hadn't seen her – there were at least two hundred students in those lectures and I was too nervous to notice any individual students anyway. We met on the 10.30 to London when it was too crowded for either of us to get a seat. Maria introduced herself and – even though we had to stand all the way – the two-hour journey passed in a flash as we got to know each other. When we arrived we each had to go our separate ways but fortunately I had the presence of mind to ask for her phone number first.

# Photocopiable tapescripts

## Unit 2, Listening exercises 2 and 3

**Part One**

**Examiner:** First of all, we'd like to know a little bit about you. So Rebecca, where are you from in England?
**Rebecca:** I'm from Nottingham, in the East Midlands.
**Examiner:** Mm. And where are you from, Amanda?
**Amanda:** I'm originally from Bath, near Bristol.
**Examiner:** And have you studied any foreign languages, Amanda?
**Amanda:** For a while I studied Spanish but I found it very difficult and gave up.
**Examiner:** Rebecca?
**Rebecca:** I did French and German at school and then I learnt a little bit of Italian when I went to work in Italy. So for a couple of weeks we had a crash course in Italian. That's about it.

**Part Two**

**Examiner:** Now, I'd like you to ask each other something about your interests and leisure activities. So ask each other questions. Rebecca, could you start please?
**Rebecca:** Er, do you have any hobbies, Amanda?
**Amanda:** Mm. My hobby is going to the theatre and going to the pictures. I know it's not much of a hobby but I don't really have a lot of time for hobbies.
**Rebecca:** Er, what are your favourite films?
**Amanda:** What kind of films do I like best?
**Rebecca:** Yeah.
**Amanda:** I like thrillers, suspense. That's my favourite.
**Rebecca:** Oh, I don't like those. I'm no good with those. I get too scared. I don't watch any of it because I have my hands over my eyes.
**Amanda:** So what are your favourite hobbies, Rebecca?
**Rebecca:** I want to take up self defence. I'm starting new hobbies because I haven't really got any at the moment apart from reading and music but I'm going to take up self defence and dancing classes, something like that.
**Amanda:** I've done a sort of Middle Eastern dancing. It's like an Egyptian belly dancing but it's not Egyptian, it's a kind of, um, country form where your hips actually go down instead of upwards. And you're dressed in lots of clothes, you're not showing any stomach or anything. So, yeah, I did that for a little while but I get fed up with things really, get bored and move on. I did yoga and that annoyed me. It used to make me anxious.
**Rebecca:** Did it? Yoga made you anxious?
**Amanda:** Yeah, because you have to go and relax all your body and then ... you go right from your toes, up your body and then you go down it and relax it again and I used to think, Oh my God, I've got to relax it all again and it made me anxious.
**Examiner:** Right. Ask each other about things you hope to achieve in the future. Rebecca, what would you like to achieve in the future?
**Rebecca:** Er, I want to be rich. I've got a little dream, and this won't be until I'm sixty and I don't know what I'm going to do until I'm sixty, but when I'm sixty, I'm going to have a donkey sanctuary.
**Amanda:** She wants to be Brigitte Bardot!
**Rebecca:** I'm going to live on a Greek island and wear the same dress and the same straw hat every day and wander around on the craggy stones, in the heat and under the olive trees with my donkeys and my goats.
**Amanda:** That sounds lovely.
**Rebecca:** Oh, I really fancy that. What about you?

**Amanda:** I want to be happy. I want … I don't know really. I think I just want to be happy more than anything else. I mean ideally, I'd like to carry on with further studies. I wouldn't mind doing my PhD. I'd like to do that. But I just haven't got time.

**Rebecca:** Mmm.

**Amanda:** But I will. I'll be a wacky old lady in jeans and blue rinse hair and do my PhD aged seventy or eighty.

**Rebecca:** I'd like to do another degree because I did English and I'd like to do one in History and then do a Masters degree from that rather than a Masters in English. History is more interesting to me at the moment. And I want to travel.

**Examiner:** How would you feel about living or working abroad permanently?

**Amanda:** Absolutely love to.

**Rebecca:** Yeah, I'd like to, definitely for a few years. That's one of my ambitions.

**Amanda:** I'd like to end my days in a foreign country. I think in England we like, work all the time, and really people, especially in Mediterranean countries, people work to live and we live to work and we need to get back to that same kind of ethos that they have.

**Rebecca:** It would just be nice to live somewhere where it's always sunny and warm and more relaxed. As you say, you can get like stressed out if you're at work, but then when you've finished work, you know, you've got a good few hours of sunlight left and you can go to the beach.

**Amanda:** Unless you went to Iceland of course!

**Rebecca:** I wouldn't do that though. I'd move to a hot country.

**Examiner:** And then what are your earliest memories of school?

**Amanda:** My earliest memory of school is when I was in the infants, I was about four or five. I went to a very strict school and every term you got a report to take home. And I remember the teacher saying, whatever you do you must not open this report, it must go home to your parents. And well, you know, I just thought that's a cue to open it. So I remember opening up the report and then she hit me, whacked me, hard with a ruler.

**Rebecca:** Really?

**Amanda:** Yeah, I really hated her. That's one of my earliest memories.

**Rebecca:** My earliest memory is in infant school again. And I was doing this maths problem and I really couldn't work it out. And everyone else had gone off to watch this TV programme that we were allowed to watch once a week. And the teacher said, you've got to stay here and finish this. And I thought, right then. I got up and I walked home. It was a good mile back to my house. And I got there and my mum was, what are you doing here? And at the school they had everyone looking round the school grounds for me and the headmaster was looking in the street for me.

**Amanda:** Did you get told off?

**Rebecca:** Yeah, absolutely, by everyone …

## Unit 6, Listening exercise 2

**Speaker 1:** Hi, this is a message for Andy. I wanted to know about our homework. The history project. Can we word process it or has it got to be handwritten? I hope we are allowed to type it! Please could you ring me back? Oh, this is Eddie, by the way, I don't think I said. In case you've lost my number, it's 245908. I've got to go out at 7-ish, so I hope you get back before then. Bye.

**Speaker 2:** Hello, is that Michael Removals? Richard Johnstone gave me your number and suggested I contact you. I was wondering if you could move some stuff for me on the 22nd, or the 21st if you don't work on Saturdays. It's not a lot of stuff, just some beds and chests of drawers and bits and pieces into a house I'm going to rent out and it's only moving about a mile. Oh yes, and there's a fridge and a washing machine too. Would you be able to plumb those in for me as well? Could you get back to me and let me know your charges and availability? My name is Robert Smith and I'm on 0207 562 4957.

**Speaker 3:** Hi, Nicky. It's Leila, just ringing for a bit of a gossip. Nothing important but there's some news you might be interested to hear. Jo's decided to resign. And wait till I tell you why! There'll soon be nobody left there at all! Anyhow, give me a ring when you get back and I'll fill you in on all the gory details. Bye.

**Speaker 4:** This is a message for Nicola Smith. It's Paolo calling about the seminar you're doing for us next Tuesday. Could you get here for 11 rather than 2 and then we'll finish at 3.30 not 5. So you'll still be doing three hours but it'll be broken up by lunch. And I'd better warn you that the group are really on the ball. So come prepared with loads of stuff to keep them going. They like doing things rather than just listening so make sure you come with plenty of stretching activities. They're very nice but pretty hard work. So don't say you haven't been warned. Ring me back if you've got any queries. It's probably easiest to catch me on my mobile – that's 0802 334 567.

**Speaker 5:** Hi, Michael? This is John, I've been trying to catch you all day but your machine's been on all the time and I don't really like talking to these things. Seems like I've got no choice now as I won't be near a phone for the next hour or so. Er, we're meeting for Bob's stag party in the *Red Lion* tonight not the *Slug and Lettuce*. Er, hope you'll get this in time. If you haven't turned up by 8.15, I'll try ringing the *Slug*. Cheers.

**Speaker 6:** Andy? This is Alex. I've got this brilliant new PlayStation game. I only got it today and I'm already on level 6. Do you want to come round and try it later on this evening? Dad says I've got to get my homework done first but that should only take ten minutes. Come at 7 if you can. Bye.

## Unit 7, Listening exercise 1

**Speaker 1:** When I was at school I decided I definitely wanted a career and I thought of what I could do that involved working with other people. I'd had various Saturday jobs working as a hairdresser and it was only until I got an apprenticeship that I really thought this is what I want to do with my career. I love the work because you meet different people every day. You can be creative which is important to me. I suppose if there are any downsides it's that some of the times you can get other people's hair on your clothes and that can take some picking off. But on the whole it's something I really love doing.

**Speaker 2:** Well, this job found me really. A friend recommended me and so I did a job for somebody and it seemed to work out quite well. I never fancied doing a run-of-the-mill job, sort of nine to five sort of thing, and I quite like the secrecy of the job, I think really. You do have to do some boring office work but the best bit's out on the street. I'm quite a private man by nature so it sort of suits me and detective work, well, it's laborious at times but quite rewarding too.

**Speaker 3:** Well, initially I wanted to be an actress and then I realised that wasn't going to happen so I've always been keen on fitness and I used to go to a judo class every week, then got more and more interested and sort of went three or four times a week, and it was my teacher there that sort of suggested to me why I didn't become a stunt woman? So he introduced me to somebody and I've been on sets ever since really. There's a lot of travel which sometimes gets me down but I do get to meet the famous people which is great and I travel the world, which is something I've always really wanted to do, so I've involved everything that I really love – travelling and fitness, and meeting famous people – so I really enjoy my work.

**Speaker 4:** Well, I sort of got into it by accident really. I needed a bit of extra money in the summer holidays and I've always liked the, you know, the outdoors and getting out in the mornings and all that sort of thing so I just decided to give it a try and keep on going. It was reasonably lucrative, you know, it's not a great sort of one for money but you do get cash which is the one thing I like in this job. You know, it goes straight in your hand and I like the exercise, you know, it is, it's quite sort of strenuous work and you know, you get out in the mornings, have a bit of a scrub around and the nice thing is the satisfaction, is people's faces, looking at people's faces afterwards when they realise they can actually see outside again.

**Speaker 5:** Well, at school I'd always been really interested in fitness. I was actually a gym champion when I was young and then I decided what to do when I grew up and yeah, it was, it was a really good choice in the end because what I really like is helping other people to get fit and to actually bring the best out of them. I can advise them what to do and what not to do, what's best for their muscles and yeah, it's really worthwhile. I suppose the thing I don't like about it is that it's sometimes a bit insecure, like I did have a job actually in a health club once but I didn't like that so much so now I'm just freelance and I suppose it's a bit insecure but on the whole, I really like it.

**Speaker 6:** Well, first of all I did an English degree and then I didn't know what to do really after that, and I wanted to sort of get out and you know do a job where you sort of meet a lot of people and so I fell into this job really. It's great, you know, because the hours are sort of very long but, you know, you get to sort of meet a lot of interesting people and, you know, the things I really like about it is that, you know, you're always breaking a story so whatever you get involved in is, you know, is really sort of quite interesting and it's quite sort of cutting-edge, you know. And I mean, I suppose the thing I don't like about it is that people always say that journalists are sort of, you know, the scum of the earth sort of thing but, you know, I don't agree really. I think we do a very worthwhile job. I think that, you know, if someone stands up, sort of sticks their head, you know, above the parapet and that, it sort of – and they're famous, then you know, it's in the public's interest to sort of find out as much as possible about them, you know, and that's what I do.

**Speaker 7:** I think it was clear to my family what I was going to be when I grew up from quite an early age. I'm the eldest of five and my brothers and sisters always came to me for advice, and in the end actually my mum used to come to me for advice, or she'd like to talk things over or as a family we liked to try and find out why things happened as they did and that sort of thing, so at school we didn't really study psychology as a subject on its own but as part of biology we did look at the way people work and why they do what they do. It was a long training but something that's absolutely worthwhile. My belief and commitment in human beings, I suppose, is what made me become a psychologist. I suppose if there's anything that I find disappointing, at the same time it has to be a benefit, and that's that if I've had a chat with someone or I've helped someone, I can't necessarily see the changes in them in their everyday lives so I suppose I just have to look very closely when they come and see me next time. But it really is the best job in the world to me.

**Speaker 8:** Yes, I was an only child, no brothers and sisters. My mother left my father when I was about seven years old so every holiday from school I used to be with my father. I used to follow him everywhere and his job was a sports commentator for motor racing, Formula One, and so he travelled all over the world following the races and I went with him. I suppose it was inevitable in a way that I was going to follow him into that. He, a couple of times he actually gave me the microphone when I was a little boy to – and I spoke and it went out on television. I met all the famous drivers and the smell of the pit lane and the noise from the cars and everything was, was a very powerful thing that led me into, into this profession. Now, now I don't like it. I feel under pressure, I don't see enough of my own family. I'm travelling all over the world. I have two children and as soon as I can, as soon as my children are old enough – they're at school – I'll pack it in. I'll retire, I'll, you know, go past the chequered flag because I've had enough.

## Unit 26, Listening exercise 2

Located on the northern tip of Australia's East Coast, the tropical city of Cairns is internationally recognised as the gateway to the Great Barrier Reef, one of the seven natural wonders of the world. The city is home to 100,000 people and also boasts the fifth busiest international airport in Australia with many carriers flying directly into Cairns from countries around the world. Cairns is a tropical city with many outdoor restaurants and cafés and great shopping for all tastes, as well as offering a complete range of accommodation options from budget right through to five-star.

Great Adventures cruises have been running trips to the Great Barrier Reef for more than 100 years and, as a result, are recognised as an industry leader. Great Adventures offer daycruises to Green Island, a beautiful 6,000-year-old coral bay. It is perfect for lazing on white coral sands, swimming or snorkelling on the surrounding coral reef or relaxing around the luxurious day-visitor facilities – all just 45 minutes crossing from Cairns. A full range of options on the island include introductory scuba diving, certified scuba diving and guided snorkel tours, as well as a crocodile farm, parasailing and private beach hire.

For those wanting the ultimate reef adventure, cruise from Cairns to the luxury of Great Adventures multi-level pontoon on the Outer Reef. The pontoon features undercover seating and tables where you can enjoy a sumptuous buffet lunch. There's also a sundeck, full bar facilities, an underwater observatory, a semi-submersible coral viewing tour and a swimming enclosure for children. You'll be able to snorkel or dive among the reef's spectacular coral gardens and diverse marine life. A once-in-a-lifetime experience!

# Photocopiable activities

## Unit 4, Vocabulary exercise 4

### Teacher's words

| respect | short  | king    | point   | interview | quick  |
| ------- | ------ | ------- | ------- | --------- | ------ |
| tend    | London | cigar   | mouth   | neighbour | talk   |
| boy     | guitar | similar | modern  | rest      | child  |
| love    | resent | kind    | outrage | bed       | member |
| fail    | fact   | home    | trust   | clock     | hair   |

### Student's suffixes

| able | age  | dom  | ed     | ee     | en   |
| ---- | ---- | ---- | ------ | ------ | ---- |
| ency | er   | ette | ful    | hood   | ing  |
| ish  | ist  | ity  | ise    | less   | like |
| ly   | ment | ness | ous    | ridden | ship |
| ure  | ual  | ward | worthy | wise   | y    |

# Unit 6, Listening extension activity

| |
|---|
| Invite ............. to do something with you at the weekend. Give plenty of information about what you are proposing. Don't forget to give your name and contact details. |
| Tell ............. an interesting piece of news you've just heard. Suggest getting together some time soon. Don't forget to give your name and contact details. |
| Ask ............. to help you do something this evening. Give details about exactly what it is you want to do. Don't forget to give your name and contact details. |
| Tell ............. about some change to a plan you had made. Explain very clearly what the change is and why it has to be made. Don't forget to give your name and contact details. |
| Tell ............. about a TV programme on this evening that you think s/he will be particularly keen to watch. Give full details of when it is on and why you think s/he should watch it. Don't forget to give your name and contact details. |
| Tell ............. about a party you're planning. Give full details of when, where and why you're holding this party and invite him/her. Don't forget to give your name and contact details. |
| You've had to miss a lesson. Explain the situation and ask ............. to give you full details of the lesson and any homework. Don't forget to give your name and contact details. |

# Unit 14, Speaking exercise 1

## Role cards

---

**A  Rain forests**

High temperature and high rainfall throughout year.

World's most biologically diverse ecosystem.

Less than 7% of land surface but between 50% and 90% of plant and animal species found here.

One hectare of tropical rainforest may contain approximately 60 species of trees. (*incorrect*)

More species of ant live on one tropical rainforest stump than exist in all of the UK.

---

**B  Homelessness in the USA**

2 major factors: shortage of affordable rental housing and increase in poverty.

In 1997, 13.3% of US population lived in poverty; 40% were children.

Secondary factors: declining opportunities for employment and decrease in public assistance.

When an economy is growing, homelessness increases too. (*incorrect*)

Health care and education also suffer as a result of homelessness.

---

**C  Computer use**

Statistics from 2007 show that 69.2% of the population of North America use a computer.

76 million people use a computer at work, 67 million use a computer at home and 15 million use a computer at school.

Men use computers more at work than women. (*incorrect*)

70% of children in North America have a computer at home.

---

# Unit 19, Speaking 2

## Examiner's instructions

**Part 1** Ask Candidate A to introduce him or herself and talk about his or her study plans for the future. Candidate A should also ask Candidate B about his or her study plans for the future. Then ask Candidate B to introduce him or herself and talk about his or her work plans for the future. Candidate B should then ask Candidate A about his or her work plans for the future.

**Part 2** Ask Candidate A to compare pictures a and b and to talk about how the different people in these pictures are feeling. Candidate A should also say which picture appeals to him or her most and why. At the end, ask Candidate B to comment on whether he or she agrees with Candidate A's choice of favourite picture.

Ask Candidate B to say what the advantages and disadvantages are of each of the two pictures as a record of family life. He or she should also comment on which he or she would prefer to have as a record of their family life and why. At the end ask Candidate A to say whether he or she agrees with Candidate B's choice of picture or not.

**Part 3** Ask both candidates to discuss whether they feel each of these issues will change in the future – for better or for worse (i.e. technology, transport, housing, education, health care, employment).

**Part 4** Ask Candidate A to say some more about any one of the topics in Part 3 (select any one that Candidate A did not say much about in Part 3).

Ask Candidate B to say some more about any one of the topics in Part 3 (select one that Candidate B did not say much about in Part 3).

# Unit 22, Speaking 2

## Diary A

| Diary of life now | Diary of life 2020 |
|---|---|
| Start school 5 | Start school 3 |
| Leave full-time education | Start first business 20 |
| Leave home 19 | Leave full-time job/education |
| Start first job | |
| Return to full-time education (mature students) 24 | First career job 25 Launch second business |
| Start own business | Have first child |
| Get married | Get married 35 (m) 31 (f) |
| Have first child 28 (f) | |
| Return to work 29 (f) | |
| Buy first home 32 | Return to full-time education |
| | Launch third business 55+ |
| | Return to full-time education 60 |
| Retirement | Launch hobby-based business 62 |
| Become grandparent 50 | Become grandparent |
| Life expectancy 75 | Retirement 80 |
| | Life expectancy |

## Diary B

| Diary of life now | Diary of life 2020 |
|---|---|
| Start school 5 | Start school 3 |
| Leave full-time education 18–25 | Start first business |
| Leave home | Leave full-time job/education 21–25 |
| Start first job 20 | |
| Return to full-time education (mature students) | First career job Launch second business 30 |
| Start own business 25 | Have first child 32 |
| Get married 29 (m) 27 (f) | Get married |
| Have first child | |
| Return to work | |
| Buy first home | Return to full-time education 48 |
| | Launch third business |
| | Return to full-time education |
| Retirement 65 (m) 60 (f) | Launch hobby-based business 62 |
| Become grandparent | Become grandparent 63 |
| Life expectancy | Retirement |
| | Life expectancy 120 |

# Unit 23, Speaking 2

## Customer role cards

**A** Problem: You bought tickets for a concert which were very expensive. The concert was cancelled at the last minute.

What you want: Your money back plus a free ticket for another concert as compensation.

**B** Problem: You have been staying at a hotel and the room is not as clean as it should be. The service both in the restaurant and at reception is below standard.

What you want: A reduction in your bill.

**C** Problem: You bought some software for your computer. You were assured that it would be compatible with your computer. When you got home, you discovered it wasn't.

What you want: Other software which will do the job you want, however, this is much more expensive.

**D** Problem: You went to a disco and tripped over a box which had been left on the floor. You fell and cracked your elbow.

What you want: £3,000 compensation and a letter of apology from the company.

**E** Problem: You bought an item of clothing which was very expensive. When you washed it, the colour ran and it shrank. There were no washing instructions on the item. You have lost your receipt.

What you want: Your money back.

## Company role cards

**A** Argument: You did not know that the concert would be cancelled. It was due to sickness. You are very sorry for the inconvenience caused.

Your offer: A refund of the ticket but you cannot offer another free ticket as future concerts will be given by different people/companies.

**B** Argument: You have been having staffing problems and the cleaning has not been done as thoroughly as it is normally and the restaurant and reception are understaffed too. This is regrettable but not your fault.

Your offer: The room will be cleaned immediately and you can offer a free dinner in the restaurant.

**C** Argument: No member of your staff would have told a customer that the software was compatible with their computer if it was not. You believe the customer mistakenly gave the wrong information about their computer.

Your offer: You can only offer other goods of the same value.

**D** Argument: You cannot understand how a box could have been left on the floor. You are very concerned about the reputation of your disco.

Your offer: You offer £3,000 on condition that the customer does not go to the press.

**E** Argument: The customer must have washed it in hot water and common sense should tell them not to do that. You are not sympathetic.

Your offer: As the customer has no receipt, they cannot even prove the item was bought at your shop. You can offer nothing.

# Acknowledgements

The authors and publishers acknowledge the following sources of copyright material and are grateful for the permissions granted. While every effort has been made, it has not always been possible to identify the sources of all the material used, or to trace all copyright holders. If any omissions are brought to our notice, we will be happy to include the appropriate acknowledgements on reprinting.

p. 31a–32a (Test 1): BBC Worldwide History, www.bbc.co.uk/history; adapted from 'Interesting Facts About Domain Names' by Dennis Forbes, 29 March 2006, www.yalfa.com; adapted from 'What's in A Name?' by Patricia McLinn, www.simegen.com, ©1995 Pat McLaughlin; p. 33: adapted from an article by Chris Brown, first published in *The Independent*, 10 August, 2001; p. 34: text from 'The hills are alive with the sound of music' by Anthony Thorncroft, *Financial Times*, 10 August 2001, © The Financial Times Ltd; p. 35a (Test 1): text from 'We fell in love with a lighthouse' by Patrick O'Hagan, *Guardian Weekend*, 16 December 2006, © Guardian News and Media Ltd; p. 58: text from 'Keeping up with the new English' by Michael Wright, *The Sunday Times*, 26 August 2001, © N I Syndication; p. 61: extract from 'Feminism still fails in the house' by Neil Tweedie, *The Daily Telegraph*, 6 March, 2000, © Telegraph Media Group Ltd; p. 63: text adapted from 'As easy as XYZ', *The Economist*, 1 September 2001, © The Economist Newspaper Ltd; p. 84: text from 'The bananas world of food packaging' by John Vidal, *Guardian*, 24 August 2001, © Guardian News and Media Ltd; p. 88: adapted text from 'Low water' by Vanessa Houlder, *Financial Times*, 14 August 2001; p. 112: text adapted from reviews of Margaret Drabble's novels from www.redmood.com; p. 114: 'Knieval Jr jumps Grand Canyon' by John Hiscock, adapted from *The Daily Telegraph*, 22 May 1999, © Telegraph Media Group Ltd; p. 115: adapted text from 'The cost of team building' by Colin Eastwood, *Observer*, 25 August 2001, © Guardian News and Media Ltd; pp. 138–9: article adapted from 'How do they do it?', *Guardian*, 22 August 2001, © Guardian News and Media Ltd; p. 141: adapted text from 'Creative juices' by Sandra Deeble, *Financial Times*, 7 August 2001, © Sandra Deeble; p. 142: article adapted from *Thoughts on Conducting* by Adrian Boult, Weidenfeld and Nicholson, an imprint of The Orion Publishing Group (London); p. 144: text from 'Going down, going down' by Andre Freiwald, *BBC Wildlife Magazine*, September 2001; p. 168: text from *Daughters of Britannia* by Kate Hickman, reprinted by permission of HarperCollins Publishers Ltd, © Kate Hickman, 2000; p. 175: adapted text from *Just Six Numbers* by Martin Rees, published by Phoenix, 2001. p. 170: adapted from 'New on video' by Steve Grant, *The Sunday Times*, 26 August 2001; pp. 170-1: text from 'The rest of the week's films' by Edward Porter and Cosmo Landesman, *The Times*, 25 August 2001; p. 173: text adapted from 'London's cuisine is among the best' by Robin Young, *The Times*, 30 August, 2001, © N I Syndication; from 'Ageing: only a matter of time', *The Economist*, 1 September 2001, © The Economist Newspaper Ltd.